Time for Christmas!

Chicken Soup for the Soul: Time for Christmas
101 Tales of Holiday Joy, Love & Gratitude
Amy Newmark

Published by Chicken Soup for the Soul, LLC www.chickensoup.com
Copyright ©2023 by Chicken Soup for the Soul, LLC. All Rights Reserved.

The publisher gratefully acknowledges the many publishers and individuals who
granted Chicken Soup for the Soul permission to reprint the cited material.

Front cover illustration of snowman and background courtesy of iStockphoto.com
(©maroznc), illustration of small cardinal courtesy of iStockphoto.com/Bastinda18
(©Bastinda18), illustration of pine tree courtesy of iStockphoto.com/Rustic (©Rustic).
Back cover and interior illustration courtesy of iStockphoto.com (©maroznc)

Photo of Amy Newmark courtesy of Susan Morrow at SwickPix

Cover and Interior by Daniel Zaccari

Distributed to the booktrade by Simon & Schuster. SAN: 200-2442

Publisher's Cataloging-In-Publication Data

Names: Newmark, Amy, editor.
Title: Chicken soup for the soul : time for Christmas , 101 tales of holiday joy , love &
    gratitude / Amy Newmark.
Description: Cos Cob, CT: Chicken Soup for the Soul, LLC, 2023.
Identifiers: LCCN: 2023939365 | ISBN: 978-1-61159-108-8 (print) | 978-1-61159-
    344-0 (ebook)
Subjects: LCSH Christmas--Literary collections. | Christmas--Anecdotes. | Gratitude
    -Literary collections. | Gratitude--Anecdotes. | Self help. | BISAC SELF HELP
    / Motivational and Inspirational | SELF HELP / Personal Growth / Happiness |
    RELIGION / Holidays / General
Classification: LCC GT4985.C378 2023 | DDC 394.2663/02--dc23--dc23

Library of Congress Control Number: 2023939365

PRINTED IN THE UNITED STATES OF AMERICA
on acid∞free paper

30 29 28 27 26 25 24 23   01 02 03 04 05 06 07 08 09 10 11

Time for Christmas!

101 Tales of Holiday Joy, Love & Gratitude

Amy Newmark

Chicken Soup for the Soul, LLC
Cos Cob, CT

Chicken Soup for the Soul

Changing lives one story at a time®
www.chickensoup.com

Table of Contents

❶

~Christmas Miracles~

❷

~Tales of the Tree~

3

~Feeling that Christmas Spirit~

4

~Holiday Hijinks~

5

~The Perfect Gift~

❻

~Family Fun~

❼

~Gratitude and Grace~

~Holiday Angels~

9

~The Joy of Giving~

10

~Around the Table~

⑪

~Four-legged Family Members~

Chapter 1

Christmas Miracles

In the Nick of Time

Every traveler has a home of his own, and he learns to appreciate it the more from his wandering.
~Charles Dickens

Unpredictable doesn't begin to describe our lifestyle when my husband was flying C-5s. By choice, we lived in a rural area of Dover, Delaware. We could have lived on base, but we always made it a priority to try to live out in the community so that our family could integrate and experience "regular" life as opposed to base life. So we were living on a small farm complete with sheep, chickens, the occasional pot-bellied pig and Amish neighbors.

I learned early on that life would be very different here. Four-day missions turned into month-long excursions with little or no direct contact with my husband. Well-meaning base personnel would call and give us updates that frequently led to tearful disappointments when missions would change, and children who were bouncing with anticipation would have to be told it would be another week... at least. Eventually, I asked them not to call unless they knew for a fact that his plane had crossed that golden line over the ocean that meant it couldn't turn back.

It was situation normal when my husband announced that he would be leaving the day after Thanksgiving for a four- to six-day mission. No big deal, status quo, so we got our Christmas tree early, enjoyed Thanksgiving with friends, and then said our goodbyes. By this time, the farewells barely left a ripple in our days, and we got on with whatever we were doing. Our children were young and homeschooled, so this meant diving into projects and keeping a fairly normal schedule.

This also meant I was on 24/7 duty, and it was getting critical after about two weeks. He wasn't back, and I hadn't had a second to do my Christmas shopping, let alone bake all the goodies my children were dreaming about. Three weeks in, it looked like we were going to be on our own for the holiday. This realization landed me on the front porch of our nearest Amish neighbor, tearfully asking if they would please watch my youngest while I ran out to get everything I needed for Christmas.

Mattie was a beautiful Amish woman, probably in her sixties then, and more than happy to take him in for a few hours. This is someone who helped me chase my sheep when they snuck out of their fence on more than one occasion, taught me about Rhode Island Reds, and shared eggs, canned fruits, baked goods and the occasional recipe. I thought she hung the moon. I tried my best to return these favors, but I was more the type who had to explain that I had baked them a beautiful pie, which had looked great until my youngest son accidentally sat on it.

Over the course of December, I received a couple of calls indicating that my husband might or might not be on his way — which I did not relay to the kids. I wanted to avoid any unnecessary heartbreak. We went ahead and made sugar cookies and a gingerbread house with full gumdrop trimmings, and planned our traditional Christmas Eve dinner of homemade bread and New England clam chowder. The gifts were wrapped and ready to be placed under the tree on Christmas Eve.

Christmas Eve morning, the phone rang. It was a ham radio operator letting me know he had a MARS (Military Auxiliary Radio System) patch call for me. It was my husband letting me know that they had crossed that golden line, and he would be home. I knew he wouldn't call unless he was positive, but I also knew better than to say anything because things change when you least expect it.

I proceeded with our normal Christmas Eve activities. Christmas music and sugar cookies fueled the day while the smell of baked bread filled the house. I put the finishing touches on the table and our soup as the kids played out the Christmas story in the living room. They couldn't wait to take their baths and get into their Christmas pajamas so we could have dinner and read *The Night Before Christmas*.

We sat around our carefully set farm table and said grace, prayed especially for Daddy, and dug into our favorite meal of the year. From where I was sitting at the table, I could see our front door clearly, and there framed in the window stood my husband — tired, scruffy-faced and still in his flight suit. My heart skipped a beat as he raised a finger to his lips to keep me from saying anything. I held my breath as he knocked on the door. Three heads snapped up from their bowls, and our home erupted with shouts of "Daddy's home! Daddy's home! He's really home!" They were at the door before he could get it fully open and were all over him in a second.

We laugh about our "Hallmark Card Christmas" now, but the feelings are still fresh — even twenty-five years later — and all that joy wells up in my heart all over again. Being a military family has its challenges and hardships, but it can have its sweetness, too. I won't pretend it was easy being the one left behind, to hold down the fort or whatever phrase we use to describe the day-to-day. It could be downright hard, but it made those homecomings all the more significant and memorable.

— Susan Mulder —

Gramma's Gift

A grandmother is like an angel, who takes you under
her wing. She prays and watches over you,
and she'll gift you anything.
~Author Unknown

The Christmas season could only really begin once my grandparents arrived for their annual December visit. The moment they pulled into our driveway, our home would light up with their love and delight in spending time with their family.

Gramma, in particular, relished the joy of the season. She'd hum Christmas carols as she wrapped gifts and addressed her hand-painted cards. We would bake chocolate kringle cookies and read stories in front of the tree. On Christmas Eve, we'd sing "Silent Night" on the ride home from church, while I snuggled against her in the back seat and looked for Rudolph's red nose in the dark sky.

Years passed, and Gramma shared our traditions with my three children, her great-grandchildren. They learned how to melt chocolate for the kringles and roll out the pie dough without handling it too much. They read the same Christmas stories, curled up on Gramma's lap.

We always said Gramma was the closest person to a real angel on earth. She was serene, patient and always positive. She never, ever spoke a bad word about anyone. She was devoted to her family, and Christmas was the time of year when her beautiful spirit really shined.

When Gramma had a stroke at age ninety-seven in February 2019, we knew it was time to say goodbye. She'd lived a full and happy life. I drove to Pennsylvania with my fourteen-year-old daughter Lucie to see her in hospice care. During the two-hour drive, I tried to prepare Lucie for what was happening. We talked about life, death, and the afterlife. I told her how some people believe that our spirits carry on and are still present after death. I shared with her some of the stories I'd read in my job as a Chicken Soup for the Soul editor, putting together our latest book of stories about angels and miracles, *Chicken Soup for the Soul: Angels All Around*.

We said our goodbyes. Gramma wasn't able to speak or respond, but we could tell she was listening. Lucie handled it with composure beyond her years, and in our final parting, she said, "Send us a sign when you're gone, Gramma, a sign that you're with us."

Months went by, and one day Lucie asked me if I'd seen any signs from Gramma. No, I hadn't seen any signs. I wondered if I should have told her those angel stories and created those expectations. Now she was waiting for a sign, in the literal way that a teenager would. What if there was no sign? I worried that she'd be disappointed and think Gramma was just gone forever.

The Christmas season arrived, and it seemed that Lucie had forgotten about watching for Gramma's sign. But we all felt an emptiness in the season without her. We tried baking chocolate kringle cookies, but they turned out flat and didn't quite taste as good. We sang "Away in a Manger," but it sounded off-key.

December festivities kicked into full swing, and I became too busy to dwell on missing Gramma. In fact, I was too busy even to enjoy the spirit of the season. It flew by without a moment of appreciation for my bright-eyed children and their excitement for our family holiday traditions.

On Christmas Eve day, I saw our mail carrier deliver a stack of cards to our mailbox, but I was frantically doing all the things a mom does the day before Christmas — wrapping, cleaning, baking, cooking, and preparing. *I'll collect the mail tomorrow,* I thought.

After hosting dinner for thirty people, I collapsed into bed. But instead of falling into a dreamy Christmas Eve slumber, I tossed and turned in my regret that I had been too busy to even pause and enjoy my family during this special time of year.

Christmas morning, I was exhausted. I had a cup of coffee and smiled through the flurry of unwrapping. Once it was over, my husband took the kids to his parents nearby to see their cousins and open more gifts. At last, I had some time to myself. I went for a quiet walk and reflected on all the wonderful Christmases I've had. I thought about Gramma and promised myself to be more positive like her, to take more time to enjoy the small moments in life.

Back home, I went by the mailbox and grabbed the mail before jumping in the shower. I stopped short when I saw the card at the top of the pile, addressed in Gramma's distinctive cursive handwriting. And then my eye went to the return address: Thelma A. Church, with her home address. I ripped open the card. It was Gramma's hand-painted Christmas card, a lovely watercolor she did every year:

> Dearest Jamie, Tom, Lucie, Emmett and Clara,
>   To all 5 of you —
>   What a precious family! It will be so nice to see you on Christmas. Save a few hugs for me.
> Love you,
> Gramma

It was last year's Christmas card that hadn't been delivered. It had a December 2018 postmark, and there was a slight error in our address, so it hadn't made it to our house last year. Somehow, it had ended up in our mailbox on our first Christmas without Gramma.

There was no logical explanation. I quizzed family members and even asked our mail carrier what happens to undelivered mail. Was there a chance it was in a box of lost Christmas cards that were redelivered the following year? She shook her head. "No way," she said. "That's just a Christmas miracle."

Gramma gave me the gift of knowing she was with me on Christmas Day and every day. I slept like a baby that night for the first time in weeks, with Gramma's card propped next to my bed.

— Jamie Cahill —

The Night Santa Claus Cried

Every day holds the possibility of a miracle.
~Author Unknown

Four-year-old David was giddy with excitement as we drew near to the front of the line to see Santa Claus. He stood on his toes to see over the shoulder of the taller boy in front of him. "We're next, Mama," he said, grabbing my hand and pulling me forward.

Santa gently patted the back of the little boy who scrambled off his lap and turned to us. He held his hand out to David, barely giving me a glance. "Come, sonny. Tell Santa what you want for Christmas." He smiled indulgently as David rattled off an impossibly long list of toys he'd seen advertised on TV. "You know, son, I have many boys and girls to bring gifts to. I may not be able to bring you everything you want, but I think I can bring the things you'd like most."

David looked puzzled. "How will you know which things I want most?"

Santa gave a low chuckle. "Santa knows." For the first time, he really looked at me. The twinkle left his green eyes, and he swallowed. He turned to Mrs. Claus, who was passing out candy canes to the kids as they left. "I think I need a quick break."

Something in his face made her react quickly. "Boys and girls, Santa will be back in a few minutes. He just needs a little break."

Santa gently slid David off his lap and stood to follow Mrs. Claus. Although he tried to turn his head away from the kids, I was standing right in front of him, and I saw the tears in his eyes as he hurried away. I saw him grab Mrs. Claus by the arm and say something to her just as I was turning to leave. She looked back at me and motioned me to come forward. For a moment, I was too stunned to move, wondering what was happening and how it could involve me. She gestured again, this time almost frantically.

I grabbed David's hand and followed them into a small storage area in the rear of the store. Without saying a word, Mrs. Claus abruptly left the room. Santa stood staring at me, his green eyes glistening with tears that he somehow managed to keep from falling. I knew that if David had not been there, this man would have been sobbing. But why? And what did he want from me?

"Beth?" he whispered hoarsely. "You are Beth. I know you are." He swallowed. "I've looked for you for years, honey." He saw the confusion on my face, and he took the cap off his head and tore the fake glasses from his nose. "My hair and beard used to be red, but they turned snow-white quite some time ago. I'm your daddy, honey."

I reeled back on my heels. Daddy was an alcoholic, and Mama left him when I was seven years old. I saw him once in a while for the next few years, whenever he managed to stay sober long enough to come for a visit. Then Mama was transferred to another state with her job, and I never saw him again. He was always good to me, even when he was drinking, so I missed him terribly. But Mama was bitter toward him, and she never let him know that we were moving.

As I stared at the man in front of me, I began to see remnants of the father I once knew and loved. I especially remembered his green eyes that always seemed to shine when he looked at me. My own eyes were filling with tears, but I couldn't speak past the huge lump in my throat. I had resigned myself to the fact that David would never know his grandfather, yet here he was standing in front of us in a Santa Claus suit, of all things. But I had some of my mother in me, too, because I instantly doubted if I wanted my son to grow close to an alcoholic grandfather or not.

As if he could read my thoughts, he said in a rush of words, "I've been sober for ten years, honey. I started playing Santa Claus when I worked for the mall during the Christmas season one year to make extra money. The man who usually had the role got sick, and they couldn't find a replacement. My manager looked over at me and said, 'Joe, you'd make a good Santa with all that white hair and beard. How well can you do a ho, ho, ho?' I found that I actually liked it, and I've been doing it ever since."

He swiped at his eyes to knock back a stray tear. "Honey, I've searched for you everywhere. But I never dreamed I'd look up and see you in one of my lines." He looked down at David, who was utterly perplexed and not understanding anything that was being said. A huge smile spread across his face, and dimples that looked exactly like David's creased his cheeks. "I'm a grandfather," he whispered, reaching out for me.

I stepped into his arms, and as we embraced, I could smell the familiar scents that I had forgotten until that moment. The clean, familiar smell of his soap and after shave filled my senses as I clung to him.

David, eyes big with surprise as Mama and Santa embraced, stepped forward and put one arm around Santa's waist and one arm around my waist. Santa and I both laughed. David didn't yet know it, but he was meeting his grandfather. Ten minutes ago, I thought that my son would never know this man. But as I watched him place a big hand lovingly on David's head, his eyes sweeping over the boy as if he couldn't get enough of him, I instinctively knew that this man was in our life to stay.

I invited Dad over for dinner. David was overjoyed that Santa would be having dinner with us. I had a lot of explaining to do, but as I watched the small boy and the man in the Santa suit grin at one another, I knew that everything was going to be just fine. I could already see the beginning of a bond between them. Dad's green eyes shone when he looked at David, just as they always did when he looked at me when I was a girl.

When we got home, my husband, Glen, was making spaghetti for dinner. "Did you two have a good time?" he asked.

David ran to him and jumped into his arms. "Daddy, guess what! Santa Claus is coming for dinner tomorrow."

Glen looked at me over the top of David's head, his eyes full of questions.

I laughed. "I'll explain later," I said.

— Elizabeth Atwater —

The Christmas Diamond

Miracles come in moments. Be ready and willing.
~Wayne Dyer

I remember holding my mother's hand when I was a little girl and being mesmerized by the bands she wore on her right ring finger. The rings had belonged to my mother's mother, and her mother before that, and had been handed down through the generations. They were the only things remotely of value that any of the women had ever owned.

The engagement ring consisted of a small center stone surrounded by even smaller diamonds. I remember using one finger to gently trace the outline of that delicate gold band, so thin and frail from years of wear. None of the women ever had the means to have it repaired.

As a teenager, I used to beg my mother every single day to let me wear those rings, and she never would. Then, one sunny Saturday when I was seventeen years old, she gave in and let me borrow them to wear on a date. That very morning, my mother had announced that — after twenty-three years — she was finally filing for divorce from my abusive father. As she slipped the rings onto my finger, she made me promise that I wouldn't let anything happen to them, and that I'd return them to her the second I came home. Eager to finally have a chance to wear them, I gave her my word, childishly crossing my heart as I did so.

I never had a chance to keep that promise.

That night, while I was away, my father came back to the rundown rental house we had all shared, armed with a revolver. Without saying a word, he shot everyone in the house, killing my mother and brother and badly injuring my sister before taking his own life.

I wore those rings every single day for seventeen years.

Then, a few years ago while decorating the Christmas tree at work, I looked down to find that the center stone was missing from my mother's ring. For three days straight, I searched everywhere for the diamond. I swept the entire room where I had been decorating, pulling everything apart and retracing every step. I methodically sifted through every speck of dirt and debris, and checked every sequin, bead, and piece of glitter three or four times. The stone never did turn up, and finally I had to accept that it was just gone forever.

Thinking about the situation in the days that followed, I realized something. Although I had really hoped to find the diamond, I never felt desperate about the situation. The minute that I noticed it was gone, my very first thought was, *If you don't find it, you'll just have it replaced. No big deal.*

Had the same thing happened to my mother, I know exactly how she would have felt — we would never have had the money to fix that ring, and it would have been lost to her forever. These were her mom's rings, the only thing handed down to her, and they were probably the nicest things that my mom had ever owned. She meticulously cared for them and wore them with great pride. Knowing how much they meant to her, it would have been a huge blow, and she would have been frantic over the whole ordeal. I could picture the desperation in her eyes as she looked for that tiny stone, and I knew she would have been crushed when she didn't find it.

All that my mom ever wished for us was that we would have it better than she did. She wanted more for us. She wanted us to leave behind that poverty and desperation she so often felt. In many ways, that wish has come true, and I know she'd be proud that I didn't have to worry over that little diamond or anything else. So, even though I really hoped that I would find the stone that had been hers, I decided that I would have the rings repaired, and she would understand.

That Christmas, when it was time for the decorations at work to come down, I was in a terrible mood. It had been a chaotic several weeks, and I was busy and tired. I took the decorations from the tree and wrapped the ornaments for storage. But when it was time to put away the tree, I couldn't find the box anywhere. Agitated, I grabbed the tree by the base and dragged the entire thing across the property, outside and to the storage building fifty or so yards away from my office area. There, I threw it into the corner and slammed the door, leaving it forgotten for an entire year.

When the following Christmas season rolled around and it was time to pull out the tree and put it up, I found it exactly where I had left it. By then, it had been covered up with other discarded junk — empty bags, a broken weed eater, and a piece of water hose that had been chewed up by a lawn mower. I kicked all these items out of my way and dragged the pathetic artificial tree out of its corner and into my office. There, I began the painstaking process of shaping this battered and abused piece of junk into something that slightly resembled a pine tree.

While doing so, I thought about my mom — about those rings and the day that she gave them to me — and breathed a silent apology to her that I had lost her diamond. Suddenly, just as I had that thought, I got so cold that I physically shivered, and the skin on my arms broke out in goosebumps. All at once, as I pulled up one of the little branches of the tree, a sparkle caught my eye. It was a tiny diamond, just lying there, as if someone had put it on the branch of the tree, stood back and waited for me to find it.

Scarcely daring to breathe, I reached out with a shaking hand to pick up the stone. Gently, I laid the diamond in the palm of my left hand, convinced that I was imagining the entire thing, that I would blink and nothing would be there after all. But it was there.

Somehow, after having been up for the entire season the year before, after all the abuse that I had bestowed upon that tree, after having been pulled across a parking lot and abandoned in a pile of garbage for an entire year, the diamond was there. It just didn't make sense. How could that tiny speck of stone still be on the tree, perched on a branch without having fallen out anywhere? It was a miracle, plain and simple.

That day, I got the best Christmas present I ever received. It was not the diamond, although I am thrilled to have the same stone that my mother cherished back in my possession. No, the best present was the confirmation that my dear mom, whom I miss so much that it hurts, never left me at all. She is here, every second, watching over me still. I know it, as sure as I know that diamond was never in that tree until the second that I felt a chill come over me, and my mother laid it there for me to find.

— Candy Allen Bauer —

Merry Christmas, Mum

A mom's hug lasts long after she lets go.
~Author Unknown

M y parents were both actors. My father passed away only a few years ago at the age of ninety-one, but my mother died in 1973 at age fifty-three, when I was only seventeen years old.

The theatre was their particular sphere of influence. While not exactly stars, Hilary and Leslie Yeo were often recognized by knowledgeable theatregoers in both Canada and their native England. Even more to their delight, they reached the point where they were recognized by their peers as very accomplished and respected actors. The fact that they both possessed an energetic, devoted love of their craft (not to mention each other) had a great deal to do with their success.

In my mother's case there was also her undeniable physical and spiritual beauty, which friends, audiences and cameras alike found irresistible. Her effect on me was no less profound — I adored her.

As radio, television and film grew in popularity they both expanded their repertoire to include them. The television cameras were particularly fond of my mother and she appeared in several CBC shows — the *Festival Series* among the most popular in the 1960s. Dad found a great deal of TV and stage work as well, but had even more success as a Producer Director in a new phenomenon called the *Industrial*.

I was an only child, and our small family was very close. They would often make sure they were both offered parts in the same production, and as much as possible, I would travel with them to various "seasons" at different theatres. When they did television, I would accompany them to the studio or the location whenever possible.

In the late 1960s Mum began to develop some inexplicable aches and pains. As time progressed, so did her pain. Then the doctors discovered the lump. A small thing, really. A little lump in her breast. It seemed those years of discomfort had been real after all.

The cancer that took her was not swift. It took two years to waste away one of the most beautiful and special people I'm ever likely to know. She died just after Christmas in 1973. I was a seventeen-year-old boy who adored his mother, and I did not deal with it well.

Her death altered my feelings and attitudes about many things. Predictably, Christmas was one of the things that was ruined for me. Dad and I each had to deal with some personal realities. He had lost his companion, lover and partner of over twenty years. I had lost my mother. Thankfully he and I had each other, and our warm loving relationship grew stronger with every passing year. But after Mum died, Christmas for me was never the same. In fact, it became a time of year when I really had to work at just staying level, let alone cheery. The reality was I wanted to skip the whole thing.

Ten years after Mum's death, the young woman I was living with was determined to alter my feelings about Christmas. But the harder she worked at making the house cheery and getting me into the spirit, the more I thought about Mum and how much I missed our family Christmases. I tried my best, but as usual, it was a very difficult time.

Fast forward to Christmas Eve. Not to be uncharitable, but thank goodness it was almost over. Val and I stayed up late wrapping gifts for family and friends and then it was time for bed.

I'm an early riser at the best of times, and as sleep was somewhat elusive this night, I was up even earlier than usual. I puttered around in the living room for a couple of hours — doing what, I don't remember. All I remember is that sometime around 6:30 or 7 a.m. I turned on the TV. And as I moved away, I heard something that stopped me in mid-turn. I hadn't heard that voice in over ten years. I hadn't seen a rerun, heard an audiotape — nothing. But in the early hours of this Christmas morning, the voice I was listening to was unmistakably that of my mother.

I quickly turned and saw an old black and white show appearing on the screen. It was unmistakably a Christmas winter scene. There was a barnyard where two men were standing, looking off to one side. And Mum's voice. The camera panned over to one side, revealing a door. As it opened, my mother stepped out.

I don't even remember sitting down, but I must have, because that's where Valerie found me, mesmerized, tears streaming down my face. She had never met my mother, but had seen photos. As soon as she looked over at the screen she knew. She sat down with me and together we watched my mother in something she had done at least ten years before she died. What made it even more incredible is that it wasn't a videotape. In those days television was live. The only way to record a live show was to actually film it off a television monitor. Rarely would the networks go to the trouble and expense of doing this. Apparently this was one of those rare occasions.

As much of an emotional shock as it was, I wouldn't have stopped it from happening if I could have. And I like to think that knowing how much I missed her, this was her little Christmas present to me. She was letting me know, that at this special time of year, and on this most difficult of days for me, she was with me, even as she always is.

One would think that having parents in that kind of business you would expect to see them on TV at some point. I constantly see my father's movies and series work on TV without warning. But I truly never even thought of the possibility of accidentally seeing Mum, and until that morning, in the ten years since her passing it hadn't happened even once.

It's been forty years now since her death, and I have yet to inadvertently come across another of her performances. But even if I do, it's unlikely to mean as much to me as that one special performance, on that Christmas morning in 1983.

— Jamie Yeo —

A Matter of Hours

*Believe in miracles. I have seen so many of them
come when every other indication would say that
hope was lost. Hope is never lost.*
~Jeffrey R. Holland

It was nothing more than a plaster five-and-dime-store nativity, but to me it was as perfect as fine china. During the Christmas season, I loved nothing more than rearranging it over and over, moving animals closer to Baby Jesus or positioning the angels to keep a careful watch over the tiny figurine in swaddling clothes. I remember the glow on my mother's face as she'd turn from the kitchen sink to see me at the piano, strategically placing the sheep in a circle around the shepherd or arranging the three wisemen in a triangle as they carried their precious gifts to the manger.

The small figurines had belonged to my dad's grandparents, and I was touched when the nativity was given to me the January I moved into my first apartment. My mother was boxing up the Christmas decorations when I stopped for a visit. She placed the aged pink shoebox in my hands and told me she wanted me to have the family heirloom I loved so much as a child. I was getting married that September and moving to Massachusetts, and she wanted to ensure I would have the set to display the following Christmas. I lived in the upstairs apartment of a home owned by two very kind senior citizens who lived downstairs, and they generously allowed me space in the attic to store items. That is where the pink shoebox containing my childhood treasure was

Christmas Miracles |

safely tucked away.

Our first Christmas as husband and wife came, and I couldn't wait to decorate our tiny apartment. We purchased a table-top tree and a few decorations to brighten our home. I began searching the closet where items I'd brought from home were stored, but I couldn't find the pink shoebox that held my treasured nativity. A great sadness poured over me as I realized I must have left it in the attic of my apartment in Pennsylvania. I called my landlord and she agreed to look for the missing box. Only a few minutes passed before she returned to the phone to report she couldn't find it. I felt confident it was there, but pleading my case got me nowhere. I was devastated.

A few years later, we moved back to my hometown in Pennsylvania. As Christmases came and went, I reflected on the memory of my simple nativity. I wondered if my daughters would have loved it as much as I did, and I visualized them arranging and rearranging it as I had.

Thirty-four years had gone by since I left my apartment when I picked up the morning newspaper one day and saw my landlord's husband's name in the obituaries. His wife had passed away long before him, and now they were both gone. Immediately, panic set in. What if my nativity was still tucked away in the corner of the attic? What if the house was put up for sale, and all the contents were cleared out? I would never see my beloved family heirloom again.

My head was spinning when a name popped into my mind. Of course! The name was that of my landlord's grandson's wife. She was close to my age, and I vaguely knew her in high school. Maybe she could tell me what was to become of the house. Perhaps she could solve the mystery of the missing pink shoebox.

I quickly found her on social media and sent a message spilling out the whole story of the lost nativity. In no time at all, I got a response stating her son was moving into the house, and he was in the process of cleaning out the contents. She was more than happy to have him look through the items he had ready to donate to a charitable organization.

The next day, I received another message from her. She believed her son had located the missing box. The anticipation I felt as I drove to the house was almost overwhelming, and my hand was shaking as I reached for the doorbell. A young man came to the door, and I identified myself. He politely asked me to wait while he went to another room to retrieve what he suspected belonged to me. As he returned, he was clutching a familiar pink shoebox. I nearly gasped at the sight of it, and I profusely thanked him. He told me it was a good thing I hadn't waited any longer; the box was just hours away from becoming a charitable donation.

I loaded my precious pink package into the car and joyfully transported it home where I sat down on my living-room floor and gently opened the lid. There it was, each piece wrapped in tissues just the way my mother had given it to me that January day so long ago. Tears streamed down my face as I unwrapped the delicate figurines, smiling at each one the way one would smile when reunited with an old friend. After the tearful reunion, I mindfully placed my precious nativity in a safe place in my own home, never to be abandoned again.

Every Christmas since that day, my beautiful treasure has been placed in a spot that can easily be reached by my young granddaughter. I derive such joy from watching sheep being herded, angels watching over the Baby Jesus, and the wisemen bearing gifts — from whatever position she chooses.

— Tamara Bell —

The Magic Red Sweater

Christmas is the day that holds all time together.
~Alexander Smith

When I slipped the new crimson-red sweater over Mom's head and gently pulled it down for her, she magically came to life just like Frosty the Snowman. "It's Christmas Eve, Mom," I whispered joyfully.

She slid her frail fingers over the silky-smooth wool and smiled up at me to show her approval. This was the first time I'd seen her genuinely happy in months. My heart melted!

I'd moved in to become Mom's full-time caregiver ten years earlier after a stroke robbed her of the ability to speak or adequately communicate by other means. It also left her with diminished use of her right side.

Although the journey hadn't always been easy, it had most certainly been a wonderful opportunity to give back to a special loved one. Mom was a trooper and tried to make the most of every day. Her never-give-up attitude made my job far less strenuous over the years.

Sadly, symptoms of dementia began to present themselves two years earlier, when she was ninety-five. In addition to her poor communication skills, Mom was nearly deaf, which made it difficult to determine the severity of the dementia in the beginning — or perhaps I just didn't want to see it. Now, unfortunately, it was crystal clear to me, evidenced by her lack of interest in her surroundings, her withdrawal from family and friends, and her bouts of frustration and paranoia.

Because we were never sure how Mom would be feeling from one day to the next, we hadn't hosted our family's traditional Christmas get-together at her house since I moved in. Instead, the kids had been taking over the hosting festivities at their homes.

But this year was different. With the realization that Mom was experiencing fewer and fewer moments of clarity, along with the possibility that she might not be with us for another year, I decided that she deserved the best Christmas possible — one celebrated in her own home surrounded by her loved ones.

When I mentioned this idea to the kids, everyone loved it. We decided to gather on Christmas Eve since it had always been Mom's favorite time of the season.

My son found us a beautiful ten-foot fir at the neighbor's tree farm and helped me string lots of brightly colored lights. I dug out all the ornaments Mom and I had used on our trees throughout the years and hung them one by one until the entire tree was adorned with beautiful, precious keepsakes.

We even moved the living-room furniture around and faced Mom's recliner toward the tree so she could enjoy the warm, festive atmosphere from the best vantage point. This also gave her an unobstructed view of the front door, which would allow her to see each of our guests as they arrived for the big night. Things were looking good!

To my disappointment, however, Mom was not in her best form for the entire week prior to Christmas Eve. Her yelling was nearly constant, and I worried that she wouldn't be able to experience all the joy and love I so wished for her. I also worried that others wouldn't have a good time if they saw Mom either extremely agitated or completely withdrawn.

But, to my overwhelming delight, things changed miraculously just hours before our family began to arrive. I'll never know for certain if it was the magic in the red sweater or some other remarkable intervention, but Mom was instantly transformed into her formerly vivacious self. She truly sparkled with the spirit of the season!

Mom's complexion glowed, as did her bright eyes and rosy cheeks. Even without make-up (which she gave up wearing years ago), she was absolutely beautiful.

After brushing out her thick, wavy white hair into soft curls, I fastened her favorite diamond necklace around her long, slender neck and handed her a mirror. Her smile reflected it all.

"Wow, Granny looks amazing!" "You look so bright and festive, Granny!" "She looks happy, Mom!" "Your smile is so beautiful, Granny!" "She is so alert!" "Granny looks younger than the rest of us!" Sincere, astonished compliments flowed freely as each of our guests walked through the door and headed straight for Mom to give her a warm hug. Each was in turn rewarded with a huge, radiant smile as Mom's frail, soft hands clasped lovingly around theirs.

She not only recognized everyone but was delighted to see them, contrary to the past year when she hadn't acknowledged those around her. All five of my children and their families were able to come, which thrilled me beyond measure. It was a priceless night to say the least. We took lots of photos, including several of our five generations, and Mom's smile was (for the first time in years) genuine and from the heart, rather than forced. She loved every moment, including our visit from Santa, who hadn't made an appearance at our home in years.

After the last of the kids trickled out the door shortly before midnight, Mom and I sat together looking at the tree lights and soaked up the beauty of the silence. I reflected on Christmases past when my father, brother and husband were still with us. It saddened me, but at the same time, I was so thankful that we still had Mom.

Deciding it was time to call it a night, I made my way over to get Mom up from her chair and ready for bed, and noticed unexpected tears trickling down her rosy cheeks. My heart melted as I guided her walker to the bathroom. It had been a big night with lots to take in.

As I tucked her into bed and whispered, "Good night, Mom. Merry Christmas," she was still crying but unable to tell me why. I wondered if she somehow sensed that this beautiful evening of clarity would end soon, and she'd once again slip back into the clutches of the devastating dementia.

But that would be okay. We were blessed with the best Christmas gift ever — having Mom back for the most magical night of the year.

— Connie Kaseweter Pullen —

Room at the Inn

The gift which I am sending you is called a dog,
and is in fact the most precious and
valuable possession of mankind.
~Theodorus Gaza

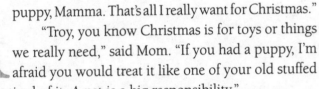

"**A** puppy, Mamma. That's all I really want for Christmas."

"Troy, you know Christmas is for toys or things we really need," said Mom. "If you had a puppy, I'm afraid you would treat it like one of your old stuffed animals and get tired of it. A pet is a big responsibility."

My shoulders sagged. I'd been asking for a puppy for more than a year and, even though I was only seven, I knew I would never treat it as a toy.

Christmas Eve arrived. My parents were of modest means, but always managed to make the holidays happy. I knew they wouldn't get me a puppy, but I would act thankful for whatever gift I did receive this year. And I had faith that some day, somehow, I would get that puppy.

The family was finishing dinner when I heard something. Sometimes, raccoons rustled around our porch, especially on a cold night. I excused myself from the table and opened the front door. I was shocked by what I saw — a small, very round, fluffy dog. It looked up at me and whined.

My mother soon stood next to me. We both looked at the little dog, then at each other. Mother opened the storm door and the dog waddled in without hesitation.

"Okay," Mom said. "It's too nasty for an animal to be out in this weather. We'll give it a place to sleep until your father can find out who it belongs to... before we open our presents tomorrow."

"Mom, he has no tags. Maybe someone just left him 'cause they couldn't feed him. Maybe he has no home."

My mother sighed. "He is a she, Troy, and she looks well fed, as stuffed as your teddy bear, I'd say. She's certainly no puppy."

"Can I play—"

"She could be sick or have something wrong with her. You need to get to bed, young man. Tomorrow is a big day, you know."

My father agreed we could put our guest up for the night. I asked to stay up long enough to help Mom find a wicker basket in the basement and a woolen blanket to place inside it.

Mom lifted the pooch into the makeshift bed and set a pan of water nearby. She also put newspaper on the kitchen's linoleum floor in hopes the animal would understand its purpose. I peeked at the visitor one last time as Mom closed the kitchen door.

"She'll be fine. Just remember that we must find out who she belongs to. Now get up to bed and dream of sugarplums."

Mother kissed my cheek as did my father as I trundled up the stairs. "But she has no tags," I murmured as my parents remained downstairs as always on Christmas Eve. I had difficulty getting to sleep. If the excitement of Christmas Day wasn't enough, I kept thinking of the round fluffy dog shut in our kitchen. She hadn't barked or whined once since she came inside, and she seemed happy to be given a warm bed. Maybe no one wanted her anymore. Maybe...

Finally, I was asleep, dreaming of the lost dog in its basket rather than sugarplums or presents under the tree.

***

"Troy, wake up. It's Christmas." My mother gave me a little shake. "Get dressed and come down."

It took me a moment to remember our overnight guest. Fear struck me. What if my parents had taken the dog away before waking me? I pulled a robe over my pajamas, stepped into my slippers (a gift from the previous Christmas), and padded down the stairs.

My parents were not next to the Christmas tree in the living room as I would have expected, but rather by the kitchen door. They waved me toward them.

"What's wrong?" I asked, concern in my young voice.

My father led me into the room. I cautiously looked at the basket. My eyes grew large as I tried to comprehend what I was seeing. Next to the little dog were two squirming smaller creatures no bigger than my hand.

Newborn puppies, their eyes tightly shut, nestled against their mother's tummy.

"It seems a miracle of sorts happened overnight," said my mom. "Maybe this little mother-to-be was sent to us for safety."

Like Baby Jesus, I thought.

The subject of what to do with the little mother and her babies did not come up during the day. Presents under the tree were opened later, almost as an afterthought.

No one ever claimed her, so she and her pups became part of our family. The mother would be named Love for bringing more of it into the Seate household. I named the pups — Faith for the female and Hope for the male because I'd had faith that my wish would somehow come true.

And so it came to pass that on this night of miracles, a miracle occurred. Not only did my dream come true, but a new family of three had found a home full of warmth and love.

— Troy Seate —

The Visit

Just a thin veil between this world and that world
of beauty and love. Just a thin veil that hides
the view of our Spirit loved ones above.
~Gertrude Tooley Buckingham

n Christmas Eve, Dad struggled a bit while holding the front door open to welcome us, his smile half-hearted after months spent mourning Mom. With each hug from me, my husband, and the kids, his melancholy seemed to lift. We followed him into the familiar living room, and it immediately struck me that the traditional decorations Mom always loved to display were nowhere in sight. My throat tightened.

My two sisters and their families were already sharing the latest family gossip over Dad's blaring television set. After Dad got himself settled back into his well-worn easy chair, everyone milled around sipping the rich eggnog Trish served. The aroma of Kelli's cookies baking made my stomach rumble, and I hurried to get my version of the Christmas chili simmering on the stove the way Mom always had. We, each in our own way, rallied to reproduce Mom's epic Christmas cheer, but trying to recreate our past merriment without Mom was exhausting. We all ended up going to bed early.

I'd been sound asleep for most of the night when I looked up to see my mother, as real as though she were alive, hovering above me. I was filled with love, peace, and joy.

Mom wore a flowing robe with colors streaming away from her center.

White clouds hovered around her, filled with what seemed to be a galaxy of beings. Floating among them, I basked in their affection. Harmony and wellbeing enveloped me. I was no longer aware of my physical body. I wanted it to last forever.

Still tingling with awe, I was confused when I saw a regular ceiling above me. I felt the firm mattress beneath me and realized I was lying in bed, dawn's light edging through the bedroom window. Beside me, my husband slept, unaware of my incredible epiphany.

I closed my eyes, yearning, almost aching to continue the encounter. Instead, I lay awake, savoring my new serenity, then watching through the gap in the curtains as yellow and pink rays strengthened into daylight.

As soon as I heard my sisters awaken, I hurried to tell them about Mom's visit. Trying to use mere words to describe something incomprehensible, I finally stopped talking and took a breath.

Kelli, my younger sister, said, "Well, here's what happened to *me* last night. I dreamed I was back in our old church, watching the memorial lamp flicker. Didn't the pastor tell us it would stay lit forever to honor our departed loved ones?"

"Yes, I remember him saying that," I said.

"Well, in my dream I was so worried the light would go out, I started to cry. I kept sobbing, almost getting hysterical, shouting over and over in the empty church, 'Who will keep the lamp lit? How can it work?' Standing there so upset, I heard Mom's voice. She said, 'You will be okay. All will be well. Everything will go on.' I remember I wanted more. I wanted to see her, to hug her. Instead, there was a special silence, like she knew I would believe her. And I did."

Glancing from Trish to me, Kelli added, "Then all of a sudden, I realized I was in the bed facing Gary, and I knew Mom was standing behind me. I felt her rubbing my shoulder, like she always did. And... that's all I remember."

We stared at each other for a second, until Trish, my older sister, took a deep breath and released it with a light "whew." Then she said, "Oh, my gosh. Wait 'til you hear!"

"*Last night, a pressure, like when someone sits on the bed, woke me up. It felt so normal, I wasn't worried or scared. And there was Mom, sitting on the side of my bed with a small suitcase on the floor beside her. She was happy, very serene, and said, 'Dear, dear Trish, always my little worrywart. There is nothing at all for you to worry about… but I have to go now.' She smiled, as if she knew I would understand. And I did.*"

I found it hard to breathe, and felt goose bumps up and down my arms. I started to say, "So, we all…"

"Yeah, I wasn't accepting Mom's death. Seeing her last night, well, I'm okay now. I get it," Trish said.

Kelli said, "I've been missing her so much, wondering how I can get through life without her. It seemed so unfair. Now I know for sure she's always going to be with me."

Each time I recall Mom's visit, decades ago, I marvel at the gift of faith I received that Christmas Eve. Mom's visit woke me up spiritually. Where before I doubted, I now believe. Where before I was drifting, I now have a life filled with purpose and meaning.

All I have to do is close my eyes to remember that night. And, eyes wide open, I am filled with gratitude for life on this earth and for Mom's visit, which showed me the glimpse of eternity that changed my life forever.

— Wendy Keppley —

Chapter 2

Tales of the Tree

The Christmas-Tree Kitty

Taking down the Christmas tree makes it feel official:
time to get back to joyless and cynical.
~Greg Fitzsimmons

My five-year-old son came running frantically into the kitchen. "I can't find Zorro, Mommy!" I dropped my dishtowel to help in the search. Zorro was an indoor-only cat and did not know how to fend for himself.

Together, my son and I made a thorough search of the house, but still no Zorro. As my son grew closer to tears, and I edged toward his earlier panic mode, I remembered that we had decorated for Christmas the night before.

"Did you check under the tree?" I asked my son. He looked up at me with wide eyes, and then dashed into the living room to check as I followed him. Sure enough, we found a very sleek and elegant black-and-white gift underneath the tree. His green eyes blinked up at us with a look that could only be described as pure rapture. My son petted him happily, and we were relieved that the crisis was over — for the moment!

Despite all the colorful Christmas toys and stocking stuffers that our kitties received each year, Christmas for Zorro wasn't about the wrappings and tinsel, expensive presents and fancy feasts. It was about the artificial tree.

That year, I put away the tree a few weeks after Christmas, and I learned just how important our little tree had become to Zorro. After my son and I removed all the ornaments, we started to unfasten the branches. A restless Zorro seemed to guess what we were doing, and he lay down on the tree skirt, latching onto it with his claws and giving me the most pitiful look I had ever seen. I could almost hear his desperate pleas in my mind as he begged me silently with his eyes not to take away his "Christmas present." I wondered how it must seem to him, to think he had been blessed with such a wonderful toy, only to have it snatched away just a few weeks later.

We were moving that year, though, and I had no choice but to take down the tree. When it came time to put away the last fixture — the soft tree skirt — I attempted to distract the rather morose cat with one of his favorite toys. It didn't work. He simply lay there and stared at me. Then I tried calling him from the kitchen while shaking his favorite treat bag — a trick that always worked. It seemed he wasn't hungry for treats that day, as he held his ground fiercely.

Finally, I was forced to remove him physically from the red fabric — a dance of wills that left me struggling for breath and Zorro's claws eventually extracted from his beloved tree skirt. Quickly hiding it in the box where it would be stored, I dusted off my hands, relieved that I had accomplished my goal — for this year, at least. My son had enjoyed the intense battle between Mom and cat immensely, giggling the entire time. But we did not have the last laugh over the next few weeks, as we were forced to endure hateful glares and an extremely depressed cat who spent the majority of his time lying in the exact same spot where the tree had been.

Eventually, he seemed to forget about this major catastrophe — or at least chose to forgive us — as he gradually began to slip back into "normal cat" mode and found other interests, like pestering us for more attention or bossing the other cats around. When we moved not long afterward, his attention became focused on the huge changes in our daily schedule. He also no longer had a "tree spot" to lie on at our new place.

Eventually, Christmas rolled around again, and the first part of decorating for the holidays was, of course, the grand entrance of the tree box from the storage shed. Despite the fact that it had been many months and there had been many changes since he'd last seen this box, Zorro's ears perked up, and his eyes grew huge as he watched me carry the box into the living room. He sat down nearby to watch the proceedings while my son and I put the tree together and decorated it.

When we took a break, Zorro snuck over in his catlike way and proceeded to examine the tree. The ornaments were of little interest to him, strangely enough. It was the tree that had always intrigued him. Zorro chose a spot underneath the tree and claimed it for his own, lying there while we finished decorating, his face a picture of pure happiness. My son picked him up eagerly from underneath the tree as I added the final decoration — the much-loved and well-worn tree skirt. When the now-six-year-old placed him back down on the ground, Zorro ran over to the skirt and promptly curled into a ball, laying his little head on the fabric and looking like he had found a long-lost family member.

From that moment on, he became a permanent Christmas decoration. Whenever I was looking for him, my son would automatically run to the tree to find the soft, little Christmas present that was always underneath it.

When Christmas passed as swiftly as it always did, the time soon arrived to put away the tree. But when I dragged out the tree box to begin the proceedings, Zorro became almost desperate in his attempts to latch onto the tree and tree skirt. He looked so miserable and pitiful that I did not have the heart to take down the tree, and we decided to put the box back in storage and wait for a while.

That year, we left the tree up until Easter. Zorro didn't care which holiday it was, though. To him, Christmas was every day that the tree was there. To this sensitive, little cat, Christmas was about enjoying the things we have with a fierce intensity that sometimes defies all logic. He reminded us to take a step back and quit rushing through the holidays, something we all tend to do in our hectic lives. It didn't really matter if the tree wasn't put away by New Year's. In fact, it brought so much happiness to one caring heart that having a Christmas tree at Easter made perfect sense to us.

—H.M. Forrest—

Fit to Be Tied

A lovely thing about Christmas is that it's compulsory,
like a thunderstorm, and we all go through it together.
~Garrison Keillor

Whoever said that second marriages are twice as hard as first marriages hit the nail on the head. When I met my second husband, I felt my dreams had been answered. We both agreed we wouldn't introduce our children to each other until we knew our relationship was serious. When we got married, I had no illusions that blending two families would be easy.

We were married in May. When Christmas rolled around, we wondered how we would fare with five kids between us, ranging in age from six to fifteen. Some days were pretty hairy, but we were managing.

Shortly after Thanksgiving, we made the decision to go on a search for the perfect Christmas tree. We hit a couple of tree lots, but nothing looked good. Finally, we found a lot where the trees were reasonable and well-shaped. We had four of the five children with us. They were full of Christmas spirit and starting to get on my husband's nerves. To me, they were just being kids.

We all jumped out of the car on this cold day, and the children immediately started wandering all over the lot. My husband, getting grumpier by the minute, ordered everyone back to the car.

It was evident his patience was wearing thin. I gathered the children, and we all sat in the car while he paid for the tree we had selected. We waited patiently while the man from the tree lot placed the tree on top of the car. The lot man gave my husband some rope to tie it on. Being a dutiful wife, I followed my husband's directions as he handed me an end of the rope and advised me to hand it back at the demanded time. This process was repeated several times.

By now, he was on the verge of going ballistic, so I dared not say a word as he completed securing the tree to the roof of the car. After checking it by tugging on the rope several times, he was sure it wouldn't blow off or move until we got it home, just a few short blocks away.

Then, he attempted to open the driver's side door. He pushed the button on the door handle and pulled on it. He had tied the door shut with the rope!

The children looked terrified. I, on the other hand, started to smile. The smile turned into an audible giggle, and the giggle sparked relief and amusement on the part of the children. My husband, realizing what he had done and feeling more than a little foolish, started to relax. But the calmness turned to embarrassment as the lot attendant stood watching while he untied the tree and re-secured it, tying it to the bumpers this time.

By the time we got home, we were all laughing so hard that tears ran down our cheeks. My husband, still not happy but not enraged, laughed along with us until we got home and took the tree off the car.

That happened more than twenty-five years ago, but we still retell the story every Christmas. And every Christmas my husband begs us not to retell it! But it is a fond memory of a particularly difficult time for all of us, which we recall with affection and love.

— Ann Williamson —

Christmas Blitz

*Dogs are great. Bad dogs, if you can really call them
that, are perhaps the greatest of them all.*
~John Grogan

When Blitz, a German Shepherd puppy, came home for his first Christmas, it was fun and chaos at the Reiss household. My daughter's tree was decorated with the loveliest ornaments and lights, handed down from generation to generation.

Packages were carefully wrapped and piled neatly under the tree. Blitz had chewy toys and gifts of his own to open, but when the rambunctious puppy spotted the bows and wrappings, he dove into them without warning, like any young pup would. He crashed into the colorful boxes headfirst, legs spread out, like a sled speeding down a slippery slope. He chewed the paper, the boxes, and all the satin ribbons. In five minutes, this beautiful holiday scene was turned upside down and trashed.

Yes, it was Blitz's first Christmas, and he loved every minute of it.

The second Christmas was much like the first, only this time the tree had fewer ornaments on it, and the gifts were stacked on the dining-room table for safekeeping. A little older now, Blitz must have liked the smell of the real tree because he took a whiz on it. It wasn't "O Holy Night" but "O Smelly Night." The tree was sprayed with a pine scent, but that wasn't enough, so it was picked up and carried out to the front porch. It was viewed from inside the large living-room

Tales of the Tree |

picture window where we couldn't smell it.

The third year, after Blitz knocked over the tree, still in its stand and not yet decorated, we set it up on the front porch. It was not the cozy scene one would see in a Christmas card, but it was reality. The living room looked as sterile as a hospital, with no signs of Christmas anywhere. Blitz had stolen Christmas from my family.

This year, the decision to put up a Christmas tree was the main topic of conversation in my daughter's household. Blitz was now 130 pounds and had a mind of his own. Obedience school had proved unsuccessful, and "Blitz Rules" was the new family motto.

One afternoon, while my daughter Vicki was at work, her two adult boys decided to surprise her by putting up a four-foot tree to try and save Christmas. They wedged the tree tightly into a corner of the living room and placed a star on top. It held no dangling ornaments or lights to attract Blitz, just a blinking star.

When Blitz entered the room, he stared briefly at the tree and walked by. Maybe he thought it was dull and not worthy of attack. We looked at it as a Christmas miracle. Taking it one step at a time, packages were again assembled on the dining-room table, while cards and garlands hung from the fireplace.

Maybe Blitz finally got the message and realized that Santa would not bring him any treats if he was naughty again this year. Whatever the reason, we won't question it. Our family is just happy that Bobby and Brian saved Christmas and brought back our tree, even though it was not decorated. Well, there's always next year, depending on Blitz.

— Irene Maran —

13

The Buffy Tree

Change always comes bearing gifts.
~Price Pritchett

When I was a contrary, hardheaded teenager, my mother often said, "I hope one day you have a daughter just like you!"

"One day" came twice. I was assigned not one, but two daughters just like me. Their teen years were hard, for them and for me. Every decision was a potential minefield.

I decided to avoid any decisions at Christmastime. There were too many battles. Instead, we would have "traditions."

My traditional menu for Christmas brunch was set in stone: grits and eggs, homemade biscuits, country ham and onion sausage. The Christmas mantel had to be decorated with pineapples and white candles, cedar boughs and Nandina berries. Every Christmas Eve and Christmas morning, we had Christmas punch: equal parts apple and cranberry juice, perked through spiced apple and pineapple rings with cinnamon sticks.

The traditional tree? Cedar, of course. My grandmother always had a cedar, and the sharp smell of cedar was as much a part of my childhood holidays as hanging a stocking on the mantel, swirling sparklers on the porch, or watching *Miracle on 34th Street* on TV. Christmas wouldn't be Christmas without a cedar.

Would it?

The year we moved our family of teenagers to a new home, Buffy rode with me to Buck Cockrell's tree farm to pick out a tree. At the time she was fourteen — every bit as contrary and hardheaded as her grandmother wished her to be.

I asked to see a tall cedar that would scrape the ceiling of our "new" living room. Buffy asked to see anything but a cedar.

"Cedar stinks, the needles stick, and the ooze is icky," she said, folding her arms across her chest.

"My grandmother always had a cedar tree, and cedar smells like Christmas to me. It's a tradition!" I said, folding my arms across my chest. The wind blew cold through the firs and the cedars. I stood my ground; she stood hers.

If ever World War III erupts, my vote for mediator goes to "Mr. Buck." He ever so gently arranged a mother-daughter truce. If we wanted, he said, we could decide to have both a cedar and a fir.

It was an uneasy ceasefire, but the U.N. peacekeeping forces were otherwise engaged.

The trees arrived later in the day, and I insisted that my cedar be set in the living room. I relegated Buffy's fir to the den by the back door, where the cold winds blow.

I further insisted (according to tradition) that the cedar be decorated with ornaments from previous years: the silver drum from a high school band party... the carolers I decoupaged when Henry was in law school and we had no money... the yarn-haired, toilet-paper-roll angel that Walter Munson made in kindergarten....

As for Buffy's fir? She'd have to make do.

At first, it irritated me that she did so well. She salvaged some lights from the magnolia tree in the front yard of our old house. She bought boxes of candy canes, hung them on the tree, and voila!

Okay, the tree was sweet and sort of pretty. I could get used to it, but as for liking it? No way. I wondered: how could a child of mine not want a cedar? It's tradition.

Just because I'm contrary and hardheaded doesn't mean I can't learn. One afternoon before Christmas I was baking in the kitchen when several of Buffy's friends dropped by for a visit. When they left an hour or so later, I overheard Buffy speak to them at the back door: "Hey, take a candy cane for everybody at your house."

They were hesitant about un-decorating her tree, "Oh, no..."

"Oh, yeah," she insisted. "Take a little Christmas home with you."

They demurred but at last she grabbed a fistful of candy canes and pressed them into the hands of her friends. "Here, and tell everybody we said Merry Christmas!"

Take a little Christmas home with you.

Tell everybody we said Merry Christmas.

As I heard those words, shame flushed my face. Maybe Buffy isn't like me, after all. For sure, her tree was not like mine. My cedar was about the past; her fir was about the present. Buffy's vision of Christmas was not limited by tradition, but was focused on the present and on the spirit of the season — on the spirit of giving.

And what a joy it is.

Every year since, we've had a Buffy tree by the back door, decorated with candy canes. Some years we have a star on top, some years not. It may be decorated with Life Savers, candy canes, or old-fashioned peppermint. Whatever I can find, it doesn't matter.

What does matter is that our guests and family — over the holidays — take a little Christmas home with them,

With her generosity of spirit, my daughter taught her hardheaded mother to see Christmas in a new and lovely light.

— Sue Summer —

14

Meowy Christmas

Tree decorating with cats. O Christmas tree,
O Christmas tree, your ornaments are history!
~Courtney VanSickle

My sister-in-law Carol said she'd already picked out a kitten for me. I agreed to go with her… just to look. I made no promise to take one home. After all, only two months had passed since I lost my beloved calico, Mandi. Maybe I needed to be pet-free for a while.

When we got there, three of the four tuxedo kittens remained in the litter. Carol picked up one and handed it to me. The beautiful face and white fur on the right side of her nose reminded me of a harlequin mask. How could I resist? Then another kitten, with a more symmetrical white face, jumped into my lap and purred.

Driving home in my British sports car proved difficult with two rambunctious kittens. One clung to my left arm and shoulder, watching the scenery zip by from the window. The other paced back and forth from my lap to the passenger's seat, hindering my ability to shift gears. Both mewed in a loud duet of protest. Of course, I hadn't brought a cage. I had not planned to take home a kitten — or two.

The harlequin-masked female earned the name Squeakette with her tiny voice squeaking about each new discovery as she explored her new home. The male, lacking only a black tie in his formal attire, took the name Sebastian for my favorite composer, Johann Sebastian Bach.

A few weeks later, a neighbor helped me carry down my six-foot artificial Christmas tree from the attic. I thanked him with a batch of cookies, and then set up the tree in the corner of my living room.

Sebastian and Squeakette knocked it down before I opened the box of decorations. Propping it up, I straightened the few bent wire branches back into place. As I checked for any other damage, a flash of black-and-white fur zipped past me. Up they went, branch by branch. The tree danced a jig as the two kittens climbed it in tag-team fashion. Sebastian made it to the top a moment ahead of Squeakette.

He lunged at me from the top, paws stretched out like wings. I didn't know cats could fly. Landing on my shoulder, his hind claws dug into my upper chest. The gashes bled only for a moment and didn't require stitches.

The tree teetered from side to side, with the little female clutching the top branch. It came to rest upright, and Squeakette allowed me to pluck her trembling body from her perch. A few moments of cuddling calmed her fears.

Among the decorations, I found the eighteen-inch synthetic tree I had planned to take to my office. Aha. On the opposite side of the living room, an empty place next to the wingback chair looked perfect. I dangled assorted cat toys from the branches and topped it with a stuffed yellow mouse.

I played their game of "we knock it down — you pick it up" enough times to amuse them and divert their attention from the large tree. A sprinkle of catnip on the branches helped, too. How many kittens could boast about having their very own Christmas tree?

I made an appointment that Saturday to have their Christmas picture taken at the local animal shelter. As a fundraising activity, they brought Santa in to pose with families and their pets.

Wrestling Squeakette into the cage for transport seemed easy compared to the fight Sebastian gave me. The cardboard box, with inch-and-a-half holes on each end, served as a temporary cage. It now bore slashes from Sebastian's claws. So did my hands. Note to self: Next time, wear gardening gloves.

After doctoring my wounds and changing my clothes, we headed for the photo shoot. Squeakette emitted a few protests, crouched in the back of her cage and scowling at me. Sebastian caterwauled from his box, digging at the hole with his paw. Every traffic-light stop gave me a chance to check on him. Yowling, then digging. Yowling, then digging. Each time, he pressed his nose in the hole. By the time I drove into the facility parking lot, he had made the hole large enough to get his little white face through it.

I carried my two kittens into the building and set their carriers on the table to sign in for our appointment. Laughter exploded from the small crowd nearby. I looked down to see Sebastian's head protruding from the hole like a mounted moosehead.

With a volunteer's help, we eased Sebastian's head back through the hole. The ordeal left him in a more cooperative mood. He sat still while I put the red-and-green plaid hair scrunchy over his head and around his neck. He even let me fluff it out.

Squeakette issued a mild complaint when I slipped a red-mesh scrunchy over her head. With their colorful collars in place, I realized this would be the closest I'd ever come to dressing them in festive costumes.

Santa waited in his makeshift sled. He appeared almost agreeable as I handed him Squeakette. She gazed up at him with wary eyes and then, surprisingly, nestled in the crook of his arm and purred.

I took my assigned seat in front of Santa and hugged Sebastian against my chest.

The photographer held up a stuffed toy. "Look this way, please."
Click.
"Thank you very much."

Santa remained unscathed, at least from my kittens. Later, I wondered how he fared the rest of the day when I caught a glimpse of the Great Dane next in line.

I ordered a five-by-seven for framing and a packet of photo Christmas cards to send to friends and family.

With the kittens back in their respective carriers, Sebastian shied away from the head-trapping hole. Smart kitty. On the way home, he inched his way close enough to peek out at me and uttered a soft mew. Note to self: Get him a cage of his own.

The pictures arrived in the mail a few days later. I grinned with pride when I looked them over. My kittens had posed like professional models. They faced the same direction, holding their little heads up as though sporting angelic halos. No smiles, but neither showed any fear.

Each day, Sebastian and Squeakette gazed with wonder at the tree in my living room, decorated with blinking lights and shiny ornaments. Then they trotted to their own tree and batted the toys on the branches.

Sipping a cup of hot cocoa, snuggled in my favorite chair, I took in my surroundings. The framed picture of Santa with my kittens and me, Sebastian and Squeakette's carefree mews as they played with their tree, and classical Christmas hymns flowing from the radio reminded me of the simple joys intended for this season.

Mandi the calico would have approved. True contentment comes in moments like these.

— Janet Ramsdell Rockey —

A Christmas Surprise

Be an angel to someone else whenever you can,
as a way of thanking God for the help
your angel has given you.
~Eileen Elias Freeman,
The Angels' Little Instruction Book

Due to my Conservative Jewish background, I did not believe in angels. That is, not until Christmas Eve of 1979, when an angel brought unexpected joy to my home.

As often happens in divorce, my five- and eleven-year-old daughters not only lost the security of an intact family, but they tearfully left behind neighborhood friends, a familiar school and the comfortable amenities of a large house — all replaced by a cramped two-bedroom apartment in a poorer part of town.

I arranged to take my vacation during their winter school holiday, and we made plans for the week: cookie-baking, movie matinees, arts and crafts, games, a pizza night, and evening car rides to view neighborhood holiday lights and lawn displays. The anticipation was working its magic, and my daughters' spirits seemed to brighten.

The week before the school break, however, devastating news of multiple family disasters came in faster than we could process the pain, clouding our vacation plans. By Christmas Eve, gloom enveloped our apartment. An afternoon movie did little to improve our mood.

Upon returning to our apartment, we were astonished to see a majestic six-foot Christmas tree, aglitter with metallic icicle strands, propped against our front door. In mute wonder, we looked back and forth, from the tree to each other, and around the deserted street. Excitement built, and the girls begged to keep the orphaned tree.

"Maybe it's for us," insisted the older.

"Yeah," echoed the younger. "I bet an angel brought it to us!"

I laughed out loud at the idea of an angel bringing a Christmas tree to a Jewish family. Nevertheless, I was caught up in their newfound elation, and I pronounced the tree "ours."

We dragged it inside and headed out to the only supermarket in our small town open that late on Christmas Eve. With holiday merchandise marked down to half price, I gave a nod of approval to a tree stand, two boxes of multicolored balls, a package of six Santa figurines, a 100-foot string of miniature lights, and one lone paper angel.

Back home, we maneuvered "our" tree into a place of honor in our tiny living room. The girls snipped and glued and painted paper decorations. With an exhilaration that had been absent for months, we strung the lights, placed the paper angel on top and festooned the tree with store-bought and homemade ornaments.

Finally, with a girl snuggled in each of my arms, we sat in semi-darkness, mesmerized by twinkling Christmas tree lights. Smiles and contented sighs proclaimed the end of our long emotional crises; there was joy in our new home. I sat in thankful amazement that a Christmas tree had the power to uplift Jewish spirits.

My five-year-old whispered softly, "Do you really think an angel brought us this tree?"

At that moment, I did not know the tree and its deliverer would forever remain a mystery. All I could do was answer honestly from my heart. "Yes," I whispered, holding them closer, "I'm sure of it."

Our vacation was a resounding success — fun, laughter and the nightly wonder of our flickering tree. By New Year's Day, our spirits were healed, and we were ready to face the challenges ahead, strengthened by the bond of our shared belief in angels and magical Christmas trees.

That winter vacation became an annual family tradition, complete with a "Jewish Angel Tree" in remembrance of our heaven-sent gift. For seventeen more years, we held our breath and felt the familiar tingles up our arms when the original paper angel was placed atop each tree.

Now my adult daughters have their own homes. There are no more luxurious vacation days spent together; there are no more Jewish Angel Trees. But each Christmas Eve, they phone to sigh and reminisce about our angel, and the special childhood memories intertwined in the branches of a six-foot tree.

— Lynne Foosaner —

16

Gifts Year-Round

Yes, God will give you much so that you can give away much,
And when we take your gifts to those who need them they will
break out into thanksgiving and praise to God for your help.
~2 Corinthians 9:11

Last year, I didn't have the heart to disassemble our artificial tree covered in miniature white lights. Each time we passed the living room, we'd pause to gaze at the illuminated corner, a poignant reminder that Christmas is all about giving.

Then, something significant happened each time we looked at that tree.

It reminded us to give a gift to someone each and every day of the year.

One afternoon, our six-year-old neighbor, Hayden popped in for a visit. As he entered the living room, his eyes instantly spotted the lit tree.

"Wow! A Christmas tree! Why do you have a Christmas tree up in the middle of summer? Christmas has been over for a long time now!"

"We like to celebrate Christmas all year long!" I smiled. "Just this morning, there were a bunch of presents under that tree."

"Where are they now?" he asked, curiously. "Oh, that's one of the rules about celebrating Christmas all year long! Since it's a giving tree, the presents aren't allowed to stay here for more than a day. It's our job to see that they are given as soon as we hear of a need! That's what Jesus would want, right?"

Hayden tilted his head to one side and gazed up at me in wonder. "What kind of presents are they?"

"Well, let me think; one day, we packed up some clothes we no longer needed, and sent them to hurricane victims, and to people in other parts of the world, who aren't as lucky as we are. Of course, we always place them under the tree the night before and pray for the people who will be receiving our special surprises. Another time, I crocheted some soft baby blankets. We wrapped them up in pretty paper, and gave them to a place downtown that could use them. Then there was the day we wrapped up all of our old *Guideposts* and *Angels on Earth* magazines, and took them to an assisted living facility. There are just all kinds of people out there who could use a pleasant surprise, not only at Christmas time, but all year-round!"

The room suddenly grew so quiet; I had to look in Hayden's direction to make sure he was really still sitting next to me.

Suddenly Hayden's face glowed as brightly as the Christmas lights on the tree. "If I go home and color a bunch of pictures, would you wrap them up and give them away as presents?"

I reached out and gathered Hayden softly in my arms. "I think that's a sensational idea! I know that will make Jesus happy too!"

"And maybe we can tell others to keep their trees up all year-round, so they remember that every day is Christmas, right?"

"I'll be sure and let them know." I whispered around the sudden lump in my throat. "Merry Christmas, Hayden!"

"Father, may we keep the spirit of Christmas in our hearts year-round. Help us to teach our children that the reason we give, is because you asked us to. Thank you for sending us the greatest gift the world has ever known, Your Son. Amen."

— Mary Smith —

17

The Elves' Christmas Tree

Christmas waves a magic wand over this world,
and behold, everything is softer and more beautiful.
~Norman Vincent Peale

I n our family, the last five nights before Christmas Eve were designated as "Chimney Inspection Nights." This meant that during our single digit years, my little brother Will and I had to be in bed very early and asleep so that Santa's elves could come and check that our chimney and the Christmas tree were ready for his visit. If we passed muster the elves would leave candy canes on our bedroom doorknobs. But I think they had an arrangement with my parents, because Santa's helpers always seemed to wait until the night before Christmas Eve to visit. When I was seven, I was glad they did.

That year my public school, in Lorne Park, Ontario, sold Christmas trees as a fundraiser. Families pre-ordered, and a truckload of evergreens arrived just before Christmas break. The eldest child was given the task of picking out his or her family's tree and tagging it for pick-up. I had been carefully instructed by Mum to select a bushy, well-shaped tree with a straight trunk and at least one good side. The responsibility weighed heavily on my shoulders. The trees were Scotch pines and came in a wide variety of shapes and sizes. I examined and rejected many, but finally found and tagged one that met Mum's exacting criteria.

At dinner that night I proudly proclaimed the merits of my tree and after eating, Dad and I returned to the school to pick it up. It wasn't there. My tree had disappeared!

Dad went to ask Principal Stevens for help while I kept looking. I hadn't gone far before my heart dropped into my boots. There, lying in the muddy slush was my tag. Someone else must have taken our tree. We didn't have a tree, and with Christmas only two days away, that night was the last night that the elves could visit! What would we do? Would Santa still come? This was serious!

Apologizing profusely, Mr. Stevens led us to a lone pine standing in the corner of the yard. Even Charlie Brown would have been embarrassed to bring it home.

But with Mum waiting, ready to decorate, Dad wasn't about to return home empty-handed. On the way he suggested we not say anything about the mix-up to Mum. We had a tree and that was all that mattered.

At the house we set the tree in the stand Mum had waiting in the corner of the living room and stepped back to admire our handiwork. I heard Mum gasp. Our tree leaned drunkenly to one side, listing like a sinking ship. Its branches stuck out at some very odd angles and there were bare spots everywhere! Dad tried turning the tree this way and that, to improve the profile, but it was no use.

At first Mum was speechless and then she started to question my choice. I was devastated. I had failed her. Dad intervened and hastily explained the problem. Noting my distress, the look on Mum's face softened and hot chocolate was prescribed to ease our pain. Will and I put on our pyjamas and returned to the kitchen where, while sipping our cocoa, Dad and I told Mum the tale of our missing tree. Will and I had regular hot chocolate, but I think Mum and Dad had something a little stronger. It was now past our bedtime and of course a Chimney Inspection Night, so Mum suggested that we postpone decorating the tree until the morning. As Will and I headed off to bed, I took one last look at the tree. I can remember thinking that it looked so bad the Elves might not approve it and Santa might not leave any presents.

In the morning I found no candy cane on my bedroom doorknob.

We had failed inspection! I was heartbroken. As I moped down the hallway to the kitchen I passed the living room and looked in to scowl at the cause of my distress.

There, standing straight and tall, with candy canes hanging from many of the branches was the most perfect Christmas tree I had ever seen. Something magical had occurred!

I spotted Mum curled up asleep in the big easy chair and I ran to shake her awake and show her what had happened. Rubbing the sleep from her eyes, she smiled, hugged me hard and agreed with my exclamation that it was the best Christmas tree ever.

When I asked her what might have happened, she suggested that maybe the Elves had heard about the mix-up and decided to help out. That was good enough for me!

Santa did come and Christmas that year was wonderful as usual. I never questioned how the Elves managed to fix our tree that year, but once I was old enough to know, Dad told me the whole story.

Mum had stayed up most of that night fixing my tree. Using hammer, nails and stove wire, she and Dad managed to force it to stand up straight. Next she employed his brace and bit to bore strategically placed holes in the trunk, and then, using branches from the back of the tree Mum filled in the bare spots, holding her transplanted boughs in place with carpenter's glue and green twine. Her finishing touch was pruning the tree to shape with scissors. I guess you could say that Mum created a "real" artificial Christmas tree.

A tradition was started. Ever since that special Christmas, children in the Forrest family have risen to find candy canes hanging on their tree on the morning after Chimney Inspection Night.

This year, three generations of our family will gather to celebrate and reminisce at Christmas and the story of what is now "The Elves' Christmas Tree" will be recounted. It has been embellished a little, but fortunately Mum is still with us to authenticate and describe the details. And when the children's version of the tale is told, they will listen while nibbling on candy canes, and of course marvel at the magic of the Elves' visit.

But I will always hear in my heart, the real story and remember it fondly as a loving and creative mother's way, of preserving the magic of Christmas for her sons.

—John Forrest—

The Christmas Cat

The perfect Christmas tree?
All Christmas trees are perfect!
~Charles N. Barnard

I sat on the couch admiring our Christmas tree. My wife and I had searched several tree lots before finding the perfect blue spruce. It was about six-and-a-half-feet tall, full and plump. The tree smelled of fresh pine.

Though the tree smelled great and looked beautiful, it was a royal pain to set it up. My wife and I struggled to get the stubborn tree into its metal holder and to make it stand upright. Once it was standing, we pulled out our plastic crates full of ornaments and twinkle lights. We went to work making certain to place each ornament in its proper place on the tree. We hummed along to Christmas songs by Bing Crosby, Burl Ives and many others. We even laughed as we heard about Grandma getting run over by a reindeer.

We were young and very much in love. It was our second year of marriage and we had not yet started our family. All we had was each other and a black and white cat name Friday. This would be Friday's second Christmas with us. We had discovered the previous year that Friday really loved Christmastime. She loved batting Christmas bulbs off the bottom of the tree. She loved tugging on the stockings that hung from our mantle and she enjoyed sniffing and nibbling on pine needles. Cats are very indifferent creatures and Friday was no exception. But when it came to Christmastime, our cat was a downright festive feline!

Because of her propensity to bat at Christmas bulbs, my wife and I made sure to keep the more valuable ornaments higher on the tree as we decorated it. After we finished trimming the tree and decorating the mantle, my wife called the cat down to inspect our work. Both of us figured that Friday would be thrilled to see the condo all decked out for the holidays.

After an extensive search, we discovered the cat was upstairs napping. We decided we could show Friday the tree later and also decided that a nap was a good idea. My wife and I napped for an hour and then got up to work on Christmas cards. Once again we searched for the cat and this time we could not find Friday anywhere. I looked in each room upstairs and my wife searched diligently downstairs. Friday, the cat that loved Christmas, was nowhere to be found.

My wife became frantic as more time passed and there was still no sign of Friday. I grabbed my boots, deciding that maybe the cat had escaped and gone outdoors. Then I heard my wife laughing and saw her pointing at our newly decorated blue spruce. Our cat Friday was sitting in the center of our beautifully decorated Christmas tree. Somehow she had managed to climb into the tree and not knock off a single ornament or mess up the lights.

She peeked out at us and seemed to say, "What's the big deal? I'm just in the center of the tree enjoying another holiday season!" We laughed, and my wife grabbed a camera. She said she wanted to remember the moment forever. I thought to myself, I won't require a photograph to remember this!

That's the way it is with pets. They become a part of the family and they give you a lifetime of memories. Like all memories, some are happy and some are sad.

Several years later, my wife and I were decorating another Christmas tree. This time our daughter was around to help us. Unfortunately, this was the first Christmas without Friday. She had died a few months prior to the holiday season. We were now seasoned veterans at putting a tree safely into the stand and we had many more ornaments to cover our tree.

Once the tree was decorated, my daughter shouted, "Dad, get the stockings and candles for the mantle."

I went to the garage and opened a box full of extra Christmas decorations. At the bottom of the box sat a tiny red-and-white striped stocking that had once been filled with catnip for Friday, the cat that loved Christmas. I paused for a moment and took a deep breath. I showed my wife the tiny stocking and she cried. We both missed our cat.

A moment or two later, we laughed simultaneously as we recalled the year that Friday camped out in the center of our Christmas tree. My wife showed our daughter the picture she had taken of Friday sitting inside the beautiful blue spruce. Our daughter giggled at the photo. She told us that we were lucky to have a cat that loved Christmas so much.

Our daughter was right. We were lucky to have a cat that loved Christmas so much. We were also lucky to have a cat that gave us many great memories!

— David R. Warren —

Chapter 3

Feeling that Christmas Spirit

A Christmas Miracle

Our prime purpose in this life is to help others. And if you can't help them, at least don't hurt them.
~Dalai Lama

During World War II, my father served as a gunner and then as a copilot on a B-17 Flying Fortress, based out of England. On what was to become his last mission as a copilot, he and his crew were to drop several huge bales of anti-Hitler leaflets over Stuttgart, Germany, and then return to base.

Unfortunately, after dropping the bales on the city, my dad's plane was hit by anti-aircraft guns and so badly damaged it was unable to continue flying. The captain and my dad were able to make an emergency landing in the forest. While the plane was totaled, the crew survived the crash, although the engineer and the gunner had been badly hurt and were unable to walk. The captain decided his first priority was the health and safety of his men, and stated that they would try and make it to Switzerland where they could get medical help for the two wounded men.

It was winter, and in addition to being cold, a lot of snow was on the ground. The captain and my father had the men strip the plane for anything remotely useful and then make a sled for the injured men from the hatch door. The crew would take turns pulling the sled.

When not pulling, they would be on the lookout for German patrols.

After two days of sneaking through the German countryside, the injured men were in a bad way. The Captain and crew decided that allowing themselves to be captured and sent to a POW camp was the only way they could get help for the injured men.

The next day, the crew came across a German patrol. My dad and the captain ordered their men to drop their weapons and surrender to the Germans, and that's when the unexpected happened: The German patrol simultaneously tried to surrender to them. My dad said it was amusing and scary at the same time, as they and the Germans were all standing there with their hands in the air trying to surrender to each other.

The captain, the navigator and my dad all spoke a little French and a few words of German. The commander of the German unit — there were five German soliders — also spoke a little French. Using French and some German, the German commander (named Fritz), the captain, the navigator and my dad worked out a truce and a plan.

It was about five days until Christmas, and they were still probably a hundred miles from the Swiss border. The Germans had not been supplied with food, warm clothes or even ammo in a very long time. They were cold, hungry and sick. Having been forced to fight for a cause they didn't believe in (two were originally from Austria), they had decided it was time to desert. Fritz, wanting to save his men from freezing and starving to death, had decided they would surrender to the first Americans they saw and sit out the rest of the war in a British POW camp.

The men worked out a plan. If they came upon more Germans, Fritz would pretend that the crew from the B-17 were his prisoners, and that he was on his way to turn them in. If the group came upon an Allied patrol, the captain and my dad would ensure that Fritz and his men weren't harmed, and that they made it safely to an Allied POW camp.

The group of men spent the next five days walking together through the countryside. As the days passed, the B-17 crew and the Germans ended up becoming friends and helping each other survive.

Thanks to the navigator's skill, they made it across the border into Switzerland on Christmas Day. The captain and my dad escorted Fritz and his men to a British unit, and saw that they were safely turned in and given food and medical help. The captain and my dad later vouched for Fritz and his men, who were sent to a British POW camp. My dad was permanently grounded after suffering a back injury in the crash, and he and the other members of the B-17 crew maintained their friendship with Fritz and the others, visiting them whenever possible in the POW camp.

After the war, my dad, Fritz, and several of the men on both sides maintained a lifelong friendship, often visiting each other. When my dad told his preacher father what had happened, he said it was a Christmas miracle. The B-17 crew had survived being shot at and then a plane crash. Somehow, they had not been tracked or followed by the Germans, and had run into Fritz and his unit who were hoping to meet some Americans. They had not shot each other, and as a group they all made it alive into Switzerland. And all of them survived a German winter with almost no food, medicine, or clothes. Perhaps it was a miracle after all.

—Leslee Kahler—

The ABCs of Christmas

It is Christmas in the heart that puts Christmas in the air.
~W.T. Ellis

After fourteen years of marriage we agreed to divorce. Then came Christmas. For the sake of the children, we decided this first year they would spend Christmas Day with their dad's side of the family at the farm, far more exciting and normal than with just my parents and me. They would have the uncles and their wives, and Christmas commotion with the horses and the kittens to distract them and entertain.

For the children, it was a good plan. From my perspective as their mum... I felt lost. Empty. I had jumped into the void of divorce. How was I going to survive going back to my parents on my own? A failure. A statistic. I could not expect my friends to fill the gap. Filled with self-pity and brooding, I just couldn't get into the Christmas spirit. I must tough it out, I told myself. It was only a day.

My mother came up with an idea. She wanted to treat me to Christmas lunch at a well-known country restaurant. My thoughts raced. Wouldn't it be too obvious? Who dines out for Christmas dinner? People who didn't cook? Non-traditional types? People without kids? That was me. Not one to give up a good meal, I accepted.

Seeing my beautiful mother in her tailored, boiled wool Austrian jacket and matching skirt encouraged me to put on my Christmas sweater and dress up. It did make me feel a little better. We had something to do. Somewhere to go. A destination. That would occupy half the day, at least. My stepfather preferred to stay home, so Mum drove the two of us serenely through the snow, to the village, about a half an hour away.

Welcoming arms of snow-laced trees graced the main village street. Old-fashioned streetlamps were festooned with pine boughs and red ribbons. Boutique shops filled with antiques, art galleries, specialty bookstores and small cafés smiled gently, as we drove by. It was the kind of place where you expected to see a horse-drawn sleigh coming around the corner, with people snuggled under the warm blankets. I was beginning to feel better. Calmer. We drove through the town and arrived at the side street where the old white clapboard restaurant was situated, behind a small white picket fence. But here my bravado started to falter. I was there with my mother! On Christmas Day! How embarrassing! How pathetic at my age. Wouldn't it be obvious? My insecurities screamed inside my head.

"Come on darling," she encouraged, "this will be lovely. Chin up!"

I looked at the front door, decked in glorious fresh wreath with pinecones and tartan ribbons waving in the wind, daring me to be sad.

I told myself to breathe.

A doorman, in a velvet trimmed jacket and top hat, welcomed us into the foyer, treating us like long-established patrons. We followed him along the corridor to two enormous wooden carved doors, which he then opened with a flourish. Inside was a huge room filled with noisy families. There was laughing and the chinking of wine glasses. Kids spilled off the chairs and on to the richly patterned carpet, covered in toys and wrapping paper. A few people looked up and smiled. Most carried on with their hors d'oeuvres, happily ignoring me.

We were ushered to a table near the stone fireplace; the pine logs creating a welcoming warmth. Numerous real Christmas trees, decorated in silver and white, were positioned around the room. White linen tablecloths and pretty centerpieces added to the atmosphere of tradition and elegance. Focusing on the beauty of the room filled with happy families of all sizes, I knew I'd never forget this moment. We toasted to new beginnings.

"Thank you so much, Mum," I said, holding back the tears, knowing if I said more I would dissolve into a disgraceful mess.

"You are welcome, my darling," she said gently. "You will survive."

We carried on with the meal. The service was friendly. The food was exquisite. Savoury parsnip soup, perfectly cooked turkey with all the trimmings, and flaming Christmas pudding. Cocooned in the festive spirit of the room, I felt protected and loved. Privileged. Nourished and ready to face the New Year.

The love and support I felt from my mother that day has carried me forward into a new life filled with adventures and a new appreciation for the true meaning of Christmas. Over the years, my ex-husband and I have taken turns sharing the children at Christmas. I came to realize that being flexible was the best policy. And in those moments without the children, I remembered just how much I always wanted to be a mother. Having Christmas any day, as long as we were together, meant Christmas. Some years, I have asked single friends and their children to Christmas dinner, on Boxing Day. I call it "extend-a-Christmas," not being tethered to one day.

Since that Christmas, I have learned to do a number of things on my own: Walk into a movie theatre amongst crowds of couples and watch a movie; make new friends; enjoy my single friends. Pump gas even! And generally be comfortable on my own.

And then, just when I no longer needed anyone, along came Steve. My heart has been stretched and healed and stretched again. It now includes a new man whom I love, a pretty cool stepson and my own two beautiful, balanced adult children of whom I am very proud. Christmas has been condensed and simplified to the essentials: Appreciation, Beauty, Compassion. Love.

— Sue England —

The Christmas Cat-astrophe

Christmas is not as much about opening
our presents as opening our hearts.
~Janice Maeditere

"She's not coming, is she?" I knew by the look on my mom's face as she hung up the phone that my grandma wasn't coming for Christmas. Ever since we destroyed her decorations last Christmas, things just hadn't been the same.

It all started last year on Thanksgiving Day. We had just finished stuffing ourselves full of turkey. The twins were wrestling over the large end of the wishbone when my Aunt Melinda walked in carrying one of Grandma's old hats.

"Everyone needs to draw a name. That's who you'll buy a present for this Christmas."

"What?" Uncle Dan hollered.

"Listen," Aunt Melinda explained. "Our family has grown so large that it's hard to buy something for everyone. We thought this might help relieve some of the burden."

"Burden!" Aunt Mary Beth snarled. "I realize that I have more children than the rest of you," she went on while motioning to the twins who were still duking it out on the floor and her three daughters who were slowly lowering their cell phones to listen in on this conversation, "but I never realized that we had become a burden."

"Now, now," Grandma stepped in. "Never have any of my darlings been anything of a burden. It's just that… well… I'm not getting any younger, and you all are always so busy. Your sister just thought it might be easier on all of us if we didn't have to buy quite so much this year."

"Well, I've never heard of such a ridiculous idea," Uncle Dan bellowed. "No offense, Mama, but I thought Christmas was supposed to be a time of giving… to all, not just one person."

"So… who gets to buy Mama's present?" my mom asked.

"Well, whoever draws her name," Aunt Melinda answered.

"Humph!" Uncle Dan snorted as he pushed back from the table, knocking over half-empty glasses of water and sweet tea. Grandma's favorite cat, Snookums, had been sleeping under the table and shrieked as someone stepped on her tail. She scurried into the kitchen. My cousins and I snickered as Grandma flew after the cat, yelling, "My sweet little dumpling! I'm so sorry."

"Dan, watch what you're doing!" Aunt Mary Beth yelled, snatching up the fallen glasses and dabbing at the spills with her napkin.

"Dan, I just gave Mama that tablecloth for her birthday. Now it's ruined. Why do you have to be so difficult?" Aunt Melinda yelled.

"You know what?" Uncle Dan replied. "I'm done with this. Happy Thanksgiving everyone." He turned and walked toward the door.

"Dan, you haven't drawn a name yet."

"Oh, whatever, Melinda. Just pick one for me. I don't care."

"Fine," Aunt Melinda huffed.

"Love you, Mama!" Uncle Dan called as he stormed out the front door.

Christmas Eve arrived, and we all came to Grandma's house with our "one" present. Everyone, that is, except for Uncle Dan. He showed up with a truckload of gifts. He brought something for everyone and even a few extra, which was great since Aunt Mary Beth's girls brought their boyfriends.

Aunt Melinda was fit to be tied when she saw Uncle Dan come in with an armful of presents. She started snatching boxes and throwing them under the tree.

"Hey, watch it, Melinda!" Uncle Dan hollered. "Some of those are breakable."

"Oh, excuse me, Danny Boy. I didn't mean to ruin all your fun."

"Oh, build a bridge and get over it, Smelly Melly."

"We were having a nice time until you got here. Why do you always have to stir something up?"

"Me?" Uncle Dan yelled. "I'm not the old Scrooge who decided to be stingy with the gifts."

"Come on, you two," my mom interrupted. "It's Christmas Eve. Can't you at least try to get along? Look at the example you're setting for the kids."

"I guess you're right, sis. I'm sorry," Uncle Dan answered.

"I'm sorry, too… Danny Boy," Aunt Melinda chided while Uncle Dan glared back.

The rest of the night, Aunt Melinda sat in the corner pouting while everyone "oohed" and "ahhed" over Uncle Dan's gifts.

My dad and my uncles spent most of the night setting up the new surround sound that Uncle Dan bought for Grandma. Mom and Aunt Mary Beth sat in the kitchen discussing what to do about the neighbor who Grandma suspected was stealing her Sunday papers. Aunt Mary Beth's daughters flirted with their boyfriends. We did our best to avoid collisions with the remote-controlled helicopters the twins flew all over the house. I pretended to listen as Grandma showed me our family album for the one-hundredth time.

Dad turned on the surround sound but didn't realize the volume was on high. The blast from every corner of the room caused Grandma to wail and fling the family album into the air. It landed on Snookums, who'd been resting at Grandma's feet. The poor cat let out a howl like I've never heard before and leaped smack dab into the Christmas tree. As the tree toppled over, the red and gold angel that stood peacefully atop Grandma's tree for as long as I could remember took flight and landed right in the middle of the fireplace. It went up in flames as we all watched in horror.

The adults started fussing and blaming each other while trying to clean up broken ornaments and salvage family pictures. We just tried to stay out of the way. Finally, Grandma told us to leave. We hadn't had a family gathering since then.

So here we were a year later, and it didn't look like Grandma was coming to Christmas.

"Well, is she coming or not?" I asked again impatiently.

"Grandma… had a heart attack," my mom answered, her voice beginning to quiver. "She collapsed in the grocery store, and the paramedics are rushing her to the hospital. Go get your coat while I call Uncle Dan."

When we got to the hospital, most of the family was already there. Everyone was hugging and crying and trying to figure out what had happened. Uncle Dan rushed through the door just as the doctor came in.

"Is she going to be alright?" Aunt Melinda asked.

"Yes," the doctor answered. "We're running some tests on her heart to determine the extent of the damage. She hit her head pretty hard when she fell and has suffered a mild concussion. She's resting now, but a few of you at a time can go in to see her."

Uncle Dan and Aunt Melinda stepped forward at the same time. The rest of us held our breath. And then, do you know what happened? They looked at each other and said, "You go first."

Grandma ended up spending Christmas in the hospital, but believe it or not, we all got along. We brought presents to Grandma's room, and Uncle Dan snuck Snookums in when the nurses weren't looking. Don't get me wrong, the tension was still there just under the surface, but we all realized something important that year. Although we may have our differences, we are still family, and we need each other. We may have to work a little bit harder at getting along, but if it makes Grandma happy, it's worth it.

— Christy Westbrook —

22

Never a Bad Day

If you don't think every day is a good day,
just try missing one.
~Cavett Robert

There are few places more unpleasant than a Florida post office with broken air conditioning. Throw in the rush of the holiday season and you have a pretty good picture of where I was last year during my lunch break, two weeks before Christmas.

People crowded around me in the line, balancing boxes on hips and shoulders, all watching the three postal workers behind the counter. Red and green stars hung from the ceiling overhead and brightly colored posters advertised the latest stamps.

The wait stretched on and on.

The folks behind the counter moved as fast as they could, doling out postage, handling packages, tracking down lost mail, but they were way over their heads. As time slipped past, the mood of the line grew uglier and uglier. You know the drill: loud sighs, sarcastic comments, people tapping their feet.

In short, it was all the social unpleasantness you can imagine concentrated into one overly warm room.

The one bright spot in this whole situation was the silver-haired gentleman in front of me. Looking completely unaffected by the extended wait, he asked if I was ready for Christmas. That started a conversation and we spent the rest of our time in line chatting. He was mailing a package to some grandchildren that he hadn't seen in several months, and was nervous that he might not have picked out gifts they would like.

That led us to a discussion of gifts and gift-giving in general. As the people around us grumbled and complained, we talked about presents we'd received and given, both the hits and the dismal failures.

When his turn came, the man stepped quickly to the counter. The postal worker immediately apologized for the wait, but the man told him not to worry and they settled down to the business of mailing his package.

As he was walking away, the postal worker called out "Have a good day!"

Someone in the crowd heard and let out a cynical "ha!"

The older man turned back, smiled gently at the haggard man behind the counter, and said, "Son, I've never had a bad day in my life. And this," he gestured vaguely at the crowd of unhappy people, "certainly is not enough to make me start."

He caught my eye, gave me a wink, and walked out.

— Patrick Matthews —

23

Happy Holi-dog

For it is in giving that we receive.
~Saint Francis

My dog's personality didn't fully develop until he was about seven. By eight, Buddy was so smart that we began to suspect he'd been a genius all along, but was merely hiding it under the theory that stupid dogs get away with more fun stuff.

With dogs, old age really is a cherished gift worth celebrating, and at no time has that become more clear to me than during our family holidays.

My two children and I don't have much extended family, so we've always included the pets in our celebrations, giving them their own gifts and stockings and Easter baskets. Dogs are some of the most satisfying gift recipients in the world because they are so easy to please. Their happiness is contagious, and they never seem to notice much beyond the excitement of the moment.

Except Buddy, who had an epiphany at age eight. It happened the year Easter came right after his birthday. I started a tradition of putting refillable Easter baskets on the fireplace mantle ahead of time — like Christmas stockings — in order to prevent being stuck with cheap baskets that seem to breed faster than the bunnies that bring them.

When Buddy discovered the baskets, a look of recognition spread across his fuzzy face. He had become aware not only of our symbols of holidays, but also the pattern: we gather, we give presents and attention, and we eat. In dog world, that's pretty much the definition of heaven.

From then on, our dog learned to anticipate those wondrous occasions. He spent the following spring and summer checking the fireplace for the containers that would hold gifts. When winter rolled around and the stockings finally went up, our Christmas season took on new life. Just as parents of young children become infused with the little ones' excitement, my family's Christmas spirit was renewed by our dog.

Better yet, all of this happened just at the time when the children were getting too old to maintain the thrill of their younger years. The Budster brought it back. We took to gathering in the family room more often just to watch the Daily Stocking Check. The furry pet stockings are traditionally hung on the far ends of the fireplace at our house. Buddy began by giving his own stocking a thorough sniffing, and then strolled to the other side of the mantle to check out the competition — to make sure it wasn't just that Santa liked hamsters better.

At some point Buddy realized that cameras are often involved in these events. From then on, the appearance of a camera became cause for excitement, even if the purpose of the picture was to, say, show a new piece of furniture to a relative. It is no accident that a dog figures prominently in all of our pictures, posing importantly. He is always waiting for the celebrating to begin.

This year Buddy is fifteen, and our last Christmas was one of the most exciting we've seen since the children were toddlers. Although Santa was very quiet while making his delivery, the dog discovered his gifts shortly thereafter and getting any sleep the remainder of the night was a struggle. In the morning it was Buddy who was up bright and early and overwhelmed with excitement, and the teen-aged children had to be roused from their beds in order to allow the festivities to commence.

Recently I had my own epiphany, and I have our wise and beloved dog to thank for it. We really do create our own holidays with the anticipation, enthusiasm, and the magic we put into them. And we don't have to get more subdued as we age, either. The joys of life and family are timeless and ageless — and without regard to species.

— T'Mara Goodsell —

24

The Sally Ann Christmas Kettle

We make a living by what we get,
we make a life by what we give.
~Winston Churchill

The Friday afternoon before Christmas my art group has volunteered to take turns manning the Salvation Army Christmas Kettle inside the Orillia Square Mall. Having been raised Jewish, this is all new to me.

The kettle is strategically positioned inside the mall entrance, next to the donut shop. Repeated wafts of sweet apple turnovers and hot black coffee entice me as I attempt to focus on my task. I'm ringing brass bells to the beat of Christmas music and trying to catch the attention of passers-by as they dash by me.

My friend who preceded me estimated that she collected about seventy dollars in donations during the lunch hour. For the first few minutes I'm stymied. I can't figure out how to inspire shoppers to glance in my direction, let alone reach into the depths of their pockets for loose change.

The clock is ticking and only one toonie and one loonie have been dropped into the kettle slot. At the fifteen-minute mark, I reach into my pocket and extricate my last cash—two five-dollar bills and four loonies. I make a big show of dropping them into the kettle while jingling the bells and smiling.

Finally, I make eye contact and receive a welcoming smile from a young man who appears to be in his late thirties. He settles on the bench beside me.

"You're pretty," he says. "My name is Mark. Do you have a husband?"

My head twirls in shock. I blush, nod, and smile coyly in response. Perhaps I look younger in my runners, jeans and red sweater. Truthfully, I am more than a decade past the half-century mark. On closer examination, I realize that my new admirer is intellectually challenged. Mark's sincerity and warmth have made my day.

"I walk here every day," he continues, as he bends to tighten his shoelaces. "Do you have a sister who's as pretty as you?"

"No sisters — only brothers. Anyway, I'm old enough to be your mother. I have a son your age."

"Really?" He looks surprised.

"How about a daughter?" he asks hopefully.

"Sorry, she's married." I laugh. He smiles. I smile again. I'm in love with my new friend.

A woman in a blue coat stops and searches her pockets for coins. Overhearing our conversation she leans forward and says, "You really do look very young!"

I radiate with pleasure.

By the end of my assigned hour, I have met and chatted with dozens of kind and generous people, including: an elderly couple wearing matching jogging suits who drop in five dollars; three teenagers munching donuts who smile and drop in their change; a young mother, with preschoolers in tow, who empties her change into the kettle and then tells me how grateful she is for the help she received from the Salvation Army the previous Christmas.

"Every penny helps," I say as I thank them.

My shift ends at 2:00 p.m. As I hand over the bells to my friend, Ralph, who is sporting fuzzy reindeer antlers and a colourful Christmas sweater, I notice that somehow the coin level in the kettle has increased significantly.

I hum "Jingle Bells" and then switch tunes to "Fiddler on the Roof" as I climb into my car on this cold December evening and head home to make Friday night Sabbath dinner for my family.

I can already taste the warm challah, chicken soup and brisket, and I smell the aroma of hot apple strudel.

—Evelyn N. Pollock—

Full of Memories

*Nobody can do for little children what grandparents
do. Grandparents sort of sprinkle stardust
over the lives of little children.*
~Alex Haley

Thanksgiving was in full swing. My parents' home was filled with family, the house smelled of roasting turkey and warm bread, and the sounds of football.

Cooking with my family is one of my favorite Thanksgiving traditions. Mom was making stuffing. Dad was chopping, dicing and slicing the fruit salad. All the sisters were making pies, sweet-potato casserole, and cranberry dressing. We were sharing stories and laughing.

My two-year-old son, Jackson, was curious and underfoot, as always. He needed to taste the fruit. He wanted to see what was baking in the ovens.

"Jackson, where is your ball?" I asked, trying to redirect him.

Jackson ran to the other room for a few minutes. Shortly, he returned. He pulled on my shirt, saying, "Choo, choo. All aboard!"

"Not now, sweetie. We can play after dinner. Mommy needs to cook for our yummy Thanksgiving dinner."

"Come on, Momma," he persisted.

"Jackson, go find Daddy. He will play," I said.

Jackson sighed dejectedly and walked over to Mammaw.

"Mammaw," Jackson said, batting his sweet, blue eyes. "Choo,

choo. All aboard."

"Okay, sweet guy. Let's go see." Mammaw washed her hands and then held her hand down for Jackson to grasp. He led her proudly to the dining room.

"Wow," Mammaw said, looking at the dining-room chairs lined up in a neat row.

Jackson patted the chair in which Mammaw should sit. Mammaw sat obediently in her assigned chair. Grinning from ear to ear, Jackson and Mammaw yelled, "Choo, choo. All aboard!" several times.

"I get Papaw," Jackson said, smiling.

"Yes, he will love your train," Mammaw encouraged.

Jackson walked over to Papaw. Papaw washed his hands and allowed Jackson to lead him to the train. Papaw happily found his seat on Jackson's train.

Jackson, Mammaw, and Papaw yelled gleefully, "Choo, choo. All aboard!"

Jackson's baby brother crawled over to join the train. Jackson decided he needed Daddy and Great-Grandma on his train. Mammaw helped Great-Grandma to her chair, and Jackson pulled Daddy away from his computer.

Jackson once again came to me. "Choo, choo. All aboard?"

"Thank you!" I said. Jackson led me to his train and showed me my seat.

All our Thanksgiving cooking stopped. The pies were not watched. The potatoes were not mashed.

However, we did have a four-generation train in our dining room.

Mammaw and Baby Brother stomped their feet, yelling, "Chugga, chugga, chugga, chugga." Papaw yelled, "Choo, choo." Daddy and Great-Grandmother told Jackson that he had a wonderful train. I gasped, "Oh, Jackson, I see a cow outside my train window. Look, everyone, at that tall tree!" Jackson sat in the conductor's seat, smiling broadly.

Finally, Jackson yelled, "We are hewe!"

Everyone disembarked the train, thanking Jackson for the wonderful train ride. Jackson shook each rider's hand. He had thoroughly enjoyed every second of his four-generation Thanksgiving Day train ride.

The dining-room chairs were returned to order. Dinner was late, the pies were a bit too brown, and the homemade cranberry dressing was omitted from the menu.

After dinner was eaten and cleaned up, my mom and I sat rocking my sweet boys to sleep.

"Momma, our train ride in the dining room was so much fun. I feel a bit bad that dinner was late, though," I said.

"Oh, sweetheart. I have learned something very important since becoming a grandmother. Stuffing can always wait so that great memories can be made."

Ten years from now, no one is going to remember that dinner was a half-hour late or that the pecan pie was a bit overcooked. No one will even recall exactly which foods made it to the table. What everyone will remember is that we had a four-generation Thanksgiving Day train ride with two-year-old Jackson as our conductor.

—Marie Loper Maxwell—

26

My Guardian Angels

I would rather walk with a friend in the dark,
than alone in the light.
~Helen Keller

"Star light. Star bright. First star I see tonight." When I was pre-school age that was the way I began my nightly prayers. While kneeling beside my bed I would choose the brightest star I could see and make my wish. Then I would pray that God would bless and care for my loved ones.

When I was five years old we lived in an older home that had been inherited from my grandparents, in the Allandale section of Barrie, Ontario. That Christmas Eve the house was full of company so at bedtime I had to surrender my spot to sleep on a cot upstairs all alone. This part of the house was rarely used, and it was frightening for me to be up there by myself. My mother knew that I was both nervous and excited so she came up to get me settled in. She got down on her knees with me, and when I began the ritual she listened closely to hear my wish, which was to be safe and unafraid in the dark. Just as I started my prayers, Mom told me to look again at the star I had just wished on. I had already been told about heaven and angels and where my grandma, grandpa and baba went when they died, but that night Mom told me about a very special angel. She told me that from now on when I looked to the stars, I should direct my wishes to Robert. Robert? I had a guardian angel named Robert?

My mother explained that before she married my father, she had been married to a wonderful man named Duncan McKenzie. She and Duncan had a baby boy they named Robert. He was born in December, but tragically died Christmas Eve. Then the very next New Year's Eve, Duncan was killed instantly in a head-on train crash in Sudbury. She told me how lonely and frightened she was feeling that night too, and still did on every Christmas Eve no matter how many years passed. We cried, grieved and prayed together. I fell sound asleep that night feeling safe and comforted knowing about my special guardian angel.

The year I turned seven, another Robert came into my life. He was a Down syndrome child about eleven years old, placed in my grade two classroom experimentally. We bonded instantly. Robert sat in the seat in front of me so I could help him with his work. He became very reliant on me and would make a fuss if he couldn't stand next to me in line, or keep me in sight at recess.

One day I fell in the schoolyard before the morning bell rang. My knees were skinned and bleeding badly and I was weeping. Out of nowhere, Robert scooped me up into his arms and carried me off. The teachers were slightly alarmed and yelled at him to put me down, but I couldn't see what they were concerned about. I felt quite safe. He was much bigger than the other kids and able to push past everyone as he marched me into the school directly to the main office. There, Robert walked right into the principal's office where he laid me down on the desk and announced, "Fix her. She's my friend!"

That Christmas, King Edward School put on a pageant and invited the parents to come on the afternoon of Christmas Eve to watch. Our class did the nativity scene with Mary, Joseph, shepherds, wise men and an angel that stood out front to narrate the story. I was a pretty good reader and had long, blond curls so our teacher, Miss Shepstone, chose me to play the angel. I was ecstatic!

My mother made me a beautiful costume with delicate wings and a golden halo. While she fitted and sewed the costume, we talked more about my guardian angel. I told her my theory that her baby

Robert had not died. I felt sure there had to have been a mistake at the hospital, and that the Robert in my classroom was really her child, all grown up. I tried to reassure her that although he was different than the other kids, and lived in a special place, he was still being my guardian angel and I loved him.

She reminded me that we had often visited the baby's grave, but told me that I should be very grateful to have two Roberts watching out for me. Later that week I was able to prove just how thankful I was.

Every day before the pageant we rehearsed our nativity. I was beaming with joy over my duties and loved every minute of it. Except for one disturbing thing. Robert wasn't able to have a speaking part in the play. He would play a shepherd seated on the floor with a scratchy, grey, woollen blanket pulled over his head and body, with only his face revealed. He didn't mind that at all. In fact he took his role very seriously. He knew when he must stand up and sit down, but he desperately wanted to be closer to me.

During the course of every rehearsal he would creep up and play his part seated on the floor near me. Miss Shepstone explained over and over to him how important his part was and that it must be played in the proper spot. He said he understood, and he continued to be a wonderful shepherd, but only when he scooted forward on his blanketed behind and stayed front and centre with me.

I would take him back to his spot and sit with him a while, but to no avail. He was just too nervous on that crowded stage without me in his sight.

Two days before Christmas Eve Miss Shepstone paid a visit to our house after school. What on earth had I done wrong? I'd never heard of a teacher coming to someone's house before. My mom and Miss Shepstone had such serious faces when they told me I had a big decision to make. They said they would understand and stick by me whatever I decided.

They wanted to know what I thought we should do about Robert. The choice I had was this. I could still be the Christmas Angel and be out front to narrate the play, but Robert would have to be kept out of the production completely because he refused to stay in his shepherd's position. Or I could give up my part and the costume of the angel to someone else, and sit in the back under one of those heavy blankets playing the part of a shepherd with Robert so he could remain in the play. What a weight to place on the shoulders of a seven-year-old!

Time has passed and I still have a fascination with the stars. I gaze at the brightest ones and think of all the loved ones I have lost — including my dear mother who died suddenly at Christmas time too. My wish every Christmas Eve is that they all know how grateful I am to have known them and for their outstanding guidance. I also hope that Robert knew how thankful I was for his unequivocal friendship when we held hands under our scratchy, grey, woollen blankets many Christmas Eves ago.

— Lea Ellen Yarmill Reburn —

27

Super Bear

*Christmas is a necessity. There has to be at least
one day of the year to remind us that we're
here for something else besides ourselves.*
~Eric Sevareid

I attended university away from home and always looked forward to coming home to Halifax for the holidays. One Christmas, my mother, a store manager in a local shopping mall, was asked if she knew anyone who might be interested in some part-time work and extra money over the holiday season. Within a few hours of arriving home, I had a job.

I was hired to work as "Super Bear," sort of a superhero sidekick to Santa. Basically, it was my job to wander the mall during Santa's visiting hours and send children Santa's way. Being only nineteen years old, and a cynical university student, I thought I was well aware of just how commercial Christmas had become. But not even my jaded ears were prepared for the onslaught of "I wants" that faced poor Santa daily.

Santa was quite good about not promising anything. In fact, when one five-year-old girl appeared with a five-page typed list, Santa asked her how she would feel if he brought all those toys to the children next door and then had nothing left by the time he got to her house. In no uncertain terms, she told him exactly what she thought.

Every night when I got home, I thought about what had happened to children, to society. Had everyone, right down to five-year-olds, become so involved in "stuff" that "stuff" had become what we valued?

Was getting oodles of gifts under the tree all that mattered? What were parents teaching their children? What happened to "good will toward men" and all those kind, neighbourly thoughts in the English Christmas Carols I loved so much?

As Christmas Eve approached, I began to look forward to the end of the job. Besides losing five to seven pounds a day in fluids and earning some much needed pocket money, I was not enjoying myself. On the second to last day of work, I was on one of my patrols around the mall. I spotted a young boy, perhaps six or seven, and tried to point the way to Santa's workshop. He came up to me and said that he and his mother were just leaving and that he didn't have time to go see Santa. He asked if I could tell Santa what he wanted for Christmas. I nodded my head and bent down on one knee. He looked up at me and said, "Super Bear, will you please tell Santa that all I want for Christmas is a cure for my little sister's leukaemia?"

I was glad that Super Bear didn't talk, for at that moment, I began to cry. Here was a little boy, who like most his age, probably had several items he could have wished for — for himself. But all he wanted was that one thing, that one intangible thing. I looked at his mother, gave her a hug, whispered to her that I would see what I could do, and waved goodbye as they left the mall. Then I went to my mother's store, took off my bear head, and cried for half an hour.

That little boy and his mother restored my faith in people, and reminded me that some people do know what the holiday season is all about. I don't know whatever happened to that little boy and his sister, but I like to think their house was the first stop on Santa's rounds.

— Heather J. Stewart —

The Red Phone

Caring is a reflex. Someone slips, your arm goes out.
A car is in the ditch, you join the others and push...
You live, you help.
~Ram Dass

ack in the 1980s I was a telephone repairman in Burnaby, British Columbia. I mostly did install and telephone repair work, and over the thirty-four years of my service with the telephone company I dealt with thousands of customers. One story stands out for me, however, and still makes me smile.

It was early September, shortly after Labour Day, when one afternoon I drove up to a small 1950s style rancher on the east side of Burnaby. The homeowner, a little old lady, answered the doorbell and let me in. The problem with the telephone, she explained, was that it was very noisy, for both incoming and outgoing calls. The telephone set was red, a deep dark red like you used to see in old spy movies — you know — for the "hot line" between the White House and the Kremlin. It was in beautiful condition for an old rotary phone — indeed it looked like new.

In addition to the red phone, just about everything else in the living room was red, black or white. It looked like it had been decorated in the 1950s or 1960s and nothing had been changed in all those years. The phone fit right in with the décor and had likely been chosen for its very redness!

"Hmm, I haven't seen one of these in years," I told the lady. "They are very hard to get parts for…" I opened up the old phone, hoping for a quick fix, but it was not to be. The handset cord had an intermittent open and that was causing the crackle on the line. Shrugging my shoulders, I said, "I'll see what I have in the back of the truck." On the way out to the truck I mentally ran through my stock. I didn't think I even had a rotary phone, let alone a red handset cord. Sure enough all I had was a sad-looking beige rotary. I brought it in to show her and said, "I could pull the cord off of this set and install it on yours, but that would look really dumb." And she agreed. But then she said, "The beige phone is okay."

I could see she was really sad to see her old red phone go. So I went ahead and installed the beige phone for her, and it looked totally out of place. I handed the old phone to her and said, "You keep this old set in a safe place, and if I can find the parts to fix it I will return — but no promises." She understood, and thanked me.

Returning to the office that night I asked around if anyone had an old red rotary wall phone that was any good for parts, but no one had. Then I put a notice up on the office board and at the Phonemart Store looking for parts.

Weeks went by with no luck. But then in late October I got a call from one of the guys. He had just recovered a red rotary with a good handset cord. Fortunately I had kept the woman's address clipped to my sun visor.

Off I went the next day, and then a few days later, and then a couple of weeks after that, but she was never home. I was starting to think that something had happened to her, or maybe she had moved, so I pretty much forgot about the whole thing.

As it would happen, that year it was my turn to work Christmas Eve and Christmas Day. Christmas Eve found me working in her neighbourhood, and when I passed her house I saw the lights on. I could see friends and family gathered in her front room around a gaily-lit Christmas tree. I parked the truck and hurried up the front steps with the red phone held behind my back. When the little old lady answered the door, she didn't recognize me. So I pulled the red telephone set out to show her, and said "Merry Christmas!"

Well, she started to cry. One of her son's quickly came to her side asking, "What's wrong, Mum?" "Nothing" she said. "This wonderful young man has come to fix my red phone."

So with her friends and family looking on, I tore both sets apart on the coffee table and built one good phone out of two old ones. After more cookies, coffee and cake than I could possibly handle, I made my way back out to the company truck with her family cheering and wishing me a "Very Merry Christmas." And you know what? Even though I had to work, it was!

— N. Newell —

Holiday Hijinks

29

Dinner To Go

No chaos, no creation. Evidence:
the kitchen at mealtime.
~Mason Cooley

uckle up, because you're in for a wild ride... kind of like our turkey on Thanksgiving Eve seven years ago. These are the actual events of that day. It's the kind of experience that will only happen once in a lifetime, and no matter how many Thanksgivings we have from here on out, this will always be my family's favorite Thanksgiving memory.

Thanksgiving Eve morning, I arrived at my mom's house at about 8:30. Mom and I plunged right in and started to make the Thanksgiving feast for our family. Being of Italian descent, we not only make the traditional dishes, but we add an Italian flair. This included dishes like stuffed artichokes, fried cardones, and stuffing from scratch. So Mom and I were busy multitasking, stuffing this and frying that. I also made my famous banana split cake. Thanksgiving would not be the same without these dishes.

Since it was a very cold day, we used the garage as a second refrigerator, and put everything we finished cooking on the trunk of my parents' car. My mom got the twenty-three-pound turkey out of the fridge. We gave him a saltwater bath and placed him safely in his roasting pan. He was all set for his date with the 350-degree oven the next morning at 6:00. I brought him out to the garage and put him on the trunk of the car, next to the artichokes, cardones and banana split cake.

My dad came in and said he had to go to the store. We didn't really hear him. Although we love him dearly, we often block him out.

Hours went by, and Mom and I finished the homemade stuffing. I went to the garage to put the stuffing on the trunk of the car, but there was no car. My mind began to race. Where's the car? Where's the food? I glanced at the end of the driveway and screamed. My banana split cake was laying there — upside-down. Artichokes and cardones were in the road.

My mom came outside, saw the carnage, and began to bite on her index finger the way old Italian women do. I went to the end of the driveway in shock. My Aunt Kay, who lives next door, came outside and helped me gather the artichokes and cardones that had escaped their tinfoil homes. She tried to comfort me by pointing out that a few artichokes didn't look so bad. "Just brush off the stones. No one will know."

As I crouched there picking up all the food, it hit me: There was no turkey. I looked down the road… no sign of the turkey or the roasting pan. My mom was in a panic. Where would we get a twenty-three-pound turkey that was ready to cook the day before Thanksgiving?

I decided to search for the turkey. I drove about three miles down the road, but there was no sign of the turkey. I turned back and reassured my mom that Dad surely noticed the turkey and put it inside the car.

My mom, Aunt Kay and I sat at the kitchen table in shock. No normal person could possibly pass by all that food piled on the car and not see it. However, we were talking about my dad. Although he is the best dad in the world, he does live in a fog.

I called my four sisters and told them our turkey was missing. We became hysterical, imagining the people driving behind the "fog man," beeping their little hearts out to get my dad's attention, only to go unheard since Dad is oblivious when he's driving.

About an hour later, my dad pulled in the driveway. He walked into the kitchen holding the turkey still inside the roasting pan. Dad informed us that this poor turkey had made it on the trunk of the car all the way from Churchville to Gates (approximately nine miles). My father finally noticed it when it flew off the trunk as he was turning onto Manitou Road from Buffalo Road. He slammed on the brakes and blocked the whole intersection. He got out of his car to rescue the turkey, which, according to him, only bounced once. He picked up the turkey from the road, put it in the roasting pan, and ran back to the car. On his way home, he found the lid to the roasting pan a few miles from our house.

Once again, Mom and I were plucking stones from our Thanksgiving dinner. We gave the turkey another saltwater bath, placed him back into the slightly dented roasting pan, and put him on a shelf in the garage. My sisters showed up with bags of artichokes and cardones, and we began the task of preparing them... again.

I don't remember a Thanksgiving before or since our "road kill turkey dinner." The laughter around our dinner table that day was truly beautiful. And I am thankful for my father, who put aside his pride and chased after our turkey rolling down the road.

P.S. In my father's defense, he wants it known that he lives in a fog because he raised five daughters.

— Lori Giraulo-Secor —

30

The Gift that Keeps on Giving

*Even though you're growing up,
you should never stop having fun.*
~Nina Dobrev

For about thirty years, our family has had a love/hate relationship with a culinary wonder known as Potted Meat Product. One can find it in the Spam and Vienna sausage section of the supermarket. The ingredients appear to be meat by-products and various animal parts.

In my family, Potted Meat Product, known as PMP, became the proverbial fruitcake — the gift that keeps on being re-gifted. In the early years of our PMP days, this little can would be disguised under the Christmas tree, wrapped exquisitely as though it was an item of great desire, a package that made us wonder what treasure lay within. It has been festooned with ribbons and hung on the tree as an ornament until it was noticed. It was also found in Easter baskets, under chocolate bunnies and Cadbury eggs. Birthdays were not complete without a PMP sighting, disguised in socks or underwear.

The (un)lucky recipient of the can of PMP was then charged with passing it on to the next unsuspecting family member. We were always aware that the PMP would rear its ugly head at some point in the festivities. The burning questions were: Who would get stuck with the PMP? Which package would it be hidden in?

PMP could be wrapped in a series of smaller boxes inside a big box. It could be hidden inside a Crock-Pot or a new backpack. But as the teenage years came around, the stakes got higher. My older son, Jeff, and I were determined to outdo each other in the PMP Pass-Off.

Being a rookie at creativity and technology, I settled for inserting a can of Potted Meat Product in the center of Jeff's birthday cake. Angel food cake is especially good for this purpose.

Jeff, much more technically advanced than I was, strung up a very elaborate pulley system in my bathroom. When I opened the door, the pulley system lowered the PMP down over the toilet. We had mirrored walls in the bathroom. As I walked in, it appeared that there was PMP everywhere being lowered on pulleys, a frightening scene indeed. I screamed.

But I was not to be outdone.

I gave the PMP to a friend of Jeff's. Their class was flying to Washington, D.C. for a field trip, and she agreed to have the flight attendant serve it to Jeff as his lunch aboard the plane. Unfortunately, she forgot. She did, however, ask her dad to take the PMP with him on a business trip, and he mailed it back to Jeff from Chicago. Nice touch!

Another of my brilliant plans deserves mention. One of the secretaries from the guidance office at Jeff's school was in my bowling league. I enlisted her help and passed off the PMP to her during bowling one night. The next day, Jeff was called out of chemistry class to report to the office, causing some concern on his part and a bit of teasing from the class.

He hurried to the office at the other end of campus and was handed the PMP. He was pretty annoyed to have to walk all the way back to class and face the curiosity of the other students. Unfortunately, it was a short-lived victory. By the time I left work and got to my car, Jeff had walked from his school to my car and rigged up the PMP to my steering wheel. There it sat taunting and waiting for me.

One day, the three of us went for ice cream. As I got out of the car, I noticed some trash on the ground. Unbelievably, there was an open can of PMP among it. It had a plastic spoon in it, and a bite of the PMP was missing from the can. To this day, my boys think I arranged for it to be there, that perhaps I staged that PMP for them to see.

Over the years, our PMP days have slowed down a bit. Every once in a while, it makes a rare appearance. Not too long ago, my husband and I slipped it in an overnight bag to put it in my son's car as he and his wife left to go home after a visit with us. Unfortunately, they became suspicious and discovered the PMP before they drove out of the driveway. He put the car in reverse, stuffed the PMP in our mailbox, and roared off.

In all these years, we never opened up the can of PMP. I think we were afraid to after all the years of passing it back and forth.

The can of Potted Meat Product is currently residing in my kitchen cabinet. I am waiting for that perfect opportunity to pass it off to an unsuspecting family member. The glory of the deed is short-lived. Once it leaves my hand, I know the PMP will be back to darken my doorstep before long.

—Jeanne Kraus—

A Mysterious Angel

*I believe that prayer is our powerful contact with the
greatest force in the universe.*
~Loretta Young

It was nearing Christmas in 1987. I was a single mother of a teenager. I was on sick leave from a motor-vehicle accident, and no benefits had come in. There was very little food in the house, and I didn't know which way to turn. I had prayed for divine intervention but so far our situation had not changed.

One morning, I shed a few tears and then said, "Let go and let God." I knew that He could help me in this situation.

A few hours later, I heard a loud rap on the door. I opened it to find an old man with rheumy eyes and huge hands standing there. His beard was scraggly and unkempt. It was frigid out, and I wondered what he could want.

"Can I help you, sir?" I asked.

In a crackly voice, he answered, "Missus, do you happen to have a hot cup of tea and something to eat for a hungry old soul?"

"Well, sir, there isn't much food in the house, but I can offer you some tea and toast with peanut butter or jam."

"That would be most appreciated," he said as the water from his eyes ran down his cheeks.

I was leery about letting this man in the house, so I asked him if he minded waiting on the steps. He assured me he didn't.

I went into the house, prepared a cup of hot tea and four slices of toast with peanut butter, and took them to him. We sat on the porch as he ate and chatted a little about life and how hard it could be.

When he finished, I asked if he would like more, and he assured me he would. While the teakettle was boiling, I looked around for a pair of gloves and a scarf that had been my late husband's. With the items in hand, I took them to him, and he tried on the gloves.

"A perfect fit," he said. Tears rolled down his rosy, cracked cheeks.

We chatted a bit more as he ate, and then he politely thanked me and turned to go. When I went back into the house, I remembered a pair of boots that had been my husband's. I grabbed them out of the closet and ran outside, but there was no sign of the elderly man. I ran to the end of the block and looked up and down… nothing. I ran to the other end of the block… nothing. I jumped in my car and drove around the neighborhood. Again… nothing. Where had he gone?

Christmas Eve was just a couple of days away, and as those hours passed, the situation continued to be desperate. About 6:00 that evening, a rap came at the door. When I opened it, a man stood there with a huge box of groceries. Behind him, I saw a taxi.

"Delivery," he stated.

"From who?" I asked.

"I have no idea," he answered. "It was sent anonymously. I can tell you, I picked this up at the grocery store, and the man was old, scruffy-looking, and had huge hands."

I was stunned. The man he was describing sounded like the old man who had come to my door and whom I had fed.

With a wave and a "Merry Christmas," we parted. I took the box into the house. There was a small turkey and all the fixings for stuffing, as well as a bag of potatoes, vegetables and an apple pie.

We had a wonderful Christmas with lots to eat and gave thanks for the man, whom to this day I refer to as my mysterious angel.

— Mary M. Alward —

32

A Cruel Joke

Family time is the best time.
~Carmelo Anthony

"Mom, how soon do we eat?"

"Yeah, Mom, when do we eat?"

"John, Jerry," my mother replied, "the turkey isn't done yet."

I persisted, asking, "How much longer 'til it's done?"

"Well, let's see," my mother returned, stepping to the stove. "Boys, come here."

"Yes, Ma'am."

Mom bent over in front of the stove and flipped on the oven's light. "Look inside at the turkey," she said.

I knelt down, cupped my hands at my temples, and peered through the glass in the oven's door. My younger brother did the same.

Then Mom asked, "Do you see that little, white, plastic thingy stuck in the turkey?"

"Yes, Ma'am."

"Well, when that thing pops up, the turkey is done."

"Okay," I replied. Then I removed my face from the glass, asking, "Mom, how does it know?"

Standing erect, Mom laughed. "I don't know," she answered. "It just does."

Jerry and I looked at each other and shrugged.

Mom flipped off the oven light and added, "Now why don't you two go play and come back later to check on the turkey."

"Okay, Mom," Jerry replied.

We scampered across the kitchen's linoleum and disappeared into the family room. We didn't even notice our dad get up from the dining-room table and stride into the kitchen after our departure. Dad never went into the kitchen.

Fifteen minutes later, my mother yelled, "John! Jerry!"

"Yeah, Mom?"

"It's time to check the turkey again!"

Two young boys came tearing back into the kitchen.

As my dad leaned back against the refrigerator and watched, Mom bent over in front of the stove once more and flipped on the oven light. "Check the little, white, plastic thingy," she instructed.

Again, I knelt down, cupped my hands at my temples, and looked through the oven door's glass. Jerry followed suit. Then two boys fell back upon the linoleum with mouths wide open.

"Mom," I began, "didn't you see the little, white, plastic thingy pop up?"

"Yeah, Mom," Jerry added. "You shrunk the turkey!"

Immediately, my dad busted up laughing.

Then Mom grabbed an oven mitt and opened the oven door. She reached inside and pulled out a Cornish game hen that Dad had brought home.

Then Dad removed a turkey that was perfectly done but hidden in a kitchen cabinet.

Later, we feasted on roast turkey, mashed potatoes, bread stuffing, fresh vegetables — and one Cornish game hen.

— John M. Scanlan —

33

Thanksgiving with Mary Jane

Small cheer and great welcome makes a merry feast.
~William Shakespeare

When you're a teenager, there are a million places you'd rather be than at a family gathering. However, when I was fifteen, Thanksgiving at home with my relatives was the best turkey day I've ever celebrated.

A week earlier, the postman had delivered a package from our hippie uncle in Oregon, an artisan potter. Gathered in the kitchen, my two sisters and I watched my mother open the Christmas gift from her younger brother. Inside was a hand-crafted mini broom, a leather strap nailed to its handle for hanging at the hearth. Perfect for our 1916 bungalow's fireplace.

While we read the card wishing us a happy holiday in my aunt's blowsy writing, my mother unwrapped another present: a large freezer bag of homegrown cannabis. Our eyes widened. A resinous, earthy green scent overwhelmed the yellow-tiled kitchen.

My mother froze, holding the illegal parcel from her off-the-grid brother and his part-Blackfoot wife. My grandparents had bought the younger couple a house just so they wouldn't live in a tent on a Santa Cruz mountain, and they stocked my wild cousins with cotton panties so they wouldn't run around without underwear. Compared to that branch of the family tree, our household was conventional. Mom pursed her lips.

My Bohemian New York father swooped in from the living room.

"I'm going to put it in the stuffing," he crowed, snatching the bag from Mom.

"Oh, Charles," my mother sighed as he sprinted up the stairs with the Christmas contraband. A capricious architect, my Lithuanian father liked to bait her about the in-laws.

My traditional Italian grandparents did not embrace my father. They were in the habit of warming to respectful young men in crisp white button-down shirts when my father showed up on their middle-class doorstep in 1959. He was an art-school Beatnik in a ripped T-shirt. Still closely shorn from his stint in the Army, where he'd met my mother on a French base, in no other way was he regulation. He snubbed social convention, burying his nose in political paperbacks during my grandparents' cocktail parties with their keeping-up-with-the-Joneses neighbors. Their proper daughter, an elementary school teacher, could surely do better.

Our nuclear family usually observed holidays at their San José ranch house on a staid cul-de-sac filled with cookie-cutter residences. My dad would be gritting his teeth the entire time. But this year my conservative Chicago grandparents had accepted our invite. They didn't enjoy visiting "fruits and nuts" Berkeley, our feisty university town famous for sparking the Free Speech Movement and agitating against the government's foreign wars. My grandfather complained there were never any spots on the hilly, busy streets to park his boat-like Oldsmobile. Accustomed to La-Z-Boys and sturdy American pieces in walnut from Mervyns, my grandmother found our wicker French café chairs uncomfortable and the Joe DiMaggio giant mitt baffling. "Who wants to sit in a baseball glove?" she protested about the cult classic some Italian designer thought up. We may have lived an hour apart in the San Francisco Bay Area, but we really lived in different worlds.

Another reason my parents didn't host often: Mom wasn't a cook. In fact, my kitchen-averse mother was so grateful when my father offered to deal with the big bird that she christened him the turkey expert and let him do whatever he wanted. So the turkey was Dad's rightful domain, and this year my grandparents would be eating it. They were also bringing a recently widowed neighbor, Mary Jane. I can't say I forgot about the surprise stash, but we all dismissed the stuffing threat. Crazy talk was my father's specialty.

On the morning of November 24, 1979, Dad got up at dawn, prepared his poultry, and went back to bed. By noon, my grandparents had arrived with the sweet-natured widow. The eight of us squeezed into our places at the round butcher-block dining table, café chairs grinding against each other. The turkey was nicely done, not dry. Polite conversation flowed due to the gentle outsider, Mary Jane, who asked a lot of questions.

Suddenly, I spied a big brown bud on the edge of my grandfather's plate, speckled with bread and celery. I glanced at my sisters to see if they had noticed. Pushing food around their plate with secret smiles, they obviously had.

"Your stuffing is very spicy, Charles," effused the widow. "Is that sage?"

We kids stifled giggles.

I couldn't look at my mother. Dad was poker-faced.

"Oh, I'm tipsy! It must be the champagne," tittered Grandma, leaning in to shoulder-nudge her neighbor like a schoolgirl.

After my finicky grandfather cleaned his plate, he went to recline on the Italian baseball mitt. Soon, he was sprawled across the giant glove like Fay Wray in King Kong's hand, snoring. The seventy-something dandy in a mint-green Qiana shirt and white leisure shoes looked comfortable — and finally at home in our place.

We devoured the pumpkin pie and Grandma's anise cookies, but didn't budge from our rosy circle. For the first time, I saw my family as individuals rather than role players. In the lanky figure of Grandpa in repose, I recognized the easy character captured in a 1928 photo of him squatting in front of a baseball dugout. Witnessing chummy Grandma, I understood her life-of-the-party image from a Wisconsin lake in the 1940s, an arm slung around her ten younger siblings. Inside my strait-laced mom, I sensed a woman appreciating her daredevil husband's off-kilter view of the world. And I realized my rebel father wasn't really antisocial if he brought us all together. My sisters suddenly seemed like fellow sojourners navigating teenhood, as well as my natural allies in this normal-slash-bizarre family. They weren't so bad.

When the three seniors said goodbye, our hugs were heartfelt. My father asked Grandpa which route home he'd take, a mellow and unnecessary exchange between the two men.

"Your family is lovely," Mary Jane exclaimed, kissing each of us. "Today was the best since my husband died!"

As the five Ashmans gathered in the kitchen to do the dishes and review the day's events — with uproarious laughter and genuine shock — I found myself thinking of the untamed Oregon folk who couldn't be with us. Their holiday gift ensured they were here in spirit. In that moment, I grasped the meaning of family.

In retrospect, I realize how unorthodox this recipe for a happy family gathering was. But I'll never forget the spirit of 1979's seasoning and what I learned about my relatives that day.

— Anastasia M. Ashman —

Two Merry Christmas Widows

Shared joy is a double joy;
shared sorrow is half a sorrow.
~Swedish Proverb

In October 2017, after three years of learning to cope with my husband's death, I decided to sell my home in Panama City Beach, Florida and move to a new town 200 miles away. Although my best friend Marsha, also a widow, remained behind, we agreed we would always visit one another.

We had created a close bond since being introduced by a couple who knew both of us and believed we would find comfort in sharing our grief and coping with our "new normal" after decades of marriage. Marsha and I, both retired, became cruise buddies and sounding boards for each other.

After Thanksgiving 2017, in my new hometown of Biloxi, Mississippi, where Marsha and I had spent a few days at Christmas and Thanksgiving 2016, I meandered through Walmart. After selecting a few Christmas arrangements to brighten my new apartment, I noticed Christmas attire in the women's department. An above-the-knee, soft, A-line sweater dress particularly caught my eye. Its candy-cane-striped long sleeves, white-and-green bodice and flared skirt with a wide black belt sewn in reminded me of what Santa's elves might wear. *This is adorable and will look so cute with black leggings and knee boots!* I thought to myself.

I bought two!

Then I found a red Christmas derby that I had no doubt would look great on Marsha and a headband with candy canes for me.

Marsha and I had already agreed that she would drive to Biloxi the day before Christmas Eve and stay until Christmas Day. We planned to see the Christmas ice-skating show, have brunch and dinner, and press a few buttons at the MGM Beau Rivage Resort & Casino.

"Girlfriend, do I have a surprise for you!" I told Marsha on our next phone call.

"What is it?"

"I can't tell you!" I said. "You'll have to wait and see. But it's going to bring us lots of fun!"

After Marsha arrived at my apartment on December twenty-third, I couldn't wait to show her our matching outfits.

"Oh, my gosh! These are awesome! But where are we going to wear them?"

"We're dressing up for Christmas Eve! We are going to smile brightly this year and make others smile!"

On Christmas Eve, Marsha and I dressed in our elf dresses, black leggings, and knee boots. We added Christmas earrings, bracelets and necklaces. Marsha looked just as adorable as I knew she would with the red derby placed on top of her beautiful, silky white hair brushed down straight over her ears. I dressed, pulled my long brunette hair into a ponytail, and added my headband with bouncy candy canes. We looked each other over, laughed and agreed we were the cutest over-sixty elves in Biloxi.

Inside the MGM Beau Rivage, families snapped photos of one another among all the Christmas decorations and activities, including visits with Santa. Marsha and I, feeling happy and full of Christmas spirit, almost skipped down the hallway like children. Heads turned and smiles came our way. "You both look adorable!" said one person after another.

Just after dark, a lady approached us with a big smile.

"Hey, you two, aren't you supposed to be out helping Santa tonight?"

Marsha and I stopped for a moment. "Oh, Santa has released us for the rest of the evening. Our work is done at the toy shop till the new year! We're headed to dinner now."

"Well, you both look absolutely fabulous! Merry Christmas!"

We thanked her and looked at one another.

"This is so much fun!" Marsha said. "I'm glad you came up with this idea. It keeps my mind off past Christmases with Charlie."

"I know. Me, too," I said. "I'm so glad we have each other."

Marsha and I walked toward the restaurant for dinner. A couple stopped us.

"Are you with the ice-skating show?"

Again, Marsha and I smiled, feeling that we had really outdone ourselves with our Christmas Eve attire.

"No, we are just two best friends and widows making our way through the holiday without our husbands," I said with a smile.

"Oh, our condolences," they said. "But it's wonderful that you have one another and are able to do something like this to get through it." The couple smiled.

"We are very fortunate to have each other," Marsha said. "No one can make a grief journey alone."

"When you both wake up on Christmas morning," I said to the couple, "let your Christmas presents to one another be to look at each other, give great big smiles, hugs, and kisses, and say 'I love you.' Because no couple knows how long they'll share life together."

They both nodded in agreement. "You're right. We hope you both have a wonderful Christmas, especially given your circumstances," said the husband.

At dinner, where we continued to receive smiles and compliments, Marsha and I spoke excitedly to one another about how fabulous our Christmas Eve day had been.

"We've received a lot of smiles and sweet comments," Marsha said. "It sure makes a person feel good."

"Yes, it does. And we've provided smiles to others," I said. "It's a good health benefit, you know. Lowers stress and blood pressure, and puts people in a better mood."

Marsha said, "So, I guess we gave out lots of gifts today. And got some back!"

I agreed, and with a little laugh, I said, "You know, we have to make this an annual event and call ourselves the two Merry Christmas widows!"

Marsha agreed as we toasted one another, grateful that this Christmas was just a bit easier because we chose to do something unique in the holiday season to ease our grieving hearts.

— Deborah Tainsh —

35

The Puzzle

Great minds think alike.
~English Proverb

"Hahaha!" Dad screamed maniacally, sounding scarily like a B-movie monster as he clutched the jigsaw puzzle to his chest. "She'll hate this! Hahaha!" Dad had to clutch his sides he was laughing so hard.

It was the early 1960s, and our family was Christmas shopping. Mom had taken my little sister to the other side of the small department store, which left my brother, sister and I standing with jaws dropped, wondering what on earth had gotten into Dad for him to be acting so strangely over a 1,000-piece, non-interlocking jigsaw puzzle. The picture on the cover of the box showed mostly variant shades of a blue sky and a few small green slashes for trees.

"Who is that present for, Dad?" I hesitantly asked. He was acting really weird.

The adults in the extended family drew names to get each other presents and had a five-dollar spending limit. I knew Dad had drawn Grandma's name, and Grandma had drawn Dad's name. Even at a young age, I knew that Dad and his mother-in-law, my grandma, had "issues" with each other. Maybe it was the two-hour rant Dad went on after we left Grandma's house and were driving home that gave this away to me. They barely tolerated being in the same room together. So, it was somewhat ironic that they were the only two family members who refused to work on the jigsaw puzzle my Aunt Mary set up on a card table at Christmas time. They each made no secret of the fact that doing jigsaw puzzles drove them crazy. That was how I positively knew the puzzle couldn't be for Grandma.

Dad paused for a moment and then admitted a little defensively, "This is for Grandma. I know she doesn't normally like jigsaw puzzles, but she'll have hours and hours AND HOURS of fun putting together this great, big…" He couldn't go on as hysterical laughter overtook him again.

Back in those days, you didn't argue with your father, so I just kept quiet and watched as the clerk rang up the sale and we left the store. I was pretty sure Grandma would get Dad something not great but not bad either, possibly a box of handkerchiefs. Grandma was sure going to be disappointed.

I didn't see the puzzle again until Christmas morning. My aunt, uncle, cousins, Mom, Dad, brother, sisters, Grandpa and Grandma were all crowded into Grandma's living room amid a ton of discarded wrapping paper and ribbon. We had all enjoyed opening our presents, but the gift-opening was winding down. There were only two brightly wrapped gifts left under the small Christmas tree that Grandpa had set up in the corner. It was Grandma's turn, so she opened the next-to-last gift and pulled out her jigsaw puzzle. Everyone got a big laugh out of the gag gift, even Grandma, who giggled so hard that tears ran down her cheeks.

We found out what caused Grandma's hilarity a few seconds later when Dad opened his present from Grandma. She had the last laugh after all. We all roared as Dad took the wrappings off his present and, instead of a box of handkerchiefs, he stared at a box with a huge picture of beige sandy pyramids on the outside and 2,000 non-interlocking pieces on the inside!

— Cynthia Morningstar —

36

Christmas Mysteries

*Love is what's in the room with you at Christmas
if you stop opening presents and listen.*
~Author Unknown

Christmas morning always starts off with a little bit of chaos, especially in a house full of seven kids. The first child to wake up runs to the nearest sibling's room. First, he knocks quietly, but the knocks generally get louder and louder until the target wakes up. Then, the group builds until all seven kids are awake and knocking at my parents' door, begging to be allowed into the living room to see if Santa has visited. Once the okay is given, all seven kids rush out to see what Santa has left them. But what is unusual about my house is that we have to wait for my mother to tell us our names before opening presents.

Now, I promise we aren't all insane. We do actually know our names. But my mother discovered at an early age that we could not be trusted with our presents before Christmas morning. Patience is a virtue not abundant in my family. So, she developed a plan. Instead of letting my ruffian siblings tear through her beautiful display of presents and complain that someone received more presents or anything of the sort, she decided to change the names on our gifts. Each year, after picking a theme, she comes up with code names. The themes have included *Harry Potter* characters, candy bars, sodas, TV show characters, planets, and many more.

However, kids will be kids; my siblings and I developed our own tradition. We would take stock of all of the names. Then, from there, we would attempt to use our powers of deduction to figure out which code name matched up to each child. If there were two presents that felt alike, we would assume they were for my twin brothers. If there were a few that were identical we would conclude that they were either for the boys or the girls. Really, we developed a lot of tricks. We would all end up sitting on the living-room floor and sprawled under the Christmas tree, announcing our theories and sharing ideas.

My mother would sit and watch us climbing all around the tree, giggling to herself. When we would try to confirm our suspicions, she would merely smirk. Honestly, the month before Christmas was the time when my siblings really learned how to work as a team. Weirdly, we also all score very high in our logic and deduction skills; it is almost like we have been developing them for years. On Christmas morning, she would announce our names or give us the item that we were named after, like a specific candy bar or soda, and laugh as we all teased each other about who was right or wrong.

My siblings are all pretty much grown now. My older sisters live in another state, and my older brothers no longer live at home. But even after twenty-plus years, if you show up at the right time, you can see a couple of grown children snooping under the tree. Even this year, on Christmas morning, you can find lists of names tucked into pajama pockets and my mom smirking behind her coffee cup.

— Rose Hofer —

37

The Separation

Mothers and fathers do really crazy things
with the best of intentions.
~Rosalind Wiseman

W hen I graduated from college and moved to the other side of the state, Mom was downhearted. The next year, when my sister graduated from college and moved across the country, Mom was dejected. And when neither of us got home to visit for the next year, Mom was downright miserable.

So, I wasn't surprised when Mom called me the weekend before Thanksgiving to complain.

"It's not right," Mom grumbled. "Neither you nor your sister came home for any holidays this year — not Christmas, not Easter, not even Groundhog Day."

"Why would we come home for Groundhog Day?" I asked.

"I have no idea," Mom replied. "But it would have been nice."

"I told you I just can't make it home right now," I said.

"Then I guess I should break the news to you now," Mom sighed. "Your father and I have decided on a separation."

This couldn't be happening. Not my parents! I hadn't even known anything was wrong, but obviously it had been a while since I'd been home.

Shortly after hanging up with Mom, I received a series of frantic texts from my sister. She'd heard the news, too.

I rushed to my laptop and scheduled a last-minute flight home on Wednesday in time to meet my sister when she arrived at the airport. We planned to share a rental car to my parents' house.

Wednesday evening, my sister and I shared a long hug at the airport when she disembarked from her flight. Her arrival had been delayed due to bad weather in the Midwest, so I'd had plenty of time to claim my luggage and pick up the rental car before she arrived.

"What's going on?" my sister asked. "Mom called me nonchalantly mentioning a separation."

"Same for me," I replied as we climbed into the car. "I thought everything was fine."

Forty minutes later, we reached our parents' colonial, suburban home. The windows were brightly lit, and pumpkins lined the front steps.

"Hello," called my sister, rapping on the back door as we stepped into the kitchen. "Mom? Dad?"

"What are you doing here?" answered Mom. She was at the sink washing dishes in her apron. She grabbed us in a hug. "The kids are home!" she called to our father.

Dad emerged from the den, smiling. "What a surprise," he said, hugging us.

"You shouldn't be surprised," I responded, taking off my coat, "especially after Mom's phone call."

"What phone call?" asked Dad.

"The call about the separation," answered my sister.

"Oh, brother." Dad tucked his hands in his pockets and began walking back toward the den.

"Hold it," said my sister, folding her arms. "What's going on?"

Dad shook his head. "Your mother told me to mind my own business, or she wouldn't make pumpkin pie. And I want pumpkin pie." He disappeared into the den.

"Yes, about the separation…" Mom said as she scooped her Thanksgiving-themed salt-and-pepper shakers off the stove and handed one to each of us. "I'm giving you these."

I got the Mr. Pilgrim saltshaker; he stood at attention in his buckle hat with a musket in one arm and a turkey in the other. My sister got the Mrs. Pilgrim peppershaker; she wore a bonnet and held a pumpkin.

"What's this?" inquired my sister.

"Like I told you," Mom said, "your father and I decided on a separation — of the pilgrim salt-and-pepper shakers."

"No, no, no!" I pointed at Mom. "You said 'separation,' but you never said 'salt-and-pepper-shakers.' We thought you and Dad were getting a separation."

Mom held up her hands, laughing. "Your father and I have been married for twenty-six years," she said. "We can't separate! Your father could never survive on his own."

"I can hear you!" Dad shouted from the den.

"And you know it's true," answered Mom. She motioned to my sister and me. "Sit, relax. I'll make tea."

"Mom, you lied to us," said my sister.

Mom shook her head. "No, you misunderstood. That's all right, we'll have plenty of room at the table tomorrow." Mom put the kettle on the stove, and then shrugged her shoulders. "All I know is that I no longer have pilgrim salt-and-pepper-shakers, but my children, who haven't been home in ages, are here for Thanksgiving."

"This is unbelievable," I said to my sister. "We were outsmarted by our mother and a pair of ceramic pilgrims."

"I guess the important point is that children should come home on a regular basis," said Mom. "That way, they'll know for sure what's happening with their family."

"What are we supposed to do with half a set of shakers?" asked my sister.

"They're a nice memento." Mom grinned. "A reminder to visit home more often."

When I got home that Sunday, I placed Mr. Pilgrim on my nightstand — a token of my lesson learned. My sister keeps Mrs. Pilgrim on her desk at work.

I know Mom has a set of Mr. and Mrs. Santa Claus salt-and-pepper-shakers, so if I stay away from home too long, another separation announcement might be imminent. Just to be on the safe side, my sister and I now make sure to visit our parents as often as possible.

—David Hull—

Penguins and Polar Bears

A lot of funny stuff happens in Canada!
~Samantha Bee

I n the Vancouver area, as in a number of other areas, where cold air and colder water are a natural part of winter, a New Year's Day tradition has emerged that baffles even the most open-minded logician. It's called The Polar Bear Swim. Swim is actually a misnomer, because no one is really in the water long enough to swim; however people do don bathing attire and occasionally more bizarre costumes, and plunge into English Bay for a few microseconds. Then they return to dry land and celebrate their survival with a quick shot of something warming that they may have been drinking the night before as well.

As a keen observer of questionable human behaviour, I am drawn to understanding this odd phenomenon. My initial thoughts about the impetus behind this strange tradition center on the excessive use of alcohol the night before which, we can agree, is an even more established tradition. There are many theories. The first simply postulates that those who participate are still in advanced stages of inebriation and therefore do not have any clue as to what they are doing. They just attach themselves to some screaming herd of equally inebriated persons, and en masse head in a random direction, which ends up at the low tide mark of the local beach. However, evidence does not support this, for if it were true, we would expect to see other random herds of drunken people doing equally stupid things like cramming into busses naked or riding the baggage carousels at the airport. We don't see those, or at least not often, so clearly the New Year's dip is not a random drunken event, especially since we see it repeated reliably each and every year.

Another possible explanation is cold water as counter-irritant therapy to a severe hangover. However, this does not make a lot of sense either. I liken this to sitting on a soldering iron to distract from the pain of a toothache. In the most severe cases of post partying pain, attempting suicide by drowning might seem plausible but if one's mood were that low, one would not likely wear a Spandex Grinch costume to one's demise.

There could, perhaps, be a more spiritual explanation. The New Year symbolizes a new beginning, re-birth, starting over etc. This could provide a plausible explanation, with the ocean being the metaphoric baptismal font — a celebration of life. The fact that a number of emergency vehicles, with resuscitation equipment, are present might cloud that theory. However, it might also be supported by the fact that most men's private parts have already begun to shrink down toward neonatal proportions just by thinking of the cold water ahead.

All of this questioning and considering has now led me here, on the beach in my neighbourhood of Port Moody, where a smaller clone of the English Bay event is being celebrated. It is called the Penguin Plunge. Against my better judgment I am here with my *Nightmare Before Christmas* T-shirt, and my red Santa booties.

The ratio of observers to participants hovers around 6,000 to one, indicating once again, that jumping into freezing water is a questionable pastime enjoyed by only a special few, and that voyeuristic sadism is a very popular form of entertainment. We are relegated to a roped off area of the beach while the observers are stationed high above where they can't be splashed by any errant drops. The semi-naked shivering people around me are attired in Christmassy water themes.

There are only two emergency vehicles here. This disturbs me very much. I think that there should be a hell of a lot more. I am also deeply concerned that if someone should expire, they may face the eternal humiliation of meeting St. Peter while half naked, wearing felt reindeer antlers and a *Little Mermaid* life-ring.

The countdown takes place. I nervously turn and look at my wife Barbara, who is there with our dog Rebus, just in case some family emergency arises that would sadly take me away from this. She smiles and waves her gloved hand back at me in encouragement. Rebus is next to her in his doggy hoody and matching booties. He looks at me oddly — oh God, maybe he is unwell, maybe I need to rush him to the vet right now....

The run begins and I pray to St. Darrell, the patron saint of silly buggers. I need his help like last year in Pamplona. He must protect me. I hit the water screaming with all the others. One million stinging needles shatter my body and I feel death trying to snatch me — and then the water hits my knees and it is much worse... and then I am frigid, and iced and glacially frozen but I am not cold.

No — I am, in fact, very cool!

— Stefano Mazzega —

Chapter 5

The Perfect Gift

Bright and Shiny

Gratitude is the best attitude.
~Author Unknown

As Christmas approaches, I usually start hinting to my husband about potential gifts for me. I'll say things like, "Gee hon, that's a lovely necklace they have over at the mall." Or, "There are a ton of new books at Barnes & Noble I'd love to read."

But over the years, I have learned that this tactic is not an effective one. For many years I struggled to understand my husband's lack of ability to understand "hints." Was he just being stubborn? Were the items too expensive? Did he need to have his hearing checked?

It was last Christmas, when I finally began to understand my husband. Under the Christmas tree, was a large box wrapped with beautiful holiday paper. I was stunned. What could it be? I was pleased that my husband had finally thought of me. He wrapped the present slowly and carefully. This was unusual as gifts from my husband usually come in plain envelopes or white plastic shopping bags.

Was it a music box, a snow globe or perhaps a lovely figurine?

"Nope," my husband said. I would just have to wait to find out.

On Christmas morning, I eagerly opened the present to see what my thoughtful husband had so carefully selected for me. I ripped off the paper, tore open the box and stared at my present in disbelief. Inside the box, sat a beautiful... colander.

I looked curiously at my husband. Was this a joke? Was my real present cleverly concealed underneath this kitchen utensil? No... nothing underneath.

My husband looked at me and smiled, quite pleased with his purchase, certain that I was going to love it. Now, I must admit, it is the most beautiful colander I have ever seen. It is shiny and metallic, almost too expensive-looking for draining pasta or washing lettuce. It sparkles under the light.

"I know you need one," Pete said, "and this one looks so pretty. When I saw it, I thought of you."

It was then that I realized how fortunate I am to have this wonderful man in my life. He does not place value on material things. He does not try to impress others. He sees the beauty in things that appear ordinary. But most importantly, he knows just what I need, whether it is a long silent hug, some straightforward advice or just a single comment that breaks my tense mood and makes me laugh. By embracing the beauty of this simple colander, he made me realize that he is the perfect father to our children and the perfect husband for me, for he truly sees what others cannot.

I realized that like this ordinary colander, I too am an ordinary mom with an ordinary function. But to my husband I am not like this colander because it is ordinary, I am like this colander because I am an ordinary mom who is also bright and shiny. To him, I sparkle. To Pete I am one-of-a-kind and for that, I am grateful.

I use this colander a lot, and every time I do, I laugh out loud. I think it is hilarious how this shiny, beautiful, ordinary kitchen utensil that I use every day is what made my husband think of me.

Now, while I do appreciate my one-of-a-kind colander, this year I have a new tactic for Christmas: I'm handing him a picture of a lovely diamond necklace.

I hope this time he gets the hint.

—Lisa Peters—

40

He Listened

The most precious gift we can offer
anyone is our attention.
~Thich Nhat Hanh

Christmas was three weeks away and my husband was fishing for ideas for my present. I smiled because he is always so thoughtful when it comes to buying Christmas gifts and I have never been disappointed by his choices. "Actually," he announced, "I'd like to buy you some bras."

That got my attention and I listened intently as he explained that, while he was relatively familiar with the broader world of lingerie, he wasn't quite sure what size or kind of bra I would wear. He wanted some direction.

I paused. He waited. We sat together on the couch looking at each other with a funny smirk on our faces until I finally broke the silence.

"I would love for you to buy me a bra, but what I really need are practical bras. I don't need fancy, frilly, romantic, lacy bras for our intimate rendezvous in the bedroom. I already have a wide variety of items for that, many of which you bought for me. What I really need are practical bras to wear during the day and your timing is great… mine are almost shot."

Disappointment spread across his face as I explained what I meant by practical bras. I needed at least three, all in neutral colors: one black, one white, and one ivory. I needed bras that were comfortable enough to wear all day long, and for me that meant bras with support but no underwire. I needed bras with a little padding so that I could avoid embarrassment while wearing a lightweight and formfitting blouse to the office during the summer months when the AC kicks into high gear. I needed bras that were solid color and sparing in lace and design because the additional detail, while pretty and feminine, might show through some of my more delicate, yet professional sweaters.

My husband paid close attention, but I could tell that practical wasn't what he had in mind. Regardless, I was delighted Christmas morning when I opened one of my many presents and found three practical bras: one white, one ivory, and one black! He had done it. My husband had listened carefully to my wishes and delivered on every aspect. I was so pleased I giggled with joy, and then he handed me my next present. Gently, I unwrapped three beautiful and sexy dresses, each one designed with lots of color, lace and fabulous detail.

"One to wear over each new bra," he said, and we both laughed out loud.

Those three bras turned out to be my favorite Christmas present and a fond memory. They were not overly expensive. They were not elegant or lavish. They were not even anything I'd want to brag about to our friends and family members. But, they were everything I asked for. They were also symbolic of my husband's effort to keep his wedding vows. On our wedding day, before God and many witnesses, we promised to be loving and faithful: in plenty and in want, in joy and in sorrow, in sickness and in health, as long we both shall live. Little did he know that "plenty and want" might someday include practical bras.

— Kristen Clark —

41

The Gift that Keeps on Giving

No matter what his rank or position may be,
the lover of books is the richest and
the happiest of the children of men.
~John Alfred Langford

Christmas was always my mom's favorite holiday. She never said so, but it was easy to see in the joy she derived from giving. She'd take days off from work to bake cookies and give most of them away. The thought she put into gifts was extraordinary, and she tried to surprise us with at least one completely unexpected item each year.

The greatest gift I ever received from her, however, was my love of reading. This is the gift I took with me to Iraq during my 2008-9 deployment. I managed to read a book each week. That meant I had to regularly mail books home to make room for new ones. Shipping typically took two weeks so I had to keep about a half dozen books in order to have something fresh. Even a small number of books can be burdensome when traveling to the other side of the world. Being stationed at three different Iraq bases over the course of that year made it even more so.

I still had more than three years left in my enlistment when I came home from Iraq so I knew I had one more deployment left. By Christmas 2009, e-readers were becoming less expensive. I asked my mom for one, a simple black and white device that would be seen as clunky and woefully outdated within a few years, but which served me well.

That e-reader bounced around the U.S. with me from the California desert to the hills of Kentucky and eventually to my little lakeside home in Michigan. It also traveled with me on my next trip to the other side of the world, this time to the snowy mountains of Afghanistan in January of 2011.

Because of that deployment's timing, I had asked my mom to resist temptation and not give me anything for the previous Christmas. There was no reason for me to expect that it would be her last Christmas. As I made my way home to bury her that spring, I brought my e-reader, trying to distract myself through delays and layovers. I never thought about it being the last gift she ever gave me.

About a week before Christmas 2015, a female friend asked me for some reading recommendations. She had been offered some free e-books, but her old smartphone wouldn't work as a reading device. Excitedly, I let her know I had a perfect gift for her, a paper book that seemed to perfectly suit her request. Unfortunately, there was a big problem with that. I had forgotten about giving away my extra copy a few days before, and the one I had had been personally signed for me. I felt guilty and scrambled to find another copy.

Then I remembered my old e-reader collecting dust in the corner. It already had access to the book I offered and several others that had been recommended to her. I hardly used it because I preferred paper books myself once I wasn't moving around so much. But I had kept the device because it was my mom's last gift to me. I paused only for a moment. My mom would've been proud of me for giving it away.

I sent that old e-reader to my friend on her birthday. She would take it with her as she traveled many miles to her family home for Christmas. Giving away my mom's last gift became an incredible gift to me, helping me to feel her spirit once again during her favorite holiday.

Had the story ended there, I would still be filled with joy. It was a gift that kept giving, though. My old e-reader is once again collecting dust in a corner of my house. It's a different house this time, one I bought with my friend the following summer. A picture of my mom hangs on the wall smiling at us, and I often smile back, thanking her for the generosity that has brought me so much joy.

— Drew Sheldon —

42

Daddy's Last Christmas

*He was a father. That's what a father does. Eases the
burdens of those he loves. Saves the ones he loves from
painful last images that might endure for a lifetime.*
~George Saunders

My daddy had been sick for several years with Alzheimer's and Parkinson's disease. Before the diseases robbed him of his mind, he had earned a bachelor's, master's, and doctorate degree in theology, and had been a pastor since he was sixteen.

During the previous forty years, all at the same time, he worked as an editor, a chaplain for the local fire and police departments as well as the state highway patrol, and hosted a weekly radio show. Not only did he pastor a local church, he was considered the town chaplain and wrote for two local papers.

Last year, the months leading up to Christmas were extremely hard because we knew it would be Daddy's last. Our family loved the season, but what we usually celebrated as a joyous and eventful time had a dark cloud hanging over it.

Daddy could still walk a little but had hardly spoken since late October, and anything he did say made absolutely no sense. He didn't recognize any of us, not even my mom, his wife of sixty-plus years. His children and grandchildren were all strangers, except for me. I look so much like a younger version of my mother that he often called me my mom's nickname: "Barbs."

In early November, I sat with him listening to music while my mom took a much-deserved nap. Suddenly, he looked me straight in the eye and said with complete clarity, "I know Christmas is coming, and I want you to do me a favor. Your mom loves bracelets. I want you to find her a silver bracelet with two charms on it: a double heart and a pair of boots. (My daddy was from west Texas and constantly wore boots, even to the beach.) I also want to get the three of you kids a sterling boot charm."

I thought it might be nice to have a note from Daddy to go along with the gifts, so I asked if he thought he could write his name. But this great wordsmith had been robbed of even being able to scrawl his own name. I wrote out both words, and after many tries, he managed to scribble out "George" and "Dad." He told me what he wanted on the two notes. I would type them out and place his name on each one. One note for Mom: "For the love of my life." And for us kids: "Always remember the way I was." Then he turned on a dime and became the man we didn't know again.

Those were his last thirty minutes of lucidity. He didn't speak another word to anyone. Christmas was emotional for all of us except for Daddy. He didn't know any of us and spent the day unpacking and packing his Christmas stocking. No one knew about his gifts but me. My brother opened his first, and the tears began to flow. My sister wouldn't open hers.

A few weeks later, he was gone. But that last Christmas, we received gifts even more precious than silver or gold. We got one more look into the mind of the man who loved us so much that his last thoughts were of making us happy. While it was a bittersweet Christmas, it was one our whole family would cherish for the rest of our lives.

— Jennifer Clark Davidson —

43

Christmas Cookies

It isn't the size of the gift that matters,
but the size of the heart that gives it.
~Eileen Elias Freeman,
The Angels' Little Instruction Book

It was 1955. My dad made $47 a week as a watchmaker, and Mom took in mending for a local dry cleaning shop in order to make ends meet. Our small wartime house on Fifth Street was clean and organized, but sparsely furnished. Our blue living room rug was secondhand; a pathway of jute backing marked the flow of family traffic from the front door, through the living room and into the kitchen. We had very little, but lacked for nothing as Mom could make, grow or create whatever we needed to sustain us. My brother, Alan, and I, never knew that we were poor.

Just before the Christmas holidays, Miss Campbell, my grade two teacher, suggested we have a party. She brought a real tree into the classroom, which we decorated with coloured paper and soda straw ornaments. She passed a box around which contained folded paper slips on which was printed each of our names. We had to buy a gift for the person whose name we drew, and we couldn't spend more than three dollars.

To me, Harvey Ferguson was the cutest boy in class. He was tall, had blond hair and freckles and got into trouble almost as often as I did. Being sent to the cloakroom at the back of the class was the "time out" of choice. Harvey and I spent a lot of time in the cloakroom.

When I talked him into peeing in the rubber boots I thought he was the funniest guy on the planet, even though he also peed in mine.

When I drew his name for the Christmas gift, I was thrilled. I couldn't believe my good luck and was determined to buy him the best gift ever. I ran home and begged my mom for the three dollars, but she refused.

"I can buy enough meat for several meals for three dollars," she said. She wasn't about to waste it on a school chum's Christmas gift. I begged and pleaded. I had imagined myself going down to Orek's Five and Dime and buying an airplane, or toy gun or something that wound up, but Mom said that all I could give him was something from home. She suggested cookies. I was devastated. Anybody could have cookies — Mom baked them all the time. Cookies were nothing special. I couldn't believe she would embarrass me like this — in front of Harvey and the whole class.

Mom made a special box and covered it with patterned Christmas paper and covered the lid with bright red foil. She lined the inside with tissue. Then she made sugar cookies. She cut the dough into three pieces and coloured two of them red and green. She then rolled the dough into ropes, which she cut into short lengths. She twisted the colours evenly to make candy cane shapes. She placed them on a baking sheet and sprinkled them with sugar before putting them into the oven. They smelled great, and they looked beautiful when they were cooked, but they were just cookies and I was still mortified by the thought of giving them to Harvey Ferguson.

On the day of the party we put our gifts under the tree. We sang carols and talked about the meaning and magic of Christmas, and then the time came. Ellen, the smartest kid in class was chosen to be "Santa" and she rose to the occasion with pride. She read each name aloud as she passed the gifts out to the class. We were to open them in unison. I stared at the small package on my desk without much interest. I was too busy feeling sorry for myself. I watched as Harvey received my mother's wrapped and ribboned box, and wished I could disappear into the floorboards. When the last gift had been presented Miss Campbell said "you can open them now!" and a mad rustling of paper began. I looked down at the present I'd been given. It was barrettes.

Harvey took his time. Other kids were holding up pencil crayons and cut-outs and plastic cars. Harvey opened the box my mom had wrapped, folded back the tissue paper and stared. "Cookies!" he said. I winced and shrank into my seat. "A whole box of homemade cookies — all for me?" He didn't know who had given them to him, but when I nodded, he looked at me and smiled. "My mom NEVER bakes cookies!" he cried… "This is the best gift EVER!"

He closed the box again and held it to his chest. He said he was going to take the cookies home and share them, and that he'd tell his family they came from me. I felt strange. It was hard to believe that his mom didn't bake cookies. We had homemade bread and cookies and pies and everything — all the time. I suddenly realized how lucky I was and how rich our lives were, even though we didn't have enough money to share — even at Christmas.

Harvey talked about those Christmas cookies again and again. Maybe he was hoping I'd bring him some more. I don't know. What I do know is — I'd given him something better than a store-bought toy, I'd given him something personal; something that had taken time to make. I'd given him a gift that, for different reasons, we both would always remember.

— Lynn Johnston —

The Joy of Simpler Gift-Giving

*Gifts of time and love are surely the basic ingredients
of a truly merry Christmas.*
~Peg Bracken

Several weeks before Christmas, inspired by articles on "alternative gift-giving" as a way to take the stress out of holidays, I decided to include my entire extended family in an e-mail discussion about how we might make Christmas easier on everyone. I ticked off the reasons in my head: (a) we all had plenty of "stuff" without adding more; (b) some of us were on limited or fixed incomes; (c) most of us led busy lives and might enjoy skipping crowded shopping malls and post offices.

Nevertheless, I approached the task with trepidation. My sister, after all, had six — that's right, six — artificial Christmas trees she decorated every year, each with a special theme. I didn't know how it would strike her that I wanted to simplify gift-giving. Other family members all seemed to be fine with the traditional way of buying gifts. Would they think I was trying to ruin Christmas?

My first e-mail went out in September: "I'm starting a dialogue early this year. I know that we all have our own ideas about gift-giving but maybe we could try something different this year. Please share your thoughts." I attached copies of the articles I'd read.

As the weeks went by, e-mails flew back and forth. My son, who had recently discovered the joys of working with clay, wrote, "I think we should all give pottery!" I replied that I would welcome homemade gifts.

My mother-in-law sent a lengthy e-mail about what she didn't want to receive as a gift, including charitable donations given in her name. It didn't seem personal enough, she felt. I affirmed her willingness to speak her truth.

All of us chimed in with gift ideas that were both meaningful and simple. The declared winners were: (1) a family photograph from the past that came with a special memory, perhaps with a written explanation of that memory; (2) a used book that somehow expressed an attribute of the person receiving it; or (3) a special card. The only "ground rules" were that we could each choose any of the three ideas, and that no "store-bought" gifts would be exchanged or expected.

As the days between Thanksgiving and Christmas passed, I experienced a new spaciousness to the holiday season. Instead of making endless lists of gifts and trooping through malls looking for things my family might like, I roamed through my own bookshelves. Suitable books for various family members almost leaped off the shelves. I relaxed into the season in a new way, free from the gift-buying anxiety that had plagued me in past years.

Three weeks before Christmas, all my "shopping" had been done and I had a wonderful time wrapping my selections in beautiful pictures saved from old calendars — just the right size for books.

Inspired by my newfound freedom, I also decided to create a special booklet of favorite quotations for each family member, to go along with their books — something I had wanted to do in previous years but never found the time to accomplish.

Finally the day came. Our gift exchanges were joyous and peaceful. Each book was a treasured gift. My mother-in-law gave each of us a handmade card and asked us to write in them a wish for ourselves for the coming year. She collected the cards and said she would give them back to us at the end of the year to see if our wishes came true. From my sister I received a beautiful framed childhood photo of the two of us that brought back special memories; from my daughter-in-law came a humorous book that recalled my Southern heritage.

And my son... He gave us his best pottery creations to date — "memory bowls," he called them, each uniquely created to hold whatever family treasure or written memory we wanted to place in it.

Freedom from the tyranny of gift-buying — the tyranny of living up to cultural expectations of what Christmas "should" be like — also gave me freedom to experience the joy and diversity of who we are as a family. I can hardly wait to see what we'll do next year!

— Maril Crabtree —

45

A Perfectly Timed Gift

Blessed is the season which engages the
whole world in a conspiracy of love!
~Hamilton Wright Mabie

It was two days before Christmas and I still felt numb. Steve had passed away in late September and I was doing the best I could to celebrate the season. My two adult sons wanted to carry on some of our family traditions like our Christmas Eve Open House, but I knew others would end.

Every year, Steve and I always put a special gift for each other under the tree. I made sure he had something fun, and he made sure I had something from Saffees, my favorite women's clothing store. No matter what other additional gifts we exchanged, these were the two that mattered most.

Although Steve was no longer here to celebrate, I kept wondering what I could give him. That probably seemed strange to everyone, but for thirty-seven years we had exchanged gifts, and I just wasn't ready to stop. I stubbornly asked my sons, "What should I buy for your dad?"

I finally settled on naming a star after Steve. Because he was an avid space enthusiast, I knew it was the perfect gift, and I could envision him having fun seeking it out just to see the heavenly orb that now bore his name. I didn't mind not having a gift from him, except that it was just another sign that he was no longer with us.

Later, as I was putting the finishing touches on wrapping presents, the phone rang. It was the manager of Saffees, whom we had gotten to know quite well over the years. "Vicki, could I stop by your house after work? I've got something I need to give you."

I couldn't imagine what Bonnie might have for me because I knew Steve was too ill to have pre-arranged something three months in advance. So I waited patiently until she arrived at the door, and to my surprise, she was holding a beautifully wrapped present to place under the tree.

She explained that the owner of the store had suddenly awoken in the middle of the night and thought, "What about Vicki?" He knew our tradition and he and Bonnie had selected something they knew I would like. They wanted to make sure that Steve's traditional gift for me continued on what they knew would be a very difficult Christmas Day.

As I accepted this special act of kindness, it was difficult not to cry. For one last time, our tradition was honored — I gave Steve a gift of fun, and my package from Saffees was under the tree.

— Vicki L. Julian —

46

The Year I Was Mrs. Claus

To give without any reward, or any notice,
has a special quality of its own.
~Anne Morrow Lindbergh

I t was the most fun job I ever had. At the time I was a college student raising my then nine-year-old son, Joshua, on my own. In fact, Joshua and I had been on our own since before he drew his first breath.

Single parenting came with both challenges and joys. All too often there was no money for the extras other families took for granted.

But somehow I always managed to make Christmas special for Joshua. In addition, I was able to buy a few presents for myself, usually things I was in need of, and open them Christmas morning. It prevented Joshua from wondering why Santa brought no presents for Mum.

The year he was nine I was in college and living on a student loan. It was tight. Christmas was less than three weeks away and I still hadn't managed to buy my son the few gifts he'd asked for. A church downtown was giving away toys and clothing to families in need. Swallowing my pride, I decided to go see what I could find.

I was ushered into a back room with a group of women of all ages. A long table held slim pickings, but I managed to find a couple of board games I thought Joshua might like. A middle-aged woman with stiff bluish hair approached me and asked how many children

I had. When I said, "one little boy," she bellowed, "One gift only for each child!"

Everyone looked at me as if I had been caught stealing. I was so embarrassed I put the games down and walked away with what pride I had left.

I didn't want to repeat that humiliating experience, but for Joshua's sake I began to consider swallowing my pride and perhaps visiting another church giving away toys.

One crisp snowy day, while walking downtown, a large poster of a fat, jolly Santa with an overflowing bag of toys in front of a fireplace caught my attention. On his knee was a smiling little girl with pretty golden curls whispering in his ear. A huge sign welcomed boys and girls to visit Santa at the department store for the next three Saturdays before Christmas.

An idea hit me. Rather than seeking church donations, I'd make Christmas for Joshua using my wits and imagination. The answer to my situation was staring me right in the face. Santa was coming to town, but what about Mrs. Claus? Why should she be left behind at the North Pole baking cookies, while Mr. Claus has all the fun listening to the giggled secrets of children?

Stepping into the store, I boldly asked a saleslady if the store manager was available. There was no turning back as I headed toward the manager's office and knocked on the door. I was expecting to see a middle-aged man wearing a starched white dress shirt and tie. Imagine my surprise when I found an attractive, young female manager sitting behind a desk.

Introducing myself, I pitched the idea of Mrs. Claus accompanying Mr. Claus to the mall. The words came with ease. I was in need of employment, trying to make Christmas for my little boy and was applying for a job as Mrs. Claus. The manager mulled over the idea, asked a few questions and hired me on the spot, more or less.

"You'll need to dress as Mrs. Claus if you want the job," she said. "We can try it for a day, and if it works out, you can come back the Saturdays leading up to Christmas."

I thanked her and left. I made a quick stop at a secondhand

clothing store and purchased a red top and a matching skirt. I stopped at a sewing shop and bought a huge roll of cotton and balls of white yarn. And I went home to put it together.

The next morning, I carefully packed a paper bag with my home-made costume, and raced downtown to the department store. After ducking into a changing room, I emerged dressed as Mrs. Claus.

"Come in," called the manager when I knocked on her door. Taking a deep breath I stepped into her office. "Good Morning, I'm Mrs. Claus." If she was taken by surprise, she didn't show it.

"You have the job," she said. "Tie your long hair into a bun, and be here Saturday morning by ten. You can pass out balloons to the children waiting to see Santa. You'll get paid before Christmas, like the rest of the staff."

"Sure, I can do that," I said casually, wanting to jump up and down with excitement.

I loved the job — it was so much fun. Joshua told all his friends that his mom was Mrs. Claus at the Mall. As the month wore on, my best friend, Liz, agreed to bring Joshua and her daughter, Katie, downtown to visit Santa on the last Saturday before Christmas.

The two kids were excited about seeing Santa and getting a treat. Liz jokingly told them to behave while they waited in the line-up because Mrs. Claus would be watching, and if they weren't good, she would put their names on the naughty list.

Katie and Joshua giggled when I offered them balloons. Joshua whispered in my ear that he had a wish list for Santa.

"What's on your wish list, Joshua?" I asked, worried about being able to fulfill his expectations.

"It's between Santa and me," he replied, holding the list tightly in his fist. Later I saw Joshua pass his list to Santa, while he pointed to Mrs. Claus who was talking with the waiting children. Old Santa winked at me and tucked Joshua's wish list in his pocket.

At the end of the last day, and after an endless line-up of children, it was quitting time for Mr. and Mrs. Claus. Before I left for home the store manager gave me a substantial paycheque — which included a very generous bonus. I was overjoyed, because now I could make

Christmas for Joshua without having to resort to handouts.

Late on Christmas Eve, long after Joshua had gone to bed, there was a knock on my apartment door. "Who could this be calling so late?" I wondered. I opened the door a crack to take a peek.

"Ho, Ho, Ho," bellowed Santa Claus. "I can't stay long. It's my busiest night of the year," he said with a twinkle in his eye.

As I stood speechless at the door in a nightgown and housecoat, Santa dropped a bag of presents on the floor and then disappeared into the darkness of the night.

How did he know where I lived? Then it dawned on me that it had to be the items on the wish list Joshua had passed to Santa. Tomorrow morning, there would be even more gifts under the tree for Joshua. Boy, would he be surprised. Santa really came through for him.

But when I opened the bag, I found four beautifully wrapped presents ready to place under the tree. Tears welled in my eyes as I read the tags: To Stella, Love Santa.

— Stella Shepard —

47

Tools for Life

*A child enters your home and for the next twenty years
makes so much noise you can hardly stand it.
The child departs, leaving the house so silent
you think you are going mad.*
~John Andrew Holmes

It was December when my father had to live the moment every dad dreads—times two. I, with my bachelor's degree in hand, was officially and permanently leaving the nest for Connecticut. My sister, clutching her master's degree, was heading off to New Jersey to start her new life.

And to make matters even worse, there was a long-time boyfriend waiting for each of us. Not only was my father losing both of his girls at once, he was losing them to other men. He had us hostage for the holidays, but after that, all bets were off. The clock was ticking.

So that's the year he gave my sister and me the best presents we ever received.

A pony? No, I'd given up on that dream years ago when he bought me a stuffed horse instead. A car? Nope, my father insisted the old Buick he'd procured from our elderly neighbor was "a great car!"

Sitting underneath the tree on Christmas morning were two identical gifts my brother, muscles straining, pushed in front of his sisters. Large, slightly lumpy, and heavy enough to make me question what I'd do with a box of rocks.

"This is from your father," my mother said, eager to re-distribute

The Perfect Gift | 143

the credit. With slightly nervous glances cast each other's way (my father does not do his own shopping), my sister and I tore open the paper to reveal... toolboxes.

Just what every little-girl-at-heart wants for Christmas.

"Open it, open it!" our very own Santa announced gleefully, clapping his hands.

So we did.

Hammers. Wrenches. Nails. Duct tape. Tire gauge. Tape measure. Screws.

The fun just kept coming, and he couldn't have looked prouder.

We couldn't have been more confused.

Like your average girls, we dutifully ooh-ed and ah-ed over our loot and kept our eyes glued to the clearly denoted GAP box under the tree.

"He did that all by himself, you know," Mom confided to us later when all of the crumpled wrapping paper had found a home on the floor and presents lay scattered about. "It took him hours to pick all of that out."

Suddenly, it was clear -- tightly packed into those cumbersome, clunky toolboxes were all of a father's lessons and love. He may have been passing us on to other men, but his girls were going to be able to take care of themselves -- and always remember who it was in their lives that first built a foundation and always picked up the pieces and hammered them back together.

Yes, my father gave me a tire gauge for Christmas, along with the forethought to avoid problems before they happen.

A spare key holder -- and the knowledge that everybody's human and forgets their keys sometimes.

A hammer -- and the strength to know that girls can swing them, too.

Nails -- and countless memories to hang on the walls.

A toolbox -- and all of the love and support to get through the good and the bad in life. No matter what's bent out of shape or broken.

Thanks, Dad. For all of the tools you've given me.

—Caitlin Q. Bailey—

48

My Really Son

Truth is beautiful and divine,
no matter how humble its origin.
~Michael Idvorsky Pupin

My son was nearly ten years old when I met him and his sister in an orphanage in Russia. On that day Edward had only a few moments to decide his future. As he leapt across the room and into my husband's arms, I had no doubt what his answer would be. He had found a mama and a papa and he was coming home.

Edward and Katia devoted themselves to catching up and becoming part of the family. They each gained twenty pounds in the first two months, made friends, and began to put sentences together in English. Four months after coming home, it was Christmas, and the kids had no idea what to expect.

Not only would this be my children's first Christmas in America, it would be their first Christmas celebration ever. Seventy years of communism had relegated the celebration of Christ's birth to just another day on the calendar.

A few weeks before Christmas, Edward made a list of what he wanted to buy for everyone in the family and proudly showed the list to everyone on it. We discussed the concept of presents being secret, so he hid his list. Then he told everyone what was on it. Who could blame him? For the first time, he had a family to give presents to, presents he had purchased with his own money saved from his allowance.

The kids worked hard to save. They pored over sales ads looking for the best deals on everything for themselves and for others, and dreaming big dreams. More than anything, Ed wanted a Buzz Lightyear, but he was resigned to defeat after seeing one in the store for thirty dollars. It was, he declared, too much. Still, he was full of anticipation, insisting that every day seemed like a year.

As the preparations for the day started to overtake us, we joked that we should have told the children that Christmas was on the 26th so we'd have one more day to prepare. On the afternoon of Christmas Eve, I was frantically sewing up stockings that had not been finished, and my husband was cooking our traditional Italian dinner.

Edward asked a few times if he could help, but I told him to go play. Six months pregnant and exhausted, I thought it was easier to do things myself than to take the time to explain and translate all that was going on.

Somewhere in there, a little boy felt lost and alone and out of touch with this day he did not understand, and he had a meltdown.

It started slowly at first, just getting into a little trouble here and there, but soon he had my full attention. He started to tell me, in his broken English, that he had done without Christmas before and he could do without it again. He had been without food, he could go without food again. If I wanted him to go back to Russia, he could handle it.

"Maybe you think I can't learn how to be in family. Maybe you not want me anymore. Maybe, when the baby came, you say I not a really-son."

I thought my heart would break.

I put down my sewing and enveloped him in my arms. Through a lot of tears — mine and his — I assured him he was loved and treasured and never going back.

"You will always be my really-son," I soothed.

For over an hour, I held him, explaining as best I could that our family is for real and our family is forever. I talked about extended family, life insurance, and wills, promising him he would always be protected and taken care of by someone who loved him, no matter what.

We cemented our relationship by making a batch of fudge. His tears melted with the chocolate as he stirred and talked and finally smiled. Soon he was content to go join his sister and the neighbors for a game of football.

After attending the Christmas Eve service, we all settled in by the tree with hot chocolate and cookies and read the Christmas story from the gospel of Luke. Once the kids were tucked into bed, we dragged out piles of presents, set up the train under the tree, stuffed stockings and collapsed into bed.

The next morning we got up, set up the camera, and opened the doors. The children were amazed to the point of disbelief. And somewhere in that pile was Edward's very own Buzz Lightyear.

In the coming days, whenever someone asked Ed if he got his Buzz Lightyear from Santa, his chest puffed out with pride as he declared, "No, my mama and papa give it to me." It was a wonder beyond wonders to him that we would give him this toy, this treasure that he had so longed for.

On January 6, the Day of Epiphany, I overheard a conversation between Edward and Katia. They were speaking in English and talking about the occupations of every adult they knew.

Finally, Ed asked, "What me?"

Katia was puzzled. Ed had no career; what could he be talking about?

He persisted. "What me?" he kept asking, and still she did not answer.

He pointed to himself and said, "Me, son."

Epiphany indeed.

I never did get the stockings hemmed at the top, but I guess the mending I did do was far more important than a little finish work on a piece of cloth.

— Rose Godfrey —

Chapter 6

Family Fun

Merry Christmas, I Broke into Your House

*Perhaps the best Yuletide decoration
is being wreathed in smiles.*
~Author Unknown

Maybe it was the army of bleeding Jesus candles greeting us in our foyer. Or the suspicious pieces of tinsel squished inside our doormat. Or, perhaps, the new wreath lovingly placed on our front door, gently flecked with spray-on snow and plastic "dew."

It had finally happened. Our home had been visited by Santa Claus! And, apparently, Santa was drunk.

Let me back up. Just two days prior, my husband and I had hosted our very first family Christmas party. We were a young couple, and we'd been living in this house together for just over a year. In the past, we had gamely divided up our Christmases between two families in different cities, one pair living north of us, the other living south. No more. This year, my parents would come up for Christmas Eve, and his parents would get to see us on Christmas Day, at their home. We thought ourselves brilliant tacticians. My parents graciously accepted the invitation.

The day before the Christmas Eve party, Ross and I set about decorating our humble little Christmas tree. Up went the ornaments passed down to us from family: a pewter silver bell with our wedding date engraved, some ceramic candy canes, the store-bought colored globes. Around went the twinkly lights, white with a few burnt-out bulbs. Ross is a teacher, so we proudly hung the misshapen pipe-cleaner-and-paper creations his students had made for him. It was our first tree. We admired it with pride, a funny symbol of our still-new domesticity.

My parents arrived the next evening, presents and potluck dishes in hand. In short order, my uncles, a few cousins, and even more presents tumbled inside. We had just put on a Christmas CD and poured a few glasses of champagne when our final visitor arrived.

"HEELLLOOO!!!" came the bellow from the foyer. "Hello, excuse me! I'M HERE!"

Aunt Frances.

"Is anybody home? I brought ROLLS, people. Where do ya want 'em?"

"Frances. It's so good to see you!" I ran into the foyer, greeting my eternally wild-haired aunt. Frances is my mother's older sister and always knows how to make an entrance.

"Hi, sweetie. Your auntie is HERE! I've got BAGS of presents." (Literally. She was carrying trash bags.)

"That's so kind of you, Frances. Here, let me take these."

I led Aunt Frances into the living room, and Ross looked at me with an expression that said, "There's a pair of acid-washed jeans waiting for me in those trash bags, isn't there?"

You should know that Aunt Frances is kind of crazy. This is one of the reasons that I adore her. She tends to be what some might call an "extreme personality," with a heart that has room for both the Holy Spirit and vodka on the rocks. In fact, this combination has led to the occasional prophecy from Frances, where she sits me down and tells me what the Lord has on his mind. The last time we spoke, the Lord told me (through Frances) I would not be raped (yay?), but even so I didn't have to wear so much tacky eyeliner (boo).

Another one of Frances' quirks is her abnormally large heart.

This leads me back to the acid-washed jeans thing. You see, Frances has never been a rich woman, but she absolutely loves to indulge her family members with presents. The solution? Blowout thrift-store shopping sprees.

"You wouldn't BELIEVE the deals I got at Goodwill!" said Frances, proudly holding up the plastic bags and giving them a little shake. "Your Auntie Frances got you A FANNY PACK, and a whole box of MUGS! I think they have goldfish on them."

"Shh, we want to be surprised!" I interrupted her with a smile. "Can't wait to open them."

I handed the bags off to Ross. He carefully wedged the mass under the Christmas tree, and we led everyone into the kitchen to serve themselves dinner.

The rest of the night was a blur of clinking champagne glasses and spirited rounds of *Balderdash*. When everyone was good and ready, we opened presents. But out of the corner of my eye, I kept catching Frances stealing glances at our Christmas tree. She looked vaguely troubled.

"Tolly," she whispered raspily in-between presents, "where is the Christ child?"

"Eh, I don't think we have a Christ child," I said.

"I see."

"But we did have a star, so we decided to put the star on."

"Wait. Angels, honey. Where are the angels?"

"Hmm?"

"Well, sweet girl, it's not exactly Christmas without Jesus and angels on the tree, now is it?"

I earnestly agreed. Next year, I told her. Next year, Frances, that tree would be downright dripping with Jesus and angels.

As it turned out, we didn't have to wait that long.

The day after the party, Ross and I had a quick turnaround Christmas trip to see his family. We laughed and ate, unwrapped gifts and played with our in-laws' toddler son. In less than twenty-four hours, we were back on the road, knowing we had more guests coming to visit and a messy house to clean. We pulled up in the driveway and got out of our car. Our eyes immediately fell to the wreath.

"Um... who's been here?" I asked Ross, cautiously pushing open the unlocked door.

The tinsel. The bleeding Jesus candles. We walked farther.

Then, we saw it.

Our Christmas tree had been wholly redecorated.

Gone were the dainty candy canes, scattered around the tree's base like last night's party accessories. In their place hung large, red felt stockings, the kind one would normally hang on a fireplace mantle. They were accented with glitter and had different people's names on them: "Merry Christmas, Aaron!" "Happy Holidays, Ruth!"

Huge plastic balls with scenes from the nativity printed on them now graced our tree's branches as well, along with gilded, cut-out ornaments proclaiming "JESUS CRISTO" at various branch intervals. There was a set of star-shaped frames carefully hung on the highest branches, filled with faded photographs of smiling children... stranger children. Children we had never seen before. Our strand of white twinkly lights now served as a dual-purpose Virgin Mary hanger, with about thirty-eight thimble-sized Virgins dangling off. Tiny plastic rays shot out from behind their heads.

And on the very top, bending the highest branch under the weight of its holy mass, perched a giant ceramic angel. Playing a bugle.

You know the show *What Not to Wear*? This was like the Christmas tree version. Only I was staring at the After, not the Before.

This was the most bizarre thing that ever happened to me. I got a little weirded out. Who breaks into someone's home on Christmas Day, never mind the fact that they broke in to give you stuff? I had a hunch who it was.

"Is this a Goodwill receipt?" Ross said, picking up a piece of white paper from the floor. It was dated from the day before. Frances.

My husband laughed, holding the receipt between his fingers. "C'mon, Tolly, it's funny. And sweet."

He was right. My aunt wanted to spoil us, wanted to give us a better tree. She didn't have much, but she spent what she could to give us something that was, in her eyes, lavish. Sure, it was a little...

odd. But this was probably a tree Frances would have liked to have for herself. Rays-shooting-out-of-head Virgin Marys and all.

It's funny to admit this, but looking back, breaking and entering into my home has been one of the kindest things a family member has ever done for me.

—Tolly Moseley—

The Power of Pasta

Conscience is less an inner voice than
the memory of a mother's glance.
~Robert Brault

n the day that I was married, I took the usual "love, honor, sickness, health, etc." vows out loud. I made a few other vows to myself, one of which was to stay calm and understanding about the incredibly close bond between John and his mother. After all, he was thirty-three when I married him, and he had lived with this mother that whole time, so a few precedents had been set. The dating years had taught me that, in the choice between her and me, I might get a sheepish look followed by an apology in private later, but he would never take my side against her in front of her or others. My mother-in-law, in her own way, is a wonderful woman, and I could give her some unflattering labels such as "quirky" or "difficult," but what comes to mind most is "very loving," in a unique way.

So I vowed to stay calm whenever he took her side, knowing that the results of hurting her were far worse than the results of letting me down. Or at least I hoped so.

And so it went for many years, smoothly as can be expected. My teeth are shorter from grinding them down, and the neighbors have become accustomed to my running out in the backyard to scream from time to time, but, overall, it has been smooth, except for a random holiday here and there.

As in all families, we had holiday "traditions," unwritten rules set in concrete, never to be changed. Christmas Eve was at my sister-in-law's because she knows how to do that seven-course fish thing so well. So Christmas Eve was his family's. Each Christmas Day, we attended church and spent the morning at home. Around noon, all presents opened, we headed to his mother's for homemade cappelletti and ravioli. Around four, we went to my mother's, pretending we were hungry because she had worked all day preparing a turkey or ham dinner. These endearing, if fattening, traditions were embedded in our lives.

As fate would have it, one year we just couldn't follow that routine. It had snowed, snowed and snowed, leaving us buried in feet of white powder. Our home is situated in a large natural wind tunnel between a sizeable lake and a pond, giving us a double lake effect, plus a wind chill factor worthy of the Arctic. We could barely open the door that day and had to force the dog to go outside to do his duty. No one was traveling; the roads were barely plowed, and TV announcers urged everyone to stay put. We almost did.

I knew there would be trouble. My mother-in-law began calling at 9:00 A.M. Those bags of cappelletti and ravioli that she had created were bursting out of her freezer. It was Christmas. They had to be eaten that day. Weather had no influence on her schedule or her cooking. I said no. She called at 10:00, 10:30, 11:00, 11:30 and 12:00, frantic by 1:00.

It was Christmas! There were ravioli! About 12:00, John had started to pace. From 1:00 to 2:00, we all shoveled, trying to move at least two feet of snow off the house roof, as it was leaking more than usual. Of course, this made him even hungrier. Thoughts of ravioli obsessed his genetically-driven mind. I said no. Then I watched in amazement as his primal instinct took over. He became crazed. Christmas and ravioli had to be honored! I said no — we would not go out in that storm just for pasta. At 3:00, he lost all control. "Get into the truck! Everybody!" he screamed as he grabbed for the phone, dialed and yelled, "Put the water on. We're on our way!"

It certainly was an exciting trip. We live at the top of a one-mile hill, followed by a bit of level road, followed by a two-mile downhill fondly known as The Wildcat, then a two-mile uphill stretch. There was no "over the river and through the woods to Grandmother's house we go" because nothing could be seen but snow, waist-deep snow that sprayed out on both sides of the truck as we plowed our own path. We were on the road, off the road, in a ditch, in the opposite ditch, but my husband is a veteran of driving on roads like this, and his truck is built for this challenge. The girls were having a great time in their car seats, whooping at all the white spray. I had confidence in John and very little fear, although I realized that my mother-in-law's wishes were dominant again. In the true Christmas spirit (and because I just LOVE her pasta), I hung on and enjoyed being the only family out in that untouched winter wonderland.

We did not pass a single vehicle the whole way down, and the twelve-mile journey took more than forty-five minutes. The bleak, beautiful snow had brought the Valley to a halt — except for one blue Chevy Avalanche on an "emergency" ravioli run.

She complained as we walked in. "What took so long? The pasta is getting cold!" Unbelievable. I almost decided not to eat at all when she nagged like that, but even I could not hold out against Margaret's homemade ravioli and sauce. I felt thankful and peaceful that we could spend Christmas together — at least our branch of the family. John's two sisters and one brother never made it, thereby proving to their mother — neglected on Christmas — that their love for her was nowhere near as strong as John's. John beamed.

My mother lived nearby, but we didn't stop in. She would have been shocked, appalled, furious, unbelieving that we had left the house in such weather. The ride home was faster, the road almost hidden in the night. Our tracks were the only ones through the snow. John once again made it seem like a Sunday drive in the park, even though he was working hard to keep the truck in line. By the time we got home, we all knew this had been a Christmas to remember.

Someday, I hope I have a child who loves me, or at least my cooking, as much as John loves his mother and her ravioli. But I will insist that they stay home until the roads have been plowed.

— Anne Crawley —

51

A Burning Issue

I once wanted to become an atheist but I gave up...
they have no holidays.
~Henny Youngman

My family is Jewish. These days, many Jewish families have given in to the Christmas juggernaut by putting up Christmas trees. But when I was growing up, we weren't one of them. For a while we had a six-inch toy tree that my siblings and I attempted to decorate. But we were forced to hide it when my grandfather showed up, so it never really felt right. Besides, it could only hold about two Froot Loop garlands anyway.

Yes, we had Hanukah, but the truth is Hanukah is a very minor holiday in the Jewish religion. Just because it falls in December, it's gotten puffed up to compete with Christmas. But who are we kidding? It will never equal Christmas. How could it? Come December, the world goes Santa Claus crazy. We are deluged with images of the wonder and the glory and the letters to Santa and the many, many presents. Menorahs, potato pancakes and dreidels are fun, but they are no match for Christmas. Any attempt to make them so feels just creepy and sad. Like when we sang in the school choir and the choirmaster threw in "O Dreidel Dreidel Dreidel" as a blatant sop to the Jewish kids. It was so pathetic; we wished he had just skipped it altogether.

For the most part, playing second fiddle to Christmas didn't really bother my brother, two sisters and me when we were growing up. We knew who we were and we were proud of it. Pining for Christmas would be like a giraffe wanting the elephant's trunk. Sure it was cool, but really, what did it have to do with us? In fact, it was sort of nice to relax outside the holiday hysteria.

But we were just kids and it took us a while to get to this place. As little kids, for a while Christmas looked good. Really good. One year, when we were ten, eight, six and four, respectively, we did a full frontal push on our parents. "Just once? Puhhhleeeeeeeeez?"

Finally, they gave in — with one caveat. No tree. The little toy tree would have to do. "Sure, whatever," we said. We placed it in front of the fireplace where everyone could trip on it, and the dog could eat the Froot Loops.

Christmas Eve, we went to bed extra early at 8 p.m. Around 3 a.m., we snuck downstairs for a look, and oh! There they were! Piles of presents in four rows, one row for each kid. With ribbons and bows and fancy, unwrinkled paper that hadn't been saved from a previous gift! We just about collapsed. We went back to bed but rousted our parents around 6 a.m.

There was an explosion of energy as we ripped packages open and squealed with delight. But afterwards, a slight, slumping sadness set in. Was that it? All that build-up and it's over in five minutes? Trying to revive the momentum, we instructed our father, "You have to light the wrapping paper in the fireplace! That's part of it!"

Rolling his eyes, Dad threw the brightly colored paper in and lit it. But groggy at the early hour, he forgot to open the flue. A huge flame shot out and up, setting the mantelpiece on fire. We gawked for two seconds, then my mother grabbed my brother and me, my father grabbed my two sisters and we all ran out the front door into the frigid air. They dumped us, dressed only in our footie pajamas, into the snow, and ran back in to deal with the flames. We looked at each other in shock, all with one thought in our minds: Talk about your burning bushes! Clearly, God had spoken.

I can't remember if the firemen were called or if my parents managed to snuff it out themselves. But I do remember what came next. My father came stamping out into the snow to tell us it was okay to go back in. As we guiltily marched behind him, he turned to say, quite evenly, "See? This is what happens when Jews do Christmas!"

We never said another word about it.

— Beth Levine —

52

Sugar Plum Fairies Danced in Her Head

*It's the dream — if not a rite of passage —
of every young female ballet student to
dance the role of Clara in* The Nutcracker.
~Karen Kain

When I think of Christmas I think of many things, but one of my fondest memories was seeing The National Ballet of Canada perform the *Nutcracker.* So, it was a no brainer for me that I should take my own children to see that ballet, only this time it was in the city of Detroit, which is right across the river from Canada.

My daughter, Miriam, was four years old. When the curtain opened her eyes grew large. When the dolls that Drosselmeier had brought to the party began to dance she gasped with delight.

"They're real," she whispered in an awestruck voice. "Mommy, they're real!"

"Yes, honey. They're ballet dancers."

"I'm going to do that," she said with a conviction that was surprising for a four-year-old.

Miriam sat in her seat completely mesmerized. From that moment on all she ever talked about, dreamed about, breathed about was being one of the children in that show.

In truth she really wanted to be the Sugar Plum Fairy or Clara but she would settle for being one of the children.

Because we live so close to the U.S. and Canada border, a lot of kids took Arts lessons in both towns. This was so for Miriam when she turned seven. Her ballet instructor was the late Iacob Lascu who at the time was also the choreographer, director of the Nutcracker ballet for the Detroit Symphony.

My daughter was ecstatic when she auditioned in the fall and became one of those children.

Now, not only did she have ballet class on Tuesdays and Thursdays, she had rehearsals every Saturday and Sunday. They were long and hard but Miriam didn't care. I worried it would be too much but she refused to quit. She wanted to be on that stage. She would move heaven and earth for that chance. Neither my husband nor I had the heart to deny her this once-in-a-lifetime opportunity.

The warm autumn days soon turned into cold, bitter, winter days that darkened before five p.m. but Miriam insisted on going to rehearsals. She refused to miss any.

Rehearsal week at the Fox Theatre — twelve-hour days every day. The children were exhausted but so excited. Miriam was exhilarated.

The girls' hair had to be in ringlets for the show. Miriam's hair was thick and down to her waist. The rehearsal before opening night had ended late — ten p.m. I had to put in over 120 curlers in order to make those ringlets. Still Miriam didn't whine or cry. "Put more in the top, Mommy," she said. "It has to be poufy."

December 17th — opening night. After making sure she was dressed and ready to go on stage I joined my husband in the audience.

Curtain up — Miriam was radiant! If ever there was a child who was born to be on stage I was looking at one and she was my kid. This was not exactly the life I had planned for her.

Because Miriam was the shortest girl she had been put centre stage, right by Clara. Her little face even outshone Clara.

"I think we have a problem," said my husband. "Actors and dancers do not make a good living."

"We'll figure it out. Besides, she might lose interest."

"Are you kidding? Look at that face. I've never seen her so happy."

"Mommy did you see me?" cried Miriam. "Mr. Lascu says I was wonderful!"

"You were wonderful," I said and sniffled back my tears. "But are you really sure you want to do this all month? That's all of your Christmas holidays."

"Yes! This will be the best holiday ever!"

She flung her arms around my waist. "Thank you Mommy for letting me do this. I love it!"

Miriam went on to perform in the *Nutcracker* for three more years before Mr. Lascu retired. In all of that time she never once complained and her face became incandescent as soon as the curtain went up in every performance.

Miriam has since chosen not to pursue dancing as a career but has become an actress instead. However, every Christmas she and I sit together and watch the *Nutcracker* on TV. Over and over and over.

"Those were the best Christmases ever," Miriam says and she snuggles closer to me.

"Yes, they were," I reply.

— Pamela Goldstein —

Look Who's Here

If you would have guests merry with your cheer
Be so yourself, or so at least appear.
~Author Unknown

There was a knock at the door of Great-Grandma Smith's home in Lake Placid, New York one Thanksgiving. Since she was the hostess for this family holiday, she got up, opened the door, and exclaimed with delight, "Look who's here!"

She pulled a young man into the hallway, hugged him, and said, "It's wonderful to see you again! Everyone will be so delighted!" Great-Grandma then hurried to take off his coat and led him to the table. "Oh, just look who's here!" she announced with joy. The family murmured. She moved things around and placed him in a seat between my uncle and herself. He was surrounded by family on both sides and faced Great-Grandpa Smith across the table.

"Coralie, go get us another place setting!" she commanded. "We're so sorry that we started without you. No one knew you were coming," she explained. "But you're just going to love everything. We have turkey, potatoes, squash, and cranberry sauce. Oh, you know how Fayette always teased Coralie and told her to eat more cranberry sauce so she'd have room in her stomach for more food." She stopped to laugh at the family joke about my mother's gullible nature when she had been young. We still laugh about cranberry sauce opening up extra room in the stomach each Thanksgiving. Great-Grandma gently patted his

Family Fun | 163

arm. "Oh, and Gladys made an apple and a pumpkin pie for dessert even! So, just dig right in. My, it's good to see you." She patted his arm again and sighed.

No one had interrupted her joyful speech from the moment she had left the table to answer the door. After looking around the table at our family, the young man turned and looked straight at Great-Grandma Smith's face, which beamed with love and joy. He said in a bewildered voice, "I don't know any of you. I just stopped at your house to get directions!"

— Melanie A. Savidis —

54

My Wife Tried to Kill Me

*I did a push-up today. Well actually I fell down, but I
had to use my arms to get back up, so close enough.*
~Author Unknown

Anyone who has been married or in a relationship for a long time knows what "support" means. When your spouse is trying something new, it's your duty to help in any way possible. You may not agree with the decision or even believe it will work, but if his or her mind is made up, you need to support the effort one hundred percent.

In my marriage, these little plans usually come and go, like the time my wife decided we were going to use scent-free laundry soap or start a cardboard recycling program to help save the world. No harm, no foul. But imagine my trepidation when she included me in "our" New Year's resolution to improve our physical fitness.

It sounded simple enough at first. We were already eating fairly well, so all I had to do was join her in doing something called "planking." Since it seemed to involve staying still I was all in.

For those who don't know, a plank is basically a pushup without moving. After my wife explained it to me, I figured this had to be the easiest exercise known to mankind. "You mean, I get in a pushup position and then don't actually do any pushups?" I was incredulous. The world record for holding a plank is five hours; she suggested we start with thirty seconds. I scoffed.

While she set the timer, I confidently dropped to the floor with dreams of my new rock-hard abs dancing through my head. She said, "Okay, go!" I lifted myself up, making sure my back was straight, and waited, wondering why the world record was only five hours for this. After some time passed, I noticed that my stomach muscles were complaining a bit. Surprisingly, my arm shook a little. I refocused. Then it shook again, but more pronounced. My arms started to shake a lot. "How much time?" I asked, starting to doubt my original estimate of an hour's duration for my first-ever plank.

"Twenty seconds to go," she said.

Twenty seconds to go? Meaning only ten seconds of our easy thirty had elapsed?

My stomach muscles started to complain. I started to regret how easy I had made their life. I'd been nicer to them than I was to our kids.

My wife called out, "Ten seconds!" My discomfort turned to pain, and I noticed that my arms were no longer the only things shaking. My shoulders and legs also shook like the paint mixer at a hardware store, while my stomach started a full revolt, threatening to collapse and leave me in a heap on the floor.

"Keep your back straight. You're slouching. Five more seconds!" she barked.

She was no longer the sunshine of my life. At this point, I was convinced that she was pure evil, the root of everything that is pain in this world. I'm also pretty sure she was laughing at me.

As my wife and personal trainer counted down from five, I glanced down, half expecting to see a pool of blood on the floor. Actually, I would not have been surprised if I found myself face to face with a small alien head as it ripped itself out of my stomach like in the movie *Alien*.

"Four!" she called out as I envisioned the alien climbing free of my innards.

"As seen on TV!" crossed through my mind, and I started to giggle.

"Three!" The countdown continued, and the giggles increased. Apparently, the pain was making me delusional.

"Hi, little guy," I imagined I'd say to my new friend as he peered out of my intestines. I started laughing harder. This chuckling did not match up well with the shaking the rest of my body was doing. It occurred to me that this whole fitness thing was a terrible idea. I decided I would rather walk an actual plank at knifepoint than do these planks any longer.

"Two!"

She had to be lying about the time. She was evil incarnate.

I realized that I wasn't breathing. That was probably part of her plan.

"One!"

My face hit the ground first. As I lay in a sobbing, laughing, sweating, heaving pool on the floor, I did an assessment to see if I had a bloody nose. Apparently, the human nose is not designed to stop the body from a free fall, which is pretty poor engineering. I didn't dare look to see if any fluids were leaking onto the carpet. It was her idea. She could do the cleanup after I expired.

An hour later, after the stomach pains had subsided and I regained the use of my arms, I stood in front of the mirror, saw absolutely zero improvement, and considered moving to Tibet until my wife's fitness craze passed. But I am not a quitter! (Or I am not allowed to quit, which is kinda the same thing, isn't it?) With the same resolve that allows a woman to have another child after enduring the pain of childbirth, I decided I could press on. I mean, I'm only four hours, fifty-nine minutes and thirty seconds away from the record, right?

— Marty Anderson —

55

A Honey of a Christmas

The manner of giving is worth more than the gift.
Pierre Corneille, Le Menteur

As a young bride, I learned that I was in big trouble if I showed up at Aunt Honey's without a bag of trash. We're not talking about the coffee-grounds-and-egg-shells variety, but the kind made up of boxes, bags and labels from name brand products. Honey, who never shopped, managed to obtain gifts for the family by clipping and mailing product "qualifiers" from the packages to turn this rubbish into mounds of Christmas gifts.

Aunt Honey and Uncle Joe were quite a pair. I don't know how to describe them. How can I make all the love, pettiness, squabbling, originality, meanness, kindness and humor shine through without making them into either a pair of cranks or an affable Mr. and Mrs. Claus? They drove everyone a little crazy.

Our family party took place on Christmas Eve at the home of Honey's brother, our Uncle Harry. Once we were all assembled, we were led into the basement, blinded by the lights from Uncle Wayne's omnipresent movie camera. There, amid the washer, dryer, water pipes and furnace, was Honey's little workshop. She had once again worked her yearly magic on the family trash, turning discarded packaging into free products and cool gifts.

Honey lived for Christmas Eve, and she began clipping and mailing labels every December 26th. She'd keep it up for an entire year until everyone could count on a newspaper-wrapped stack of crazy, sometimes useful, gifts. We'd sit in our little family clusters tearing at the wrapping to discover toothpaste, laundry detergent, shaving cream, macaroni and cheese, shoe polish, and more.

In 1974, for example, she provided the first two babies in the family with stacks of disposable diapers in a variety of sizes. Each box had the product stamp carefully removed, saved for some future magic. As struggling young teachers, we found her gifts a godsend.

Since Honey was aunt to seven nieces and nephews and their families, she tried to be evenhanded about her gifts, making sure that everything was equal. If she couldn't get enough of a particular gift, she would hold what she had until the next Christmas when she might have obtained more. One year, she had a huge fiberboard playhouse for each family with kids. At the time, there were four of us. She forced Uncle Joe to assemble them — right there in the game room. As if that were not enough, she topped each house with a little doll in a crocheted dress with its legs neatly tucked into a full roll of toilet paper. The doll held the reins to a huge, inflatable dog the size of a Volkswagen. We could barely move to open our other gifts — and there were other gifts!

Each of us remembers a favorite silly gift, like the Sprout dolls from Green Giant, or the Lucky Charms T-shirts in sizes infant to XXL. There were radio hats advertising beer, nightshirts proclaiming the cleaning power of Tide, toys of every imaginable product mascot, and cookbooks featuring everything from creamed corn to crème de menthe. Not every gift was silly; there were Timex watches and silver napkin rings, tea towels, ornaments, cereal bowls, golf balls, jewelry and games. If it had an advertising slogan or product name emblazoned across it, there was a good chance it was under our tree.

We always brought stacks of gifts for Honey and Uncle Joe, but nothing we ever gave them could equal the pleasure they derived from watching us and our children open the presents they had been gathering all year long. We tried, though. We bought them TV sets and nativity sets, clothes and food. We lovingly made things for them: blankets and potholders, crayon pictures and embroidered pillowslips, homemade jam and nut bread. Honey and Uncle Joe were the heart and soul of our family Christmases, and we wanted them to feel as loved as we did year after year.

I'd like to say that they stayed in the bosom of their loving family until they died at a ripe old age, but it didn't quite happen that way. Uncle Joe, always suspicious of everyone who had the children he did not, quit coming to the family parties after an imagined slight. We tried to bring him back into the fold, to no avail.

Honey continued to enjoy opening gifts on Christmas or any morning—one morning became like another to her in her final days. I put a tube of toothpaste in my grownup children's Christmas stockings every year to remind them of Christmases past, when she and Uncle Joe were the cornerstone of our family Christmas Eves.

—Rosemary McLaughlin—

56

Midnight Madness

Mothers are all slightly insane.
~J.D. Salinger

This year I did something I once swore I'd never do — shopping at midnight on Black Friday. I know, I'm crazy. That's what I said to the gazillions of other people who were clogging up the roads when they should have been sleeping off their turkey dinner. "Why aren't these people home in bed!" I shouted, as we sat in the left-turn lane through yet another red light. After all, this is the twenty-first century. You can get great deals online from the comfort of your own bed while sipping a hot cup of coffee. So why would I endure three things I despise — traffic, cold weather, and crowds — for a few bargains?

Teenagers.

Before you shudder and mentally add teenagers to the list of things you despise, let me say that I have two of them, and despite all that entails, I still love them with my whole heart. Even though, for them, spending time with Mom is usually down on their list next to homework and picking up the dog poop. I am no longer the one with whom they want to share a secret, play a game, or just hang out. It's a fact of life, and I get it. The natural progression of things. But that doesn't make it any easier on parents who are not ready for this sudden shifting of their universe. I miss my kids.

So, when they asked me to take them shopping at the outlet mall at midnight on Black Friday, my first reaction was definitely no! First of all, I am rarely awake past 11:00 p.m. anymore. Add the fact that we're talking about midnight after Thanksgiving, when the tryptophan of the turkey meal usually kicks in at around 5 p.m. Not to mention that the outlet mall consists of designer stores where a T-shirt costs $50. I mean, it's a T-shirt! How much designing really goes into that? A T-shirt should be $10 or less, period. But my son, who usually runs the other way if I mention shopping, wanted me to take him shopping.

I felt needed. Okay, I'm not so naïve that I didn't know it was my wallet and a ride, not quality time with Mom that they wanted. But still…

There was the hour car ride. We belted out songs on the radio, laughing at who got the words wrong and who was off key. We talked about the deals we hoped to score and what my son wanted to get for his girlfriend. I still can't believe my baby boy has a girlfriend! Now that I think about it, the timing of this union coincides precisely with his desire for $50 T-shirts.

We took turns yelling at the idiots who cut us off or pulled some stupid traffic tricks. I had ample opportunities to give them lessons on what not to do when driving. The kids bickered back and forth as usual, and I had to keep the peace. That's what moms do.

And we all bonded as we sat in bumper-to-bumper traffic with crazed smiles at midnight.

The kids scanned for a spot once we finally made it into the overflowing parking lot, and we rejoiced at our luck when I randomly turned down one lane just as someone was pulling out. High-fives all around. And there's something about standing in a line that snakes around the building in the freezing cold that brings people together.

Once inside, we had to work as a team, one going this way, one the other, hoping to come together with just the right size and color. Searching for a particular shirt for my husband was proving to be a losing battle as I dug through mound after mound of disheveled clothing. Giving up in defeat, I turned to see my daughter coming toward me, shirt in hand and victory on her face. "I got the last one!"

So we emerged at 3 a.m. with some bargains. Nothing earth shattering, nothing we couldn't have found online or in stores at a reasonable hour. But for me, I got so much more. Quality time with my kids. The definition has changed since they were little, but I'll take it where I can get it.

Driving home bleary eyed and running on nothing but adrenaline, I said, "Next year, no shopping before 7 a.m." But then I looked in the rearview mirror at my children's sweet faces, both dozing in the car like they did when they were little.

The truth is… if they ask me to go again next year, I'm in.

— Lori Slaton —

The Holiday Card

Mistakes are the usual bridge between
inexperience and wisdom.
~Phyllis Theroux

I t was two weeks before the holidays, and I still hadn't sent out my holiday cards. Each year, my family gets dozens of holiday cards from friends and family, and I wanted to send one out as well that year. We get all types of cards, like pictures of an entire family, pictures of the children, vacation pictures or even professionally produced pictures. Sometimes we receive cards with no pictures at all, just wishing us happy holidays in bright, bold letters.

After giving it some thought, I decided to go with the family picture taken by a professional photographer. After dropping off my two boys at grammar school, I called the local photographer and made the appointment. The photographer told me since there wasn't much time before the holidays, he would come first thing Sunday morning and told me to have the whole family in white shirts. It sounded perfect.

Now, not only now did I have my usual five million things to do — carpooling, volunteering, buying last-minute presents, grocery shopping, cooking and making sure my family was happy — but I also had to find matching whites tops for my entire family. After visiting a bunch of stores, I decided on white polo shirts for all of us. I couldn't have asked for a smoother morning. I was able to continue doing all my other errands with a smile, knowing that my family was going to look great for the holiday photograph session.

I'm not sure where the rest of the hours went, but when I went to tuck in my younger son on Saturday night, I noticed his hair was a complete mess. OMG! He needed a haircut. With all my running around, I hadn't noticed how badly he needed one. I didn't know what to do. It was 8:00 at night, and every salon or barber was closed. The photographer was coming the next morning. I then became resourceful... or so I thought!

I got out the scissors I used to cut fabric and told my son to come into the bathroom where I set up a little salon. My younger son is very easygoing and cooperative. I wet his hair, combed it and started snipping away. When I was done, we looked at each other and both knew that the haircut was a disaster! I started to panic. What had I been thinking? I had never cut hair in my life. Why did I think it would be so simple? Now my adorable little boy was paying the price.

Now, I had no other choice but to tell my husband. When he saw my son, he went completely bonkers. He said, "The pictures are tomorrow morning, and our son has the worst haircut I have ever seen on a little boy!" I was now sweating, and words would not come out of my mouth. I had no excuse. All I could do was apologize. My husband told me to go downstairs and have a cup of tea while he took care of the situation.

I am a woman of many talents, but obviously cutting hair is not one of them. As I sipped my tea, punishing thoughts ran through my head. I was always trying to juggle everything, fix everything, and have all the answers. Sometimes, I needed to take a step back. If something didn't get done or fixed, it was not going to be the end of the world. If I had taken a breath, I would have seen earlier that my little one needed a haircut. As tears filled my eyes, my son came downstairs with his older brother.

I couldn't believe my eyes... I saw the two cutest boys with buzz cuts! And minutes later, my husband joined in with a buzz, too!

My beautiful family holiday cards went out on time—just with a little less hair!

—Jacqueline Davidson Kopito—

Serendipity

Family faces are magic mirrors. Looking at people who
belong to us, we see the past, present, and future.
~Gail Lumet Buckley

It was New Year's Eve. Eleven adults swapped stories while seven kids, ranging from six to nineteen, laughed in the living room. Right after dinner, I gathered everyone together and proposed a ritual that would connect the old year with the new.

"Think of a valuable lesson you learned in the past year and write it down as a piece of advice for someone else," I said. "Then drop it into this bag for a random drawing."

Everyone dove into the exercise, even my little granddaughter who needed help with writing.

I asked Lulu, "What was the best thing you learned this year?"

She said, "French." (She's in a French immersion program at school.)

"Why?"

"Because it's different."

I asked for clarification. "So would your advice be to learn French because it helps you to think differently?"

"Exactly," said the six-year-old.

Her advice went into the bag with seventeen other slips of paper. We all sat in a circle, excited to see what would happen next.

"Now, it's time to think of a goal for the coming year. Say it out loud, and then pick a slip at random and read the advice aloud," I said.

"Let's see if chance advice coincides with your goal."

The room was filled with positive energy as each person stated his or her goal and then chose a random piece of paper. It was eerie how well the advice seemed to fit each person's goal for the coming year.

Teenager Zach wished for his driver's license, and he pulled a slip that read: "Know all the facts. Don't be impulsive. A lack of knowledge can lead to a fatal mistake."

Rich hoped to pass a very tough accreditation. His slip read: "Don't waste time watching so much TV. It's time you never get back." It took a while for the laughter to die down since he's such a movie fanatic.

Sheila, new to college, yearned for a best friend and wondered how to go about it. She pulled the slip I had written: "One size does not fit all. Discover and encourage individuality. Be compassionate with people very different from yourself."

Danielle planned a trip to Europe in the new year, and out came little Lulu's advice, "Learn French. It helps you to think differently."

For me, I wanted to teach a meditation/journaling program for prison inmates. I had volunteered to do it in the past and enjoyed it, but I struggle with too many demands on my schedule. How would it be possible? I pulled a slip that read: "Let God fight your battles." I interpreted this to mean that the path would open when a Higher Power deemed the time to be right. My heart simply had to be in the right place, and meanwhile, I could work toward readiness. In time, I came to realize the prisoner who needed stress relief was me.

Often, we ignore guidance from other people. Yet that night, whether it was serendipity or magic or family bonds, the advice we received seemed so tailor-made for us that we all listened. And we were better off because of it.

— Suzette Martinez Standring —

A House Without a Chimney

Even as an adult I find it difficult to sleep on Christmas
Eve. Yuletide excitement is a potent caffeine,
no matter your age.
~Terri Guillemets

I couldn't sleep. Wide-eyed, I stared up at the ceiling. "It's not fair," I whispered. "Uncle Ed's house has a chimney. Uncle Marty's house has a chimney. Grandpa's house has a chimney. Why doesn't ours?"

I clutched my blue blankie to my chest.

"Well, I'm not going to lie here and let Santa Claus skip my house just because we don't have a chimney."

I kicked off my covers and sat up. With my blue blankie draped around my neck, I leapt from my bed. In the pale glow of a cheap, drugstore nightlight, I tiptoed around the pieces to Mr. Potato Head. Then I slowly pushed the door open.

I stuck my head into the hallway and peeked left.

I could hear faint noises coming from the kitchen. Who was up this late on Christmas Eve?

I stepped into the hallway, and crept toward the noises. Meanwhile, the footies in my jammies made a funny sound "skish" on the hallway's wooden floor.

At the end of the hallway, I halted and peeked around the corner.

"John?"

I froze.

Mom asked, "What are you doing up?"

I stepped into the kitchen, replying, "Mom, I can't sleep."

"Well, you better get your little butt to bed," Mom countered, "or Santa won't come."

"I know, I know."

Mom folded her arms across her chest and began tapping her right foot.

So I asked, "Um, Mom… can I… uh… take one more look at the tree?"

Mom sighed.

"Okay, I guess so," she said. "But then you go straight to bed."

"Yes, ma'am," I replied. I scampered across the kitchen's linoleum floor.

Then I hit the living room's carpet and continued my trek to see the tree — just like I had told Mom I would. But I stopped in the middle of the living room and looked over my left shoulder.

Mom was puttering around in the kitchen.

The coast was clear!

I bolted to the front door, reached up, and grabbed the knob. I silently rotated it, barely cracking open the front door.

"There," I whispered. "Our house not having a chimney won't stop Santa now."

Then I retreated from the scene of the crime and began my trek back into the kitchen. When I reached the linoleum, I actually did turn around and look at our Christmas tree. It was beautiful, but it would look even better tomorrow morning with all the presents under it.

I turned around to go back into the kitchen — only to run headlong into Mom.

"John, please watch where you're going," she commanded, balancing a glass of milk and a plate of cookies.

"I'm sorry."

Mom traipsed to the living room's coffee table, where she set those items down. Then she stood erect, and started back to the kitchen — but lurched to a halt.

Uh oh.

Mom furrowed her brow.

I bit my lip.

"I feel a draft," Mom mumbled.

"Oh no," I groaned.

Mom looked around and then asked, "Well, who left the front door cracked open?"

I hung my head. Then I watched Mom troop over to the front door, slam it shut, and lock it.

Dang it. Santa was never going to get in.

After Mom returned across the carpet, she placed her right hand upon my shoulder and steered me into the kitchen. There, she pointed down the hallway and said, "Go!"

With my blue blankie dragging on the floor, I returned to my bedroom.

Christmas morning, I awoke to find a million presents under our tree! But I wasn't surprised. To this very day, Mom doesn't know that — on the way to my bedroom — I unlocked the back door.

—John M. Scanlan—

Gratitude
and Grace

60

The Great Thanksgiving Challenge

I can no other answer make, but, thanks, and thanks.
~William Shakespeare

My friend Marilyn and I had just settled into a booth at our favorite coffee shop. "BookTalk is at my house next month," I said. "I hate getting ready for it."

"I know what you mean," Marilyn answered. "I spent a week cleaning when it was my turn in February, not to mention baking two cakes."

"Not to mention that it's all over in a couple of hours. All that work for two hours!"

Marilyn nodded as we sipped from steaming cups of latte.

"And if that's not bad enough," I said, wiping foam from my upper lip, "my entire family is coming for Thanksgiving this year. I love them dearly, but you know what that means?"

"Yep. Cooking and cleaning, changing sheets, wondering what to feed everybody for breakfast. I go through the same thing every year."

The chimes on the coffee shop door jingled and a bedraggled woman entered, carrying two super-sized shopping bags stuffed with odds and ends. Twists of gray hair escaped from the ratty scarf covering her head. Nothing she wore matched, and one black canvas high top had a hole at the big toe. As she passed us, it was evident she hadn't bathed in days.

"Would you listen to us?" I whispered, feeling ashamed of myself. "We sound like two ungrateful curmudgeons."

"That poor woman probably can't pay for a cup of coffee."

"Do you think she's homeless?" I asked.

Marilyn shrugged her shoulders. Then she grabbed her wallet, and headed for the counter where she paid for the woman's coffee and an apple fritter. The woman smiled, showing bad teeth. I heard Marilyn invite her to join us, but the woman shook her head and settled into a soft chair in a sunlit corner of the shop.

"That was nice," I said when Marilyn slid back into the booth.

She rolled her eyes. "That was guilt."

I nibbled a piece of chocolate biscotti. "You know something? Some days, all I do is complain."

"Me, too."

"Take BookTalk for instance. Those women are smart and funny. I'm honored they asked me to join the club. The last thing I should do is complain about having them come to my house for a few hours."

Marilyn glanced at the woman thumbing through a tattered *People* magazine. "I don't know why I always see the glass half empty when it's more than half full," she said.

"We should stop complaining — it's a bad habit." I said this with more conviction than I felt.

Marilyn set her cup down just as a megawatt smile broke over her face.

"What?" I asked.

When Marilyn gets that look, it always means some bold plan has taken hold of her brain — usually one that includes me.

"We'll give it up. Complaining. We'll give it up for Thanksgiving."

"You mean Lent. That's months away."

"No — I mean we'll stop complaining and start being thankful. Just in time for Thanksgiving. It takes thirty days to drop a habit and thirty days to start a new one."

"So what's your plan?"

Marilyn leaned back and crossed her arms. "A challenge. We'll keep a diary. Write down every complaint. Then think of something to be thankful for, and write that down too."

"What if we can't think of something to be thankful for?"

Marilyn pointed to the old woman who had fallen asleep in her chair. "You can think of something."

"Then how will we know we're really keeping track? It would be easy to cheat."

Marilyn stuck out her little finger. Now it was my turn to roll my eyes. Pinky swear. We'd been doing it since junior high.

"Challenge accepted," I said.

Thanksgiving Day was a month and a half away. Could we really drop a bad habit by then? And replace it with a new one?

The next morning I poured my cereal and picked up the milk carton only to discover it was empty.

"I can't eat cereal without milk," I muttered. Then I caught myself, not believing the first words out of my mouth that day took the form of a complaint.

"Great," I said, talking to the cat. "Can't even start the day right."

And there it was: complaint number two.

"This is going to be harder than I thought," I said, searching the desk shelves for a notebook. "Why can't I ever find what I need when I need it?"

Welcome to my world, complaints three and four.

I grabbed the phone and dialed Marilyn's number.

"What's up?" she asked, way too perky for early morning.

"I've been awake fifteen minutes and all I've done is complain," I complained. "This is hard!"

"No kidding. Jim forgot to make the coffee last night — his job — and I had to wait ten minutes for the pot to brew."

"Did you write that down?"

Marilyn laughed. "Can't find a notebook."

"Neither can I!"

"Okay — quick — what are you thankful for?" she asked.

"I'm talking on the phone with my best friend and the cat is purring in my lap. What about you?"

"I'm drinking coffee in a warm kitchen and about to go work out," Marilyn answered. "See? This won't be so hard after all."

But it was hard. Hard to believe I complained so much about trivial things. Hard to believe I wasn't more thankful for my family, my friends, and my health. My mind kept wandering back to the homeless woman, and I caught myself saying little prayers for her.

BookTalk met at my house the first week of November. In preparation, I cleaned and cooked and complained. But I recorded the blessings, too: my husband cheerfully moved furniture to accommodate thirty women; the cheesecakes I baked were perfect; my friends in the book club complimented my beautiful home — and I realized they were right.

As weeks passed, I noticed my notebook recorded more blessings than complaints. Marilyn reported the same phenomenon. That's not to say we didn't complain — we did. Just not as much. Maybe the complaints dwindled because we realized we had so much to be thankful for.

The Monday after Thanksgiving, Marilyn and I met for coffee again, comparing stories of the holiday weekend and sharing what we'd written in the pages of our notebooks.

"It's interesting," Marilyn said. "I don't complain as much now. And when I do, the complaints sound more like problem statements than whining."

"I feel better about myself, too. And about life in general." I took a sip of creamy latte. "I guess we owe that homeless woman a bushel of gratitude, don't we?"

"Yeah," Marilyn said. "We sure do."

— Ruth Jones —

61

The Best Gift

Love is, above all, the gift of oneself.
~Jean Anouilh

With two teenagers on the verge of college there wasn't much money left over for holiday shopping. Although I had never conveyed my concern to my daughters, somehow they knew. They had seen me glued to the news reports following the nation's economic crises. They had watched their dad grimace over the checkbook and credit card bills. They had seen me remove items from the grocery cart that we didn't absolutely need. They had witnessed me scrimp like never before. They're smart kids who are also exceptionally thoughtful.

I was on my way to the mall to do a little Christmas shopping. With a short list in one hand and car keys in the other, I asked what they wanted for Christmas. I braced myself for their reply. They looked up as if praying to God for enlightenment on what to say. If I were their age I'd ask for a curling iron, a cell phone, an iPod, gift cards, movie tickets, and new clothes. They looked me square in the eye and said, "We're good."

I stared back in disbelief. They were teenagers with final exams and SATs only one week away. The college application deadline was dangerously close. They had choir practice, volunteer obligations, and parties. They had concerts to prepare for and school projects to complete. How in the world could they be "good?"

"What are you really thinking?" I waited nervously for a reply. "There must be something you want."

They quietly deliberated and Juliana, older and wiser, swallowed hard before answering. "We don't need a thing." They nodded. "Seriously," she reaffirmed.

I stared at her in disbelief, waiting for her to smile or crack a joke, but she was adamant.

"We're really good, Mom," Andrea said. "We have everything a girl could want. You and Dad have given us everything. We're happy," she said motioning to Juliana, "just to have you."

I felt my heart skip a beat as time stood still. Her words reverberated in my head as my eyes welled with tears of joy. Both girls wrapped their arms around me and hugged me long and hard. The truth was that we didn't have much money left over for unnecessary gifts. We could barely afford the things we really needed with skyrocketing college costs looming on the horizon.

That moment was the sweetest and most tender I had ever experienced. Their words were all I needed. I didn't need a present under the tree and neither did they. I had something much better. Words spoken from the heart of the children I have built my life around for the last eighteen years lifted me to a much higher place. They couldn't have given me a better gift. I cherished their warmth and reaffirmed my love for them.

"I insist you let me get you something. We can afford it," I lied.

Juliana pulled back and her solemn voice took over. "Then get us something we can share."

"We're really good at sharing," Andrea chimed.

They were killing me with kindness. I looked at my daughters in awe and silently thanked God for blessing me with two great kids. How could I be so lucky?

I put my car keys away and assembled the Christmas tree in the family room in its usual spot. It was the one job I detested and I usually pawned it off on Patrick, my easygoing husband. This year I cherished the time together. Next year they would be on a college campus and the thought of not having them around me all of the time scared me.

I appreciated each strand of twinkle lights that we wrapped around the prickly branches. I loved every second of it.

Andrea opened the box of ornaments and dangled one on a branch near me. I remembered it fondly — a heart-shaped ornament I bought for Patrick the first year we were dating.

Andrea gave me an endearing smile. "This ornament sums up the way I feel."

Juliana peered over her shoulder and read the inscription. "Love really is the best gift of all."

— Barbara Canale —

62

A Voice Above the Vacuum

The best gift you can give is a hug: one size fits all
and no one ever minds if you return it.
~Author Unknown

I t was our first Thanksgiving in the new house, and I wanted everything to be perfect. Perfect food. Perfect house. Perfect conversation. By the time I hit the forty-eight-hour count-down, my vision of a table with pressed linens, fresh flowers, and a smorgasbord of homemade desserts had already dissolved. I was just hopeful that I'd find a clean tablecloth and eight matching dessert forks.

Our family "plan" for everyone to chip in with the necessary prep work had been torpedoed by my husband's new job in retail. To make matters worse, a critical project for me that week had claimed two days of planned vacation. John Lennon was right: Life is what happens while you are making other plans.

By Wednesday night, while my husband was selling camping gear as Christmas gifts, my children and I were at home and into full-blown vacuum-mania. I was thankful that a kid's allowance didn't constitute a salary as I put my six- and eight-year-old to work, violating all child labor laws. For my part, I was swooshing around in the toilet bowl, headed for a meltdown. I started ticking off all the ways my holiday was falling short as if it were a long list of personal injustices.

It was already too late. In my perfect Thanksgiving, there wasn't going to be any orange zest in my cranberry salad because it hadn't made the grocery list. There would be no perfect family photos to record the day because I had forgotten to buy batteries. The hand towel that matched the new bathroom paint had not been laundered. And then I saw it and exploded; it was the last straw. Someone had brought home the wrong toilet paper. Two-ply or not two-ply: that should never be the question.

I don't remember what my son asked me as he was trying his best to finish the vacuuming, but I do remember twisting into that mean-and-tight mom-face before barking out an angry answer. This combination of sound and fury is a universal signal to kids everywhere that their real mom has just been abducted by aliens, and it's best to duck and cover until she gets back. But he didn't.

Instead of darting out of view, my second-grader turned off the vacuum and walked the whole way around the stairwell to face me. He never said a word. He just wrapped his arms around me for a hug that makes me feel ashamed of myself to this very day. My son — my shrink — took a risk to teach me that sometimes we need a hug most when we are least huggable.

It was the perfect Thanksgiving. The people I loved gathered around my table where a pumpkin covered up last year's stubborn gravy stain. We dined on just one choice of pie, and my dad used a mismatched dinner fork without complaint. My daughter drew a picture of us on a paper plate where no one had their eyes closed.

I learned a lot from an eight-year-old that holiday, and I've tried hard to remember it. As the holidays approach now, I try to celebrate all of our blessings, especially those that come disguised as inconvenience. And if you find a grump circling your Thanksgiving table complaining about her job, his gallstones or her dress size, sidle up and give them all a hug. It just might be what they need most.

— Mitchell Kyd —

63

Thanks, Canadian Style

*The greatness of a community is most accurately
measured by the compassionate actions of its members.*
~Coretta Scott King

I was born and raised in Vancouver, but I have lived in Seattle, Washington, for more than forty years. During that time my American husband and I have made many trips through the Peace Arch border crossing. He learned early on that chester-fields were sofas and serviettes were napkins and that Hockey Night in Canada was as important as Monday Night Football in the U.S.

But there was one time he forgot an important Canadian tradition.

It was a cold, rainy autumn day as he drove home from one of his weekly trips to visit my mother in the hospital in Vancouver. Widowed, alone, and recovering from a string of surgeries, her prognosis was not good. In order to monitor her progress and keep things running with our family at home, the two of us alternated trips to stay with her, switching mid-week.

As he headed south from Vancouver, traffic was light. He was surprised to see his usual fast food stop closed. Hungry and with two hours of driving still ahead, he took one of the last exits before the border. A billboard directed him to a restaurant in White Rock where he assumed the nearly full parking lot meant great food. Inside, customers in heavy coats, carrying dripping umbrellas, lined up waiting for tables.

A smiling, middle-aged woman with a clipboard gently pushed through the crowd toward him. "How many in your party, sir?"

When he said "one," her expression changed.

"Sure thing, dear." She touched his arm, flashing a concerned look, then whisked him to the front of the line. "We'll get you seated right away."

Two minutes later she returned and led him to the far end of the restaurant where a man in a dark suit was setting a small table for one. The man pulled out a chair and said, "Welcome. Glad you joined us today."

"Thanks." My hubby returned his smile and sat down. Surprised by the amazing service, he chalked it up to the kind of Canadian friendliness and efficiency I always bragged about.

The woman handed him a menu. "You'll probably want one of these specials at the top of the sheet. Your waitress will be right with you."

Later, he told me his taste buds were primed for a burger until the savoury aroma from the platters of turkey and mashed potatoes with gravy coming out of the kitchen made his mouth water. He said he had no choice but to order the Gobbler Special.

The waitress hovered, refilling his coffee cup regularly. Over the din of clattering silverware and loud voices, she went out of her way to make conversation. "Quite a crowd today. It looks like the weather's going to break soon."

While he waited, he was struck by the sight of so many large groups, mostly families, sharing a meal in the late afternoon. During our months of constant commuting, the days of the week were blurring together. He checked his watch to make sure it was Monday and not Sunday.

When his turkey dinner arrived, it was as exceptional as the service. He ate every morsel and had just pushed his plate away when the attentive waitress surprised him with a jumbo slice of pumpkin pie piled high with whipped cream. "This is from your neighbours." She pointed to the next table.

He turned to the group of friendly faces across the aisle. A young woman with a toddler on her lap leaned over. "We just wanted to share some Thanksgiving cheer. You looked lonely over there."

"Oh... yes... thank you." After their kindness, he told me, he wasn't about to confess that he'd forgotten their traditional holiday. Although already full, he managed to stuff down dessert. He bid his new friends farewell and paid the bill at the counter. As he made his way through the crowd still waiting to be seated, he realized how pitiful he must have looked, all alone on Canadian Thanksgiving.

Six weeks later, in late November, my mother was out of the hospital and well enough to travel. My dear husband drove to Vancouver and brought her back the same day. We had so much to give thanks for that year when we celebrated American Thanksgiving south of the border.

— Maureen Rogers —

Christmas Without Electricity

*There is a force more powerful than steam
and electricity: the will.*
~Fernán Caballero

I was at work the day before my long awaited Christmas vacation, ready to enjoy some quality time with my family. We received a large snowfall the previous night, which was very deep, so I had a fun eight-mile ride to work on an ATV (4-wheeler).

Around lunch my wife called and said, "Honey, we have a problem. The power went off an hour ago, and we are getting cold." She was alone watching our two children. They were four and six years old. There was more snow in the forecast. I called the utility company to inquire when the electricity would be restored. The receptionist informed me that the electricity could potentially be out for several days, maybe a week.

During the long ride home, I wondered what I could do to get my family through a week without electricity. Then it hit me. "Call Dad. He will know what to do. Or, even better, he will ask us to stay with him and Mom." I knew it was a great idea. Arriving home, I called Dad. He lives five miles away, but did not have electricity either. Dad was not sure what they would do. Discouraged, my immediate reaction was, "Well great! Now what? We're on our own."

I located a flashlight, and went to the basement. I was looking for anything to help us during this crisis. I was burrowing through the junk that had collected down there when I remembered some advice from my grandfather: "Boy, don't worry about what you don't have. Do the best you can with what you got."

I keep things around the house, not like a hoarder, but rather a "Collector of Everything," like my grandfather. I located a kerosene heater along with thirty gallons of fuel I had stored for an emergency years ago. I looked at my cordless tools and pondered, "How can these help?" I always have batteries charged and ready for use in those hand tools. I discovered a plastic desk fan. I kept digging and uncovered a box of candles and a box of hurricane lamps that I picked up at a yard sale. The small, rusty wheels in my head were spinning. I was not in panic mode any longer. I was in the "I can do this" mode, and I started to feel pretty good about things. The heater worked and so did the lamps. This wasn't going to be so bad!

I made trips upstairs, like an Olympic sprinter. I carried parts to repair our life. The items were piled on the living room floor. I dug through the mound as a child would on Christmas morning. The kerosene heater started generating a bit of warmth. I placed a lamp in every room. I tore the fan apart and inserted the plastic blade into the cordless drill. I positioned the drill in front of the heater, pointed it down the hallway, and tied the trigger in the on position. Warm air began migrating down the hall into every bedroom. We had a 500-gallon propane tank for the water heater and stove. Neither hot water nor being able to cook was a concern. At least we could use the stovetop. We ate supper, watched the snowfall, and went to bed. Things were slowly getting back to normal.

I called Dad the next morning, Christmas Eve, to see how he and Mom were doing. He still did not know what they would do. He said, "We were cold last night." I asked them to come to our house. We were not at full comfort level, but were able to help. They arrived in his Jeep. It was loaded with food, clothes, and presents. He stopped to get my sister, brother-in-law, and nephew. Dad said, "The drive was slow, but it was better than freezing at home." We sat around reminiscing while the kids played games. We had a candlelit supper of hot soup. Everyone enjoyed a warm shower, hugs, and went to bed. I went to sleep thinking, "It was a pleasant day."

We awoke Christmas morning to wonderful aromas filling the house; my wife was cooking bacon, eggs, sausage, gravy, country ham, fried potatoes, and pancakes. Biscuits were atop the kerosene heater. The smells reminded me of Christmas morning at Grandma's house. The scents of hickory smoked bacon, sage sausage, and country ham were creeping through the house, like a slow, London fog. After breakfast, we sat and talked about the "good ole days." We did not realize we were reliving them. Later that evening, the snow started to melt.

Around six, as we were opening gifts, the electricity came alive. We left everything alone for an hour, making sure the electricity would stay on. We put the house back to normal and finished opening presents. After several hours of holiday enjoyment, everyone loaded up and went home.

As I look back on that Christmas, I realize what a great time it was.

Since then, many changes have occurred. My dad passed away. The children are grown, building their own lives. We have not had much snow during the winter months. Around Christmas season now, I sometimes long for another Christmas without electricity.

—Christopher E. Cantrell—

65

Finding Five

A personal journal is an ideal environment in which to "become." It is a perfect place for you to think, feel, discover, expand, remember, and dream.

~Brad Wilcox

uring my years of teaching kindergarten, my favorite lesson was about the Thanksgiving holiday. I loved introducing the students to history by sharing the story of the first Thanksgiving and allowing them to dress like a Pilgrim or Native American for a special Thanksgiving celebration.

Each child brought a snack to share with the class, and we practiced counting skills, sorting skills, and even patterning with the goodies before they were eaten. Our school cafeteria prepared a traditional Thanksgiving dinner, and the holiday felt more meaningful to me than the other holidays. I loved hearing what each child talked about when we took turns sharing our thanks.

One day, when I was online researching different ways to celebrate Thanksgiving with children, I read "The Legend of the Five Kernels." There are many versions of this story, but suffice it to say that there is a tradition that involves placing five kernels of corn at the seat of each guest. Whether this is to commemorate the fact that the Pilgrims subsisted on five kernels of corn per day during tough times, or whether the five kernels represented five things the Pilgrims were giving their thanks for, is unclear.

I became excited about using the five kernels approach with my students as a way of starting a conversation about giving thanks. Instead of using five kernels of corn, I placed five candy corns on each child's desk and asked them to share five things for which they were thankful.

That custom in my classroom led to my decision to include gratitude in my daily journal. I decided to list five blessings about each day. A sample list for one day might have included that I was blessed with all green lights when I was running late for school; the principal complimented me on my new bulletin board display; my students behaved well; my coworker surprised me with a helping of her homemade cheese bread; and the headache I had before lunch went away after I ate.

After several days of writing down my blessings, I read the lists and realized everything was all about me. Shouldn't I be blessing others?

After that revelation, my journaling changed.

Not only did I list five blessings that happened for me, but also five ways in which I had reached out to bless others. A sample list of the blessings I tried to give to others might have included that I blessed my friend by watching her class during my planning time so she could go next door to the hospital to check on her sick husband; I duplicated copies of a special worksheet for all the kindergarten teachers, not just for myself; I shared my Play-Doh rolling pins with the new teacher across the hall; I volunteered to take ticket money at the ballgame for a sick worker; and I found extra supplies for someone whose supplies had run out.

As I journaled this new way, I found myself becoming a more positive, caring person. By hunting for the blessings in my day, my mind was focused on the good, not on the disappointments. By thinking of ways to reach out and help someone, my mind was focused on others, not on my own little problems.

In the past, I often had magnified the negative and minimized the positive, but now I was magnifying the positive and minimizing the negative. There wasn't anything magical about the number five; I just chose to list five because it was the number in the "Legend of the Five Kernels." I realized quite quickly that I had way more than five blessings occur to me each day, and I even managed to perform more than five good deeds for others each day as well.

I take the time now to review my journal and reread all the blessings I've received and the blessings I've made happen for other people. It helps put things in perspective. I am much more thankful nowadays, and giving thanks is not just something I do in November. It has become a year-round lifestyle.

— Helen F. Wilder —

Gramma's Good China

The truth is, unless you let go, unless you forgive
yourself, unless you forgive the situation,
unless you realize that the situation is over,
you cannot move forward.
~Steve Maraboli

For years, every Saturday afternoon my family — Mom, my stepfather and I — had dinner at Gramma's house. We watched sporting events on TV, played *Yahtzee* and enjoyed a home-cooked meal: spaghetti and meatballs, pot roast, chicken and biscuits... you get the idea.

Anna Marie, or Gramma as we all call her, is seventy-nine years old and very set in her ways. She attends church every Sunday, never misses an episode of *60 Minutes*, completes the daily crossword puzzle in the newspaper, makes apple pie for every holiday and refuses to ever take the good china out of the cabinet because her regular dinnerware is "good enough."

However, one Saturday at the end of October things were different. My mom, my stepdad and I stayed home because my father was coming to visit. My biological father, that is, who I hadn't seen since he left town sixteen years earlier. He called asking to visit, saying he wanted to see me.

I was dreading it.

Saturday afternoon when the doorbell chimed, I peered through the blinds at my father on the porch. He looked older, heavier, grayer. For some reason, I expected him to look exactly as he did in the single photo I had of him — the two of us at the lake when I was seven. I kept the picture in my sock drawer.

My father, mom and stepfather were politely exchanging pleasantries when I stepped into the entryway. My father extended his hand to shake mine. "David," he said, smiling. "It's great to see you, son."

I knew what I should do, but I couldn't. My arm, my hand was immobile.

This man had walked out on us. He had never been there. He missed every Christmas and birthday, my basketball games, my college graduation; why would I shake his hand?

I nodded, grunted and sat on the couch.

Mom told him about her job and the vacation cruise that she and my stepdad had taken, then motioned towards me. "David's been busy lately with his job and finishing his thesis, haven't you, honey?"

I nodded. "Yeah, high school, college, getting a job. A lot can happen in sixteen years."

"David," Mom grumbled through clenched teeth.

My father held up his hands. "It's okay. I understand. You're not thrilled to see me. This was a stupid idea, but I wanted to see you."

"You've seen me." I shrugged.

"Why don't we have dinner?" Mom suggested. "I made meatloaf."

"Thanks anyway. I'm not hungry." I got up and headed for the door.

My father called after me. "I'd really like you to stay."

"But, honey, you haven't eaten," said Mom.

I walked out the door.

And that's how I left it. I didn't say another word about it. My father didn't call again. The following Saturday we went to Gramma's as usual.

Secretly, I stewed about my father, daydreamed about him, lay awake at night, replaying the visit. What should I have said or done? Why did he leave? Why did he return? Did he know how much he hurt me? Did he even care? I was angry. I couldn't let it go.

Two weeks after my father's visit, I took Gramma grocery shopping for Thanksgiving. When we returned home, I put the groceries away while Gramma sat at the kitchen table reviewing her shopping list.

"Green beans; got it," she mumbled, checking off items. "Potatoes; got it. What have I forgotten?"

I set the bag of onions on the countertop.

"Oh, the apples," Gramma said. "I forgot apples for pie."

"Okay," I replied.

Gramma reached out and caught my sleeve. "What's wrong, David?"

"I'll get apples tomorrow."

"Not apples," answered Gramma. "What's wrong with you?"

I shrugged. "I'm fine."

"You're not fine," Gramma said. "In this family, food is serious business. If I'm talking about pie and all you say is 'okay', then you're not fine."

"I'm putting groceries away."

"I know what this is about," Gramma announced. "It's about your father."

I turned away and slid two jars of olives into the cupboard.

"Your whole attitude has changed," Gramma said. "Ever since he came to visit, you're not the same."

"This isn't the time," I told her, grabbing another grocery bag off the floor.

"This is the perfect time," she replied. "You finish with the groceries. I'll make coffee."

Ten minutes later we sat at the dining room table, facing each other over a plate of brownies.

Gramma sipped her coffee. "Tell me about this."

"I'm mad," I replied. "He left us and hasn't bothered to keep in touch. Why has he come back?"

"Your father wants to make peace."

"Well, I don't want peace. I don't want to see him."

Gramma pointed at me. "This isn't good. You're tearing yourself up. And you're making life miserable for everybody else being such a grumble-bug."

I couldn't help smiling when she mentioned the name she had called me since I was a baby whenever I got upset. "My father is making me a grumble-bug."

"No." She shook her head. "You're *allowing* your father to make you a grumble-bug. You're making yourself miserable and you know what? Your anger isn't affecting your father a bit. He doesn't know you're a grumble-bug."

I rolled my eyes.

"Look at it this way," Gramma explained. "Anger is like taking that beautiful turkey we bought and leaving it on the counter until it spoils and smells bad. Then, to really show your father how angry you are, you cook the spoiled turkey and you eat it yourself hoping your father gets sick."

"That doesn't make sense," I said.

"Exactly," replied Gramma. "Neither does the way you're handling this situation. Your father goes off to live his life — you stay sick with anger. You're only hurting yourself."

I shrugged. "What do you suggest?"

"Forgive him."

"No way, Gramma." I folded my arms. "Why should I?"

"Forgiveness isn't always something you do for the other person," Gramma explained. "Sometimes you can forgive to help yourself feel better."

"What do I do?" I asked.

"Invite your father for Thanksgiving."

I shook my head. "Do you know how uncomfortable that would be?"

"I never said it would be easy," Gramma answered. "But it's better than eating spoiled turkey the rest of your life."

"Okay," I agreed. "I'll invite him to dinner, but on one condition."

"What condition?"

I pointed to the cabinet in the corner. "It'll be a special occasion. The regular dinnerware won't do. You'll need to use… the good china."

So, the following Thursday, we had Thanksgiving with my father and the good china.

"Are we actually going to eat off it?" Mom asked, stroking a plate with her fingertips.

It wasn't my best Thanksgiving, but it wasn't nearly as bad as I had imagined. We had a good meal and my father joined in the conversations. My father and I played *Yahtzee* after dinner. I discovered we both were Dallas Cowboys fans. After the apple pie, I walked my father out to his car.

"I'd like to get together again sometime, David," my father said. "I have a lot to tell you. And I'd like your forgiveness."

I nodded. "I've got your phone number. I'd like to hear what you have to say. I'll call you."

My father held out his right hand.

This time I did shake his hand. It wasn't easy, but I knew if Gramma could use the good china, I could do this. I was starting to feel better already.

— David Hull —

The Heart of a Community

*In the country, community is a loosely defined term
that starts with family, and tends to spread itself
around through a network of marriages,
friendships and other relationships.*
~Marsha Bolton

My cousin Rosaire Desrosiers was a young man when he and his wife Alice left their farm in Ste. Anne Manitoba, for a day of Christmas shopping in Winnipeg. With confidence and smiling faces, they kissed their six children goodbye that November afternoon in 1954 as they left Rosaire's fourteen-year-old cousin Simone in charge.

Late in the day, Simone busied herself with the evening meal, preparing a rather elaborate spread while the children watched and played. As she worked, the wind whistled through holes in the walls where insulation should have been. But the children didn't mind.... this was their home, a place where the family celebrated life with laughter.

As they finished their supper that evening, the lights went out with a deafening bang. Louis, the eldest at eight, went off in search of a flashlight to further investigate the problem. As he fumbled around the closet, he found it odd that something resembling a pair of cat's eyes was being reflected off the ceiling.

Simone realized in an instant what those reflections were. Without hesitating, she wrapped the baby in a blanket and yelled for the other children to get outside quickly. The roof of the house was already engulfed in flames. With snow on the ground and no shoes on their feet, Simone hurried the children to her parents' farm fifteen minutes away, carrying the baby in her skirt to keep her warm. Turning only once, she shuddered as the house disintegrated entirely in flames. What a close call, she realised with a breath of relief. At least she had got all six children to safety.

When Rosaire and Alice returned that night, they went into shock when they found their home in smoking ruins. Although they thanked God and Simone countless times for their children's safety, both Rosaire and Alice knew that difficult times lay ahead. All that they had ever owned was lost. With little insurance to rebuild, Rosaire despaired at the apparently hopeless situation. He and Alice found little to laugh about now.

Realising they had nowhere to go, Rosaire's father, Magloire, gladly opened his doors to his son's family. The children adored their pépère. Although it was a temporary solution, Rosaire knew that his young brood would benefit from the attention lavished on them by their grandfather.

Yet, even with Magloire's assistance, Rosaire was desperately in need of money. The recently purchased Christmas gifts were returned and the small insurance policy cashed. Even then he knew there was not enough to rebuild, and was resigned to renting a home.

Then, Johnny Goosen, an old school friend, came over to chat. Johnny's solution was simple: "You buy what material you can, Rosaire, and we'll all help you rebuild."

As the lumber began to arrive, so did the truckloads of people wanting to help. One truck after another showed up with family, friends and neighbours; people from both French and Mennonite communities. Together they worked in the cold and snow to build the Desrosiers a new house.

When one job was completed, Johnny Goosen would put in a word at his church for someone specialising in another trade. Sure enough, the next morning, a plumber or electrician would appear.

With Christmas only one week away, the work was suddenly finished and the Desrosiers were finally home!

As the last of the workers left, Rosaire and Alice sat back in amazement in their new kitchen. So much had happened in the last two months, and they were so grateful. But, having spent all they had on building materials, they had no money left for gifts to put under the tree.

Even after all they had been through, Rosaire and Alice still did not want Christmas morning to be a disappointment for their children. They decided to share with their children the joy that they felt from the generosity of all their friends and neighbours. Each night they worked feverishly, using imagination and leftover pieces of wood to build a dollhouse, a wooden horse, and other beautiful gifts. They were determined that Santa would come to their home after all.

Unbeknownst to them, their son Denis was watching. He would position himself nightly at the top of the stairs and watch the two elves at their secret work. And then suddenly, with two days left before Christmas, Rosaire and Alice stopped their craft, leaving some projects incomplete. This mystified Denis, but he didn't dare ask why.

On Christmas morning the children awoke to a tree magically laden with beautiful gifts and sweets. Denis noticed that many of the gifts had not been part of their parents' workshop, and quietly wondered where they had come from. Rosaire and Alice decided to keep the secret safe for the time being, as they watched their children's overwhelming joy.

It was only years later that Rosaire finally told Denis and the others the secret about that day, his eyes brimming with tears. Two days before Christmas, the local parish priest Father Laplante had arrived as an emissary. Apparently, the community's generosity had not stopped with the building of the house. They had also collected enough gifts to ensure that the Desrosiers children had all their Christmas dreams fulfilled. And so the late night work had stopped.

Good to his word, on Christmas Eve, Father Laplante had arrived at their door with satchels of presents contributed by the many well wishing families and friends.

Years later, as Uncle Rosaire reflected back on the events that transpired that cold winter of 1953, he was still moved to tears when he remembered Simone, who is my mother, Johnny Goosen, and the countless others who gave so selflessly. The Desrosiers found great joy that year, not because the people gave with their money, but because they gave with their hearts.

—Paula Meyer—

Chapter 8

Holiday Angels

A Thanksgiving to Remember

To this very hour we go hungry and thirsty,
we are poorly clad and roughly treated,
we wander about homeless.
~1 Corinthians 4:11

y husband had taken the car to see about a job and I stayed at the rest area with our six children. I kept them busy playing games and reading books. I prayed as hard as I could that my husband would get the job and this madness would all come to an end. When he came back and slammed the car door, I knew the news was not good.

My heart fell to my knees when he told me twenty people had showed up for the job and it was given to someone else.

That night, one of the churches in Portland had a free dinner, so we hurried and had the children wash up in the bathrooms. We all loaded up in our run-down car, with the muffler held up by a coat hanger, and filled the radiator with water again. I thought how good it would be to have a hot meal instead of bologna sandwiches every night. No one would get this thrilled about a hot meal, but being homeless, we all knew what a treat this would be. We all just kept eating the soup, chicken, potatoes and biscuits as if we could store them up for later use. When we were ready to leave, I asked for the leftover biscuits, as did many others who were homeless. They only served one meal a week and I wished it were every day.

That night, as we did every night, we read the Bible by flashlight. I don't think we would have been able to hang on if not for the Word of God that we read before we went to sleep. Words like, "I will never leave you nor forsake you." When you're homeless, it's as if you become invisible to the rest of the world. You do begin to feel as if you're all alone in such a big world.

In the morning, we were all just as tired as when we went to bed. It's not easy at all to sleep eight people in one car. It's hard to stay warm with only the few blankets we had to share among us. We got in the car and left to make a garbage dump run. We drove around to the back of the grocery stores and went through the Dumpsters in search of food. We found fruit that was bruised, some bread that had not all turned green. Many times on a good day, we found doughnuts and other kinds of sweets. However, standing there I could not help feeling overwhelmed at the fact that we were fighting the flies and maggots for our next meal. "God give me strength," I would say time and time again.

As my husband looked for work every day, my children and I would walk around the city picking up cans and bottles to return for the deposit. Sometimes we collected enough to get some juice and a sack of cookies to go with our bologna.

When nothing else worked, my husband and I would stand with a sign that read, "will work for food." It was an embarrassment and we felt so ashamed. I never looked up at anyone, pretending that I was elsewhere and this was not happening. Some people threw food at us and screamed horrible names. But we had to survive, and for the sake of our kids we would do whatever it took to get them food to eat.

Thanksgiving was drawing near. It was turning colder at night and we had a difficult time staying warm. My husband had not found work and we were at a loss as how to gather up enough money for a first and last month's rent as well as the deposit that all places wanted. It looked so hopeless.

We planned to go to the only place having Thanksgiving dinner for the homeless, but our car stopped running. My husband worked on it, but it was no use. We were stuck at the rest area. I wanted to give up and felt I could just not go on another day.

The night before Thanksgiving, I put my children to bed and I went and sat on the bench with my Bible and flashlight. At first, it was hard to read because I was crying and my mind was busy with what we were going to do now. I prayed for help and must have talked to God for a couple of hours before I joined my family sleeping in the car.

The next morning, Thanksgiving Day, as my husband again tried to fix the car, a truck driver who had been watching him just came over and asked if he could help. My husband told him the battery was shot and the plugs were fouled and something about the radiator. The man informed us that we couldn't get parts today, so it would have to wait till tomorrow. My husband swallowed his pride and said right now we can't afford to fix it. He said that was okay and he'd be back at 10 A.M. tomorrow with the parts.

That was the beginning of what I call a Thanksgiving of miracles.

People stopped by with food and blankets as well as some clothes. A woman brought a patchwork quilt that she had made and just gave it to us. A family brought a ham and some biscuits and a gallon of milk. Two elderly women brought some homemade fudge and two apple pies. I don't know to this day how so many people knew we were there. We just could not believe the way they were all so willing to share with strangers who were homeless. My husband and I thanked everyone as best we could but our words did not seem like much to offer them all in return for their great compassion showered upon us.

After we ate, a man talked to my husband about a job he had heard about and told him to go over there after the holiday. What a miracle this day had been, I said to myself.

That night it was hard to sleep, we were all just so thankful. I prayed and thanked God because I knew he had answered my prayer and sent each and every one of those people to help us. That next day the truck driver did come back and got our car running again. He hugged us and again off he went.

This Thanksgiving we can share what we have with others. We will be the ones to fill that void.

Now we can join you in reaching out to each other with love and kindness.

—Judy Ann Eichstedt—

69

Hear the Angels' Voices

*Pay attention to your dreams — God's angels often
speak directly to our hearts when we are asleep.*
~Eileen Elias Freeman,
The Angels' Little Instruction Book

Snow, the kind that is soundless and brings stillness to the crisp air, rarely falls in Southern Nevada. Even though decorations and lights adorn my neighborhood, this year the spirit of Christmas seems to be more than a breath away. The passing of a loved one can do that to a person. Especially when the one departed, my mom, brought the spirit of Christmas alive early every season.

Boxes of decorations stay hidden in the hall closet, way back under the stairs and out of plain sight for when the door is open. Christmas carols play on the car radio and television commercials offer enticing buys, and still the ambiance of the season escapes me.

In late November, I bought a box of Christmas cards, which still sits on my desk next to a book of holiday stamps and return address labels. I glance at them every so often without one ounce of enthusiasm. I know my mom would want the spirit of Christmas to fill our home, for us to sing carols and give praise to our Lord for all He has given us. Knowing this, still the power to embrace the season eludes me.

Yesterday, I heard her angelic voice whisper in my ear, "I am always with you. Rejoice, for you are all blessed." Then her voice faded away before I could capture it in my grieving heart.

Today I wonder if I'm simply wishful, hopeful that she is near and watching over us. If I doubt her presence, then the strength of my faith is questionable. The memory of her beautiful voice singing in the church choir on Christmas Eve resonates. "Ave Maria," her solo, hums through the recesses of my mind and restores my beliefs.

My grandson, Zack, enters the room and stands next to my desk. I look up with questioning eyes. His vibrant green eyes hold my gaze. I sense he's unsure and full of concern.

"What's the matter?" I ask.

"I want to ask you about a dream I had last night. It wasn't bad or anything… I just don't understand."

"Why don't you tell me about it maybe I can help you figure it out."

"I was asleep and the phone rang. When I got up and answered it, the woman asked for you. I recognized her voice, but I was afraid to say anything. She asked, 'Zack?' I said, 'Grammie!' I told her she couldn't be calling because she was in heaven. She said she was so happy there and she had a dog. She could see all of us and a miracle was gonna happen to our family. She promised that we'd always be together and for me not to worry so much. Then I woke up."

My heart flutters. The room goes still.

"So what do you think? Was it really Grammie?" I ask, hoping to encourage him to talk more about his experience.

"Yes, it was."

"She gave you a gift then. You were chosen to tell us her message, maybe so we'll stop crying in her absence. She wants us to be happy, happy as she is in heaven."

"Then I'm glad I had the dream. Grandma?"

"Yes?"

"She's really, really, happy."

"I'm so glad you told me about this."

Zack's eyes mist over and he offers a half grin. He leaves the room and heads back into his bedroom. I glance at the box of Christmas cards: the embossed Virgin Mary holding baby Jesus in her arms, angels in the background looking down on them. The television is on and yet the sound trails off. Above me, from a distant place, I hear a choir of angels humming "Ave Maria." One voice sings louder. Her voice is clear, her words distinct, and offers a tone so familiar and missed. The true meaning of Christmas resurrects in my heart.

I address my Christmas cards and hold my mom's love of this special time of year in my heart. I embrace her memory and all the love she showered upon each and every one of us over the years. I have received the most precious Christmas gift. I am truly blessed and grateful. Come Christmas morning, surrounded by family, I will look upon the tree strung with tiny white lights and know my mom is right beside me.

— Cindy Golchuk —

70

The Lady Who Lived Over the Hill

How beautiful a day can be when kindness touches it!
~George Elliston

My aunt was packing up her kitchen drawers in preparation for a move to a smaller home. "Oh, look at this cute pin," she said. "It must have been in there for quite a while. Do you even remember this?"

"How could I ever forget it?" I responded. Even though it had been buried deep in the drawer for years, the pin looked nearly the same as it had more than thirty years ago when a lady sitting behind my family in church gave it to my four-year-old daughter.

It was the first Sunday morning in December. My young children and I sat in our usual pew as we attended Mass. Everything was normal until the "handshake of peace"—a ritual in which participants greet those around them. On this particular morning, an unfamiliar woman sat in the pew behind us. I can't remember what she was wearing—not even the color of her coat—but I do remember the kind look in her eyes as we shook hands and embraced in the sign of peace. And I remember the Christmas pin on her coat lapel—the very one that my aunt was now holding in her hand.

My daughter had turned around to shake hands with the people behind us, and had been fascinated by the Christmas wreath pin on the lady's coat. "You like this, don't you?" the woman whispered to

Katie, pointing to the pin on her lapel. Katie nodded. Her green eyes opened wide as the lady removed the wreath and gently placed it in her hand, carefully folding her little fingers around it.

I thanked her for the gesture, but assured her that it was not necessary to give my daughter the pin even though she had admired it. However, the lady insisted, so I pinned it on my little girl's dress and she wore it proudly the rest of the day.

As the service drew to an end, I felt a gentle tap on my elbow. A soft voice whispered, "Meet me in the parking lot when Mass is over. I have something for you in my car."

"Okay," I said, a bit confused. I had never seen this woman in my life. What could she possibly have for me?

"Look, Mom, the lady parked right next to us!" one of my children shouted as we headed to our car. I drew in a deep breath when she opened her trunk and I saw what was in it. There were exactly four presents, one for each of my children. They were so excited that they wanted to rip the gifts open right there in the parking lot, but I insisted that they wait until we got home. They thanked the lady and climbed into the car.

I thanked her for her kindness and asked how she knew us and where she lived. Her eyes twinkled as she replied that she had seen us each week at church, and that she lived over the hill behind our house. I was not aware of any homes over the hill, but maybe there was a new development in the area that I was not aware of.

All the way home, the kids shook, squeezed, and passed their boxes around in the car, trying to guess what was in them. When we pulled into the driveway, they raced inside to tear open their presents.

I could hardly believe what was in them. How did this lady whom we had never met before know that I had no money to buy Christmas outfits for my kids? How did she know their exact sizes and the right style and colors for each of them?

The kids couldn't wait to try on their new clothes, and I couldn't wait to find out who this lady was. So, dressed in their new Christmas outfits, we all climbed back into the car and headed to the hill where she had told us she lived. We arrived at the location, but found no existing homes and no new construction anywhere in sight. We looked at each other, shrugged our shoulders, and then stared over the hill again. The children's eyes were big and their mouths wide open, but not a sound could be heard. My seven-year-old broke the spell and summed up what we all were thinking.

"Maybe she's an angel," he whispered dramatically in his husky, little voice. After another brief moment of quiet, a chorus of soft sighs filled the car. And then silence all the way home...

Still trying to find a logical answer to this mystery, I had the children write thank-you notes, which we took to church the following Sunday. But our new friend was not there. I asked the people sitting around us if they knew the lady who had been sitting in the pew behind us the previous week. Not a single person remembered seeing any woman there at all. Not one!

But she had been sitting behind us. She gave Katie her Christmas wreath pin. She gave each of my children their perfect Christmas outfits. And now we were sure we knew who she was.

On the way home, we passed by the hill once again, looked up, and saw only a beautiful blue sky in the crisp, winter air. I'm certain our angel had found her way back home, her earthly mission complete.

— Kathleen Ruth —

71

The Holiday Lottery from Heaven

Set me as a seal on your heart, as a seal
on your arm, for stern as death is love...
~Song of Songs 8:8

My husband grew up in a large Italian Catholic family in South Philadelphia with three families of aunts, uncles and cousins living on one block of Cross Street, and many of the other relatives just a few blocks away. Uncle Tony and Aunt Grace lived right next door to my in-laws, Philip and Rose. The two couples were especially close since Uncle Tony and Philip were brothers and Aunt Grace and Rose were sisters.

In addition to being very large, and concentrated in a three-block radius, my husband's family was unique in one particular way — the family had a category of relatives most other families do not. While the family had mothers, fathers, sisters, brothers, aunts, uncles, cousins, and grandparents, they also had a category of relatives known as "The Deads." My husband's relatives talked about the Deads as if they were still alive, especially around the holidays. A typical conversation between Rose and Grace would sound like this:

Grace: "Roe, what did you do today?"

Rose: "Oh, I went food shopping, stopped to see the Deads, and then made my gravy."

Grace: "Oh yeah? I saw the Deads yesterday."

Sure enough, whenever I went to the cemetery with my husband, all the Deads would have fresh flowers on their graves, sometimes two and three arrangements, depending on how many of the relatives had been to see the Deads that week.

My husband's family was also unique in that they had a special rule: If a Dead came to you in dream and spoke a number, you played the number the next day in the lottery.

I came to know about this rule in 1989. Uncle Tony, who had taken over his father's fruit and produce business, died unexpectedly at the end of August of that year. His death was very hard on Aunt Grace, for they had been married a long time and had been very much in love. One night, about two weeks after Uncle Tony's death, I was in Aunt Grace's kitchen with my mother-in-law when Aunt Grace said, "Tony was a great lover." The shock of this statement quickly dissipated when Aunt Grace then stated, "The week before our wedding, Tony came to my house every day and gave me a present. He was a great lover." Aunt Grace then put her head in her hands and started to cry.

As the holidays approached two months later, Aunt Grace was, understandably, a little depressed. In addition to losing her husband, money was tighter than usual and the Christmas season loomed.

At the end of November, Aunt Grace came running into my mother-in-law's kitchen one morning all excited. "Tony gave me the number last night!"

"What do you mean?" my mother-in-law asked.

"Well, last night I had a dream, and in it I dreamt that I was asleep in bed but Tony was downstairs. All of a sudden, Tony starts yelling, 'Grace, Grace, there's someone in the house! Call 911, call 911!' After that, I woke up."

My mother-in-law "remained," which is the word she used to mean that she "remained quiet and said nothing."

Aunt Grace went on. "Well that means that 911 is tonight's number! Tony just gave me tonight's number!"

Holiday Angels | 221

The news spread through the family with the speed of sound, but because Uncle Tony had spoken such an ordinary number, only Aunt Grace and Uncle Tony's best friend, Johnny Gerace, played the number that day.

That night, I was eating over at my in-law's house when seven o'clock rolled around. My mother-in-law looked at the clock and said, "El, it's almost seven. Go see what the number is."

As the houses in South Philly are so small, I only had to walk about thirty feet from the kitchen table, through the dining room, to reach the TV in the living room. After I turned the TV on, the familiar lottery music filled the room. The number started to be drawn right away. Turning my head to the left, I hollered, "The first number is... nine."

"You're full of soup," my mother-in-law answered.

"The second number is a one," I hollered a little louder.

By this time, my mother-in-law, father-in-law, and husband started walking quickly into the living room.

"The third number is a... 1. 911! 911!" I yelled.

Naturally, my mother-in-law started screaming, and we all ran back through the kitchen, out the back door, across the little yard, and into Aunt Grace's kitchen. Aunt Grace, seated at the kitchen table, her head bent and in her hands, was crying and hollering, "Tooonnnyyyy, Tooonnnyyy!"

As my mother-in-law grabbed her hands and smiled into her face, Aunt Grace whispered through choked tears, "He always gave me extra money around the holidays, and he's still finding a way."

With so many relatives living so close, Aunt Grace's house filled quickly, the coffee was made and re-made, and the story told and retold. Relatives who did not live around the corner called on the phone to congratulate Aunt Grace.

Since that night, I have known that love really does transcend time and space.

— Ellen C.K. Giangiordano —

72

A Second Chance

Wherever there is a human being,
there is an opportunity for a kindness.
~Lucius Annaeus Seneca

As I glanced at the balance in my checkbook, I wondered. What had made me think I could do this?

That morning, when Pastor Tipton spoke about the Christmas Connection program, I'd felt a tug on my heart. He painted such a heartrending portrait of needy children in our community — children who had little hope of a happy Christmas if not for the generosity of others — that I knew I had to help. When he first mentioned the program the week before, many in our congregation stepped up gladly, but there were still three names left in the basket. Although I was barely getting by on my teacher's aide salary, I was sure I felt God's urging. The suggested gift amount was twenty-five dollars, which I really couldn't spare, but wasn't sacrificial love what Christmas was all about?

When the service ended, I pulled an envelope from the basket, envisioning a little girl I would provide with a doll, book, or warm, cozy blanket. Opening the envelope, I discovered that my child was a thirteen-year-old boy. His wish list included only one item: a pair of name brand, high-top sneakers, black, size 9.

Now, sitting with my after-church coffee and my checkbook open in front of me, I was rethinking my decision. Those sneakers were going to cost twice the suggested amount. After I paid my bills, put gas in the car, and bought groceries, I would have approximately thirty dollars left. No way was I going to find name-brand sneakers for that price. But how could I let down that boy?

"God," I whispered, "please show me."

I put away my checkbook and went about my day, with thoughts of high-top sneakers following me like size-nine black shadows. The situation brought back a painful memory of another boy, another Christmas, many years before.

As much as we try not to, we educators have our favorites. My first year on the job, I fell in love with Cameron, a rough-and-tumble first-grader with big, blue eyes. His father was often unemployed, and in the four months since the school year began, Cameron's family had already moved twice. But it wasn't only that I felt sorry for him. Despite his rough upbringing, Cameron had a sunny disposition and a smile that could melt a snowman's heart. He wanted a scooter for Christmas, and I was determined to see that he got one.

Our school had a program where donated gifts were given to the parents of needy students to be opened on Christmas morning. Without a second thought, I took my entire Christmas bonus, purchased the scooter, and parked it in the school office with the other donations.

I could hardly wait for the end of the holiday break. As the morning bell rang, I helped Cameron out of his coat and boots.

"What did Santa bring you for Christmas?" I asked.

"A coloring book and crayons. And some socks."

Unable to believe my ears, I asked, "Anything else?"

"No."

"You... didn't get your scooter?"

He shook his head.

After school, I paid a visit to the principal.

"Cameron said he didn't get the scooter I bought. I don't know quite what to think."

"You didn't by any chance leave the price tag on it, did you?"

"Yes, I even included the receipt, in case there was anything wrong with it. Shouldn't I have?"

Then Marybeth told me something shocking. It was possible

Cameron's parents returned the scooter to the store and pocketed the money.

I stared at her, feeling sick.

"It's an unfortunate reflection of the society we live in. But remember, no act of love is ever wasted. We can't get discouraged. We can't stop trying."

I'm ashamed to say that I did stop trying. My entire Christmas bonus had been blown on Lord knew what. That was the last time I bought a gift for a needy child. Until now.

The next day, after work I stopped at a shoe store. As I perused the aisles, I got a sinking feeling in my stomach again. The high-top sneakers ranged in price from $59.99 to $129.99. Checking the price tags, I wanted to cry.

"God, I really want to do this for this boy. Please… help me find a way."

After another pass down the aisle in the hope I'd somehow missed something, I decided to give up. Maybe I could find something similar at a discount store.

"They're all so expensive," I murmured.

"Ma'am, try the bargain aisle."

I hadn't seen the man approach. Startled, I said, "Excuse me?"

"There's a clearance rack in the back. You might find what you're looking for there."

He was an ordinary-looking man, but somehow his presence was calming. His voice, like honey, soothed my frayed nerves.

I thanked him and headed for the clearance aisle, knowing I would not find these particular sneakers there. Dutifully, I checked each shelf. To my utter amazement, in the bottom row, stuffed behind a pair of work boots, was a large, beat-up box bearing the name-brand logo I was searching for. With trembling hands, I lifted the lid. Nestled inside, I discovered a pair of black, high-top sneakers, size 9. The price tag said $24.99.

I almost fell to my knees right there in the clearance aisle.

Cheerfully, the clerk rang up my purchase. "Find everything you need?"

"I sure did," I said, smiling widely. "I don't know if your salespeople work on commission, but there was a gentleman who pointed me in the right direction. I didn't get his name, but he was tall with reddish hair."

"I don't know who that could have been," the girl said. "There aren't any male sales associates working today."

I glanced around the empty store. "Maybe it was a customer then."

The girl gave me a quizzical glance. "Ma'am, you're the only customer who's been in for the last hour."

How strange, I thought.

At home, I wrapped the sneakers in bright red paper, adding a candy cane and a heartfelt prayer that the boy would receive and enjoy the gift.

It wasn't until that evening, when I thought about my strange experience in the shoe store, that I remembered a Bible verse about entertaining angels unaware. All at once, I was chilled with goose bumps. Surely God wouldn't dispatch an angel for something so trivial... Would he?

The answer whispered across my heart in Marybeth's long-ago words: No act of kindness is ever wasted. Who knew what long-reaching impact a simple pair of sneakers might have on a needy young boy?

Weeks later, a thank-you card arrived at our church. Tucked inside was a photo of a boy proudly wearing a pair of black high-top sneakers — a boy with big, blue eyes and a smile as wide as the sky.

— M. Jean Pike —

Thanksgiving Angel

I do all this for the sake of the gospel,
that I may share in its blessings.
~1 Corinthians 9:23

I was fifteen when my world took a bleak turn for the worst. My mom was diagnosed with cancer... again. The first time had been devastating. She underwent surgery and chemotherapy and she beat the cancer. Then the cancer came back. This time however, there was more to worry about than just the disease my mom was battling. Because of the medical bills she was paying from her previous cancer, this illness left her on the brink of financial ruin. My dad had died years before. It was just Mom trying to hold down the fort. My mom made too much to qualify for any type of assistance and too little to pay the mounting medical bills. I was too young to get a job.

That winter was the worst. We didn't have money to pay for electricity, so we did without. We had a little gas stove that provided heat, and our neighbor let us plug in an extension cord to his home so that we could have one lamp on in our home. The gas stove in the living room was the only heat in the house. I slept on the floor in the living room, as close as I could to the stove without setting myself on fire. Mom slept in her cold room, with as many blankets as we could pile on her.

Every day and every night my mom prayed and often asked me to pray with her. She thanked God for our blessings, thanked God for each other and always asked God to give us the strength to get through the hard times we were experiencing. She was never bitter, angry or demanding. She believed God would see us through it. I, on the other hand, wasn't so sure. If God was so good and great, why were we suffering like we were? Why had my mom, who still walked to church every Sunday no matter how cold it was or how sick she felt, gotten cancer again? Sometimes it was hard for me to pray. I was angry at God; I was angry at the world. Life just wasn't fair.

Thanksgiving Day came. I searched our cupboards for food and there wasn't much. I started slamming doors as I looked through the cabinets for a can of food we might have missed. The more I searched the angrier I became. The noise must have woken my mom, because she came to the kitchen wrapped in a blanket. She looked worried for me and she asked, "Baby, what's wrong?"

I retorted, "I'm hungry. That's what's wrong." I wasn't angry at her. I was angry at our situation. I knew I was acting like a jerk but I couldn't help it.

She opened her arms toward me and said, "Come here. Let's pray."

I rolled my eyes. "Like that ever works." I knew my words had hurt her but I was too upset to take them back.

She looked at me. The sadness in her eyes killed me. "God hears our prayers. We have a million blessings if you just open your eyes to them. Right now things are hard, but God is here helping us through this. Whatever we need, God will provide. All you have to do is have faith. Pray for what we need and God will answer."

"Oh really, is that so?" I turned on her. "If God is so great, why are we starving? If God is so wonderful why are we freezing to death in our own house?" The hurt look on her face was more than I could bear. I was sickened by my outburst at her but I was too angry at God to stop. "Hey God," I yelled up toward the ceiling, "if you are so powerful and almighty why don't you send us something to eat? In fact, since it's Thanksgiving, why don't you send us a fat juicy turkey with all the trimmings? Or are we not good enough for you to send us some food?"

I looked at the table scornfully. "Yeah, that's what I thought. I don't see any Thanksgiving dinner. Do you?" I sassed my mom. She stood there, silent tears running down her face.

I was deeply ashamed of what I had done and said, but I was still extremely angry at God and our circumstances. I walked fast, practically running to get out of the house. I yanked the door open, almost colliding with a stocky man in a blue striped shirt carrying an armful of boxes.

"Oh, just in time!" he said and walked in. "Happy Thanksgiving to you both!" he said cheerfully as he put all the boxes on the table. "This big box here is the Thanksgiving turkey, cooked of course. And this one is mashed potatoes; this container has gravy. Oh, and this one here is pumpkin pie, and this one pecan pie...."

Suddenly my ears felt full of cotton. I couldn't hear a word he was saying. I could smell the turkey, the stuffing, all the food in those containers. I could see our little table piled with boxes of food. "So you all have a great Thanksgiving. Now ma'am, if you'll just sign here for the delivery." He handed my mom a pen.

Mom stared down at the paper, but the entire time the deliveryman was staring at me. He had the bluest eyes I'd ever seen.

He took the pen from Mom, thanked her and as he passed me he touched my shoulder and said, "And God bless you, my child."

I stood there dumbfounded as he walked out of our house and closed the door.

It took a few seconds for me to snap out of it, but I bolted after him. Who was he? Who had sent the Thanksgiving dinner? There had to be an explanation. I ran out to our porch and down the steps, but I slipped and fell because frost covered the steps. I ran to the gate at the end of our cement walkway and out to the sidewalk. There were no cars in sight.

As I turned back towards the house, one thing stood out in the morning sunlight. There was only one set of footprints in the frost that covered our walkway. I stepped closer to the walkway, examining it closely. My footprints were the only footprints that disturbed the

Holiday Angels |

frost in our yard.

Whenever God seems far away I remember that Thanksgiving. I remember the angel God sent to cool my anger. That angel, for I have no doubt that is what he was, showed us that God cared enough to bring us food at our time of need and bring faith back to one girl's heart.

— Cynthia Bilyk —

74

Stranded

Not all of us can do great things. But we
can do small things with great love.
~Mother Teresa

My mind started wandering. I had been driving on I-79 North in our newly acquired used Jeep Cherokee with my pregnant wife through the mountains of West Virginia for nearly two hours. No radio. No cell phone service. No stop lights. No rest areas. No vehicles on the road other than ours. The only noise we heard was the slow drone of the wiper blades moving back and forth, reminding me of the metronome my fifth grade piano instructor used to keep me on tempo. The slushy mix of snow, rain, and sleet started picking up, making it harder and harder to focus on the seemingly endless road before us.

It was the night before Christmas Eve and we were making the long trek home to rural Pennsylvania. I was attending graduate school in Kentucky and our winter break had finally arrived. My wife and I had to work earlier in the day so we got off to a later start than we would have liked—forcing us to drive in utter darkness the entire trip home. We didn't really mind the drive though, knowing that in eight hours we would be enjoying eggnog in front of a warm fireplace with our family.

BOOM!!!

"Did you hear that?" I asked my wife.

"Yes. What happened?"

"I must have hit something," I said.

I pulled the vehicle off to the side of the road to check out the damage. I grabbed the flashlight from under my seat.

"We got a flat!" I yelled. "I'm going to put on the doughnut."

One by one I grabbed our Christmas presents, placing them on the sloppy ground. I finally made it the bottom of the pile, grabbing the jack, our only source of hope on this wintry night.

"Great, just our luck, it's broken! The car dealer sold us a vehicle with a broken jack! Now what?"

One by one I placed the saturated Christmas gifts back into the vehicle, replaying in my head how I could have made such a mistake. I returned to my seat and started wondering what our next move might be. We took a moment to assess the situation and offer up a quick prayer.

We laid out our options:

Option 1 — It looked like there was a house way off in the distance. I could ring their doorbell.

Option 2 — The next exit was fifteen miles. I could walk to the exit and my wife could stay in the car until I returned.

Option 3 — We could wait it out in the warmth of our car until the gas ran out — hoping that another vehicle would stop and perform a modern-day Good Samaritan deed on our behalf (even though we hadn't seen another car on the road for nearly two hours).

Neither one of us liked options one or two, considering the fact that we were in the middle of nowhere in West Virginia — so we decided on option three.

I reclined in my seat, not expecting to see another vehicle for several hours, if at all. I shut off the wiper blades so I could have a normal conversation with my wife. But before I uttered the first sentence, I heard what sounded like sirens. I looked in the rearview mirror and shouted as if I had just won the lottery: "A police car!"

The policeman pulled alongside our vehicle, asking us how he could be of service, telling us that his name was Officer Anderson. I told him about the flat tire and that we didn't have a working jack or cell phone service. Without hesitation, Officer Anderson hopped out of his vehicle, grabbed the jack from his car, plopped down on the soggy grass, and started changing the tire. He then told us to stay inside where it was warm while he found us a mechanic. He eventually found us one, but it was forty-five miles away. He told us that he would follow behind us until we made it to our destination. So for the next hour and half, Officer Anderson followed behind our vehicle, even though it was way out of his jurisdiction.

When we finally arrived at our exit, Officer Anderson told us to follow him to the mechanic and that he would give us a ride to a hotel. Before he left, I felt compelled to ask him for his police station address so I could send him a proper thank you, and to ask him a question that I had been mulling over since the moment he stopped to help us several hours before:

"So why did you stop?"

After a long pause, he looked me directly in the eyes and said:

"I stopped to help you and your family because someone stopped and helped me and my family when we were in need many years ago."

Officer Anderson's words have been reverberating in my heart and mind ever since that night. His words (and actions) have provided me with much hope in my life when we have been in difficult situations and needed help — and there have been many. His words have also been the driving force behind my mission in this life — to reach out and help those who are in need, to those who are hurting, to those who need compassion, to those who need someone to help carry their burdens.

The truth of the matter is that we all need an Officer Anderson from time to time. Life gets challenging — a flat tire, a broken relationship, an unforeseen illness, a sudden job loss, or an unexpected bill to pay. But like Officer Anderson mentioned, he stopped and helped us because someone stopped to help him first.

The day after Christmas I decided to contact the police station to properly thank Officer Anderson for his service. The police chief answered and I started recounting the amazing act of kindness we had received from one of his officers. The police chief responded, "I'm very glad you received the help you needed the other night but there isn't an Officer Anderson at our station."

To this day I'm not sure if there really is an Officer Anderson who roams the mountains of West Virginia on I-79 north or if he is simply an angel, but I do know that this amazing act of kindness has drastically changed the course of my life.

— Tom Kaden —

The Joy of Giving

75

The Angel Tree

We are not put on earth for ourselves, but are placed
here for each other. If you are there always for others,
then in time of need, someone will be there for you.
~Jeff Warner

My husband had left our family unexpectedly and I was struggling to keep the roof over our heads. It was going to be the worst Christmas ever. After re-arranging bills, there would be maybe fifty dollars left to spend on my three children.

Never in my life had there been so little money for Christmas. I stayed up at night making a few gifts so that the space under the tree would not be so bare.

My older son, Justin, sixteen at the time, had told me weeks before that he did not want anything for Christmas. Justin had always been sensitive to our situation. He told me to spend whatever money I had on his brother and sister. This display of love from someone so young was extraordinary, and I was thankful for Justin's generous sacrifice.

My middle child, Tristan, was only nine years old, and he was oblivious to our situation. Numerous times, Tristan mentioned that he wanted a portable CD player for Christmas. Fortunately, this particular item had dropped in price, and I would be able to afford it with the money I had scraped together.

The week before Christmas, we went to Walmart to pick up a few food items. My heart fell when I saw the Angel Tree, which had just been put up. It had been our tradition to go to this store, pick tags off the tree and buy gifts for children in need. I wondered if I should have looked into getting the names of my own children on that tree. While I was thinking that, my younger children ran toward the Angel Tree. They had no idea how bad things were. Now they were going to ask to buy things for the children from the Angel Tree. If I was worried before, I was terrified now. How was I going to explain our situation without making them feel like Christmas was going to be horrible?

As quickly as I could, I caught up with them. The youngest, Gerrie, was only six, and she really did not understand the meaning of the tree. To her, it was just another Christmas tree. My oldest gave me a look of horror, knowing what was going to happen next. Tristan ran frantically around the Angel Tree, glancing from tag to tag, looking for something. At that moment, someone from our church walked up and engaged me in a conversation. She asked me what we were up to, and when I turned back around, Tristan was holding a tag. He was grinning from ear to ear.

"Look, Mom, I found it."

I replied, "Found what, honey?"

His exuberance was overwhelming. "This boy wants the same thing I want for Christmas — a CD player — so I choose this one." My friend was still standing in front of me, but quickly excused herself.

I bent down slightly and told Tristan in an almost-whisper, "Honey, we can't afford to do the Angel Tree this year. If we buy a CD player for this child, I will not be able to get one for you."

Tristan tilted his head and then looked me right in the eye. "Mom, I don't need anything. Can we please buy the CD player for this kid?"

Every parent should have a moment of complete pride like that. I agreed that if he wanted to give up his gift for this child, we would do so. Through teary eyes, I helped him pick out a CD player and a CD. We took the items to the desk where the toys were to be turned in for the Angel Tree. I let Tristan give them to the woman behind the counter. He was beaming as he said, "Here is the tag and the gift."

The woman smiled and said, "Wow, thank you. You are our first donation this year."

Tristan was proud to be the first donation. He did not seem the least bit concerned that he was not going to get his CD player.

As it turned out, at the last minute, I was able to use a gift card I received from my company to buy gifts for all three children, including a CD player for Tristan that he would find under the tree Christmas morning. When we visited my brother's family for Christmas Eve that year, they gave him a CD player, too. When we came home, someone had left gifts at our front door, and Tristan received another CD player. The night of Christmas, Tristan's father dropped off a gift for him... a new CD player.

Tristan ended up with four CD players that year. He gave one to his little sister and one to his best friend. Ever since then, we have referred to this story as the parable of the CD player. Tristan is twenty-three now. He has maintained that the CD-player Christmas was one of the best Christmases ever. What we give, we will truly receive. I learned this from the good heart of a small boy who was willing to sacrifice his Christmas for someone he never met.

— Michelle Jackson —

76

Solid Rangers

*Uncles and aunts, and cousins, are all very well, and
fathers and mothers are not to be despised; but a
grandmother, at holiday time, is worth them all.*
~Fanny Fern

I t had been more than twenty years since I had gone back to
my mother's for Christmas. After I had children, and then
grandchildren, the holiday was spent where the children
were. But in 1987, my mother was unable to travel, so my
daughters and I decided to spend Christmas with her. My stepfather
had recently passed away and we couldn't bear the thought of her
being alone.

My grandsons were Chris, five, and Ben, seven months. They
were the children of my older daughter Karen and her husband Ralph.

We left for Ferriday, Louisiana on the day before Christmas Eve.
We took two cars for the trip from Orlando, Florida. My younger
daughter Linda and I were in one car, with Karen, Ralph and the boys
in the other, except when Chris "visited" our car.

Even though we got an early start, we didn't arrive until nearly
eleven o'clock that night, and by the time we decided on sleeping
arrangements, made up roll-aways, and got everyone settled, it was
nearly one in the morning. The adults were still sleeping soundly when
the boys were awake and hungry. It wasn't yet eight o'clock when
Karen, Linda, and I met in the kitchen and started to make breakfast.

I was standing at the stove in my mother's kitchen when Karen whispered, "Mom, I know you were really good at hiding Christmas presents from us when we were small, but Ralph and I can't find the stuff from your house."

"Stuff from my house?"

"You know. In the front bedroom closet?" Her eyes widened in panic.

Linda, not one to let a conversation go unheard, came over. "What are you two whispering about?" I looked over my shoulder to see that Chris was trying to hear our discussion, too. I motioned for the girls to follow me.

In the guest bedroom, I turned to Karen. "I wasn't supposed to get the presents from the closet, was I? I thought you got them."

"No, remember I asked you to bring them? We were looking for them because Ralph wanted to start wrapping while we made breakfast."

Oh, no. I thought she got those things. My breathing was shallow and I was suddenly cold.

"Karen, I'm sorry I didn't understand. What's back there? How hard would it be to find the same things here?"

"Ben's presents aren't a problem. But Chris expects one thing in particular — a special set of walkie-talkies. They're called Sonic Rangers, but he calls them Solid Rangers. That's all he's talked about for weeks. The stores at home are sold out. What are the chances of finding them in a small town like this?"

I vaguely remembered Chris talking about solid-something in the car, but I hadn't paid attention at the time.

Linda's face registered shock as she began to understand the situation. "Mom, could you and I drive to Monroe or Jackson? How long would it take?"

"We could. But if we go to Monroe and don't find them, it'll be too late to go somewhere else."

"Mom, Chris will be brokenhearted if he doesn't get those Solid Rangers. We promised him Santa would find us here. We even wrote a letter to Santa explaining where we'd be. We have to have those walkie-talkies."

"I know, sweetie. Let me think a minute."

Ralph came in and we explained the situation.

"I'm so sorry about this, Ralph. I don't know how I could have been so oblivious."

Ralph said, "It was just a misunderstanding, Mom. It could have happened to anybody."

I knew he was trying to make me feel better, but the look on his face showed how troubled he was.

I thought about the options. The longer I thought, the more I knew there was only one answer — get the toys from the closet in my house. If only I could. I reached for the phone book and started dialing.

"What are you doing?" asked Karen.

"I'm calling airlines."

"But there aren't any airports near here."

"There's New Orleans. I can drive down and fly home. If I can get a return flight tonight, we'll be all right."

"But what are the chances of getting there and back on the same day? Even if you can, that'll cost a fortune."

"Well, it was my mistake and I'm the one who needs to fix it. If I can get the flights, that seems like the only thing to do."

"Mom, you can't be serious," said Ralph.

"Yes, I am. I'm willing to do anything in my power to make sure that little boy isn't disappointed in the morning."

On my third call, I found a roundtrip from New Orleans to Orlando that would work, if I could be quick enough in Orlando. I'd have barely enough time to take a cab from the airport to my house, retrieve the packages, and get back to the airport in time for the return flight. Once in New Orleans, I'd then have to drive back up to Ferriday. It was going to be a long day.

I left as soon as I could get dressed. The drive time to New Orleans was ordinarily about four hours, but I knew the roads would be busy with people trying to reach their destinations before the end of the day.

At the airport in New Orleans, I went directly to the ticket counter. When I asked to buy the round-trip tickets, the agent looked up with surprise. "You don't want to return tonight, do you? Didn't you mean another day?"

The Joy of Giving |

"No, I need to get back here tonight."

"There's got to be a story here." She raised her eyebrows expectantly.

I told her about the forgotten toys and she said, "You're some determined grandmother, and you're lucky that today is Christmas Eve. If you'd wanted to do this yesterday, you'd have been out of luck. All the flights were full."

In Orlando, I got a cab, explained my mission to the driver and off we went. At my house, I rushed to the closet in the front bedroom. Sure enough, there sat two large bags of toys. I grabbed them and returned to the cab. We got back to the airport with only minutes to spare before the flight boarded.

The drive back to Ferriday was magical; people everywhere seemed to have stepped out of a Norman Rockwell painting, radiating merriment and good wishes. Grandma Santa was "over the hills and through the woods" making her delivery.

I made it back to Mother's at around two in the morning, with only hours to spare. Ralph and Karen still had wrapping and preparing to do.

I was the last one to join the family gathered around the tree on Christmas morning. Chris greeted me with, "Look, Grandma! Santa found me. He brought me Solid Rangers."

"He sure did, Chris." Winks and grins were shared around the room.

A few days later, as we used the Solid Rangers to talk between the cars during the drive home, I knew that flight had been worth every penny.

— Bettie Wailes —

77

Tender Mercies

Happiness isn't complicated. It is a humble state
of gratitude for simple pleasures, tender mercies,
recognized blessings, and inherent beauty.
~Richelle E. Goodrich

alty tears stung my tired eyes. I couldn't bring my husband home for Christmas, but I was determined my six-year-old son would get his other wish — a new bike.

Wiping my eyes, I studied the instructions and surveyed the assortment of bicycle parts scattered on my bedroom carpet. Never mind that it was Christmas Eve and midnight was an hour away.

"You can do this," I said.

Not that I had a choice. Since my husband's deployment with Desert Shield, I'd learned to do many things on my own. Assembling a bike would be simple compared to raising kids. Right?

I grabbed a wrench and the bike frame while Christmas carols played softly in the background.

Eight weeks earlier, I'd been blindsided when I met with my son's kindergarten teacher. She had more on her mind than his academic performance.

"You do realize children aren't allowed to bring stuffed animals to class? And yet your son brings his elephant every day."

"I don't see the harm," I countered. "He keeps King Tusk in his cubby hole."

"Yes, but…" She looked over the rim of her large framed reading glasses. "Mrs. Foster, is your husband in the military?"

What did King Tusk have to do with my husband's job?

"My husband's a pilot in the Air Force Reserves. His unit was activated last August. Why do you ask?"

The teacher spread Jonathan's artwork on the table. "That explains why your son keeps drawing camels and Army tanks during his free time. Does he talk about his dad?"

I shifted in my chair. "He knows his dad transports military troops and cargo to Saudi Arabia. But we don't talk about what's happening. You know, Iraq's invasion of Kuwait and what happens if they don't withdraw."

"Maybe Jonathan knows more than you realize," she said, sounding more like a family counselor than a teacher. "Perhaps he's worried and draws these pictures as an outlet for his emotions."

I picked up one of his drawings and studied the desert landscape filled with soldiers. Using brown and green crayons, my son had captured an image that reminded me of the evening news.

"You're right," I said, blinking back tears. "That explains it."

However, I didn't mention that one night when I tucked Jonathan into bed, he had asked me if Daddy was going to die. My stomach lurched. I wanted to hold my son and assure him that everything would be all right. That Daddy would come home soon, and we'd go to Sea World again.

Only, I didn't know if that was true.

I'd grown up in an Air Force family during the Vietnam War. I'd lived on base and seen black smoke rising in the distance after a cargo plane crashed at the end of the runway. My schoolmates and I had worn POW/MIA bracelets with the names of soldiers who'd never come home.

No, I wouldn't promise my son that Daddy would live.

"Mrs. Foster?"

I looked up and waited for her to finish speaking. Instead, her eyebrows went up expectantly.

What did she want me to say? Did she want me to describe the ballooning pressure to maintain a house and yard, and raise two children while my husband was gone? Maybe she needed to know that we didn't live near relatives. My friends at church were my local support network. Or maybe I could tell her that trusting the Lord — no matter what happened — consoled me when I lay awake at night on the verge of a crying jag.

I didn't know what the teacher expected. But the silent gulf between us disappeared when she touched my hand and said, "I'll make an exception. Jonathan can bring King Tusk to school."

Thank God for tender mercies.

The memory of that conversation warmed my heart as I tightened the last bolt on my son's bicycle. Walking the bicycle downstairs, I parked it next to the Christmas tree. Strings of multicolored bulbs crisscrossed helter-skelter within the pine-scented branches. I chuckled, remembering how the tree had fallen twice before I had been able to tighten the bolts in the tree stand to the trunk.

Now the tree and the bicycle stood upright. Grinning, I gave myself two thumbs up. And then I filled the stockings and added the wrapped gifts beneath the tree.

The wall clock chimed twice by the time I dragged myself upstairs. My body ached from fatigue, but also for my husband's arms. I hated for him to be without family on Christmas. Hated the thought of him not seeing the children's animated faces as they unwrapped their gifts. Videotaping would never do it justice. And back then, Skype and FaceTime didn't exist.

Had I known my husband would be home by June, the night would have seemed less cold. Instead, I warmed myself with the anticipation of our children racing downstairs.

Pausing at my son's bedroom, I peeked inside. The nightlight cast a golden glow on his peaceful brow. His lips curled in a half smile. And tucked in next to my son lay his cherished friend — King Tusk.

Thank God for tender mercies.

— Karen Foster —

78

In My Genes

As the purse is emptied, the heart is filled.
~Victor Hugo

I've always thought of my mother Lee-Ann as a superhero. Not that she can fly or shoot lasers out of her eyes, but because she never runs out of room in her heart for anyone or anything.

I could write about all of the wonderful things she has done, but I want to focus on the one project she does every year that has shaped my whole family and everyone around us: She collects money she finds in the washer and dryer, and she puts it in a little jar that we refer to as "The Charity Jar." Every year, she takes this money and puts it toward something—a cause, an act of kindness, anything that can help someone. Sometimes, she buys coffees for the next people in line at a coffee shop. Other times, she buys something for an organization that needs it.

If you ask her about this tradition, she will tell you that she is carrying on something that her mother used to do around the holidays. If you ask anyone else who knows her, however, they will tell you that she has a huge heart. She manages to get our whole family involved in this movement every year. Last year, she helped an organization where I volunteered — Ruth's Place — a homeless women's shelter in Wilkes-Barre, Pennsylvania.

I had been helping a professor run a writing workshop in the shelter when I noticed the wish list on the wall: comforters, a DVD player, a coffee maker and supplies. I told my mom, and within a day she had already asked if our family wanted to help Ruth's Place. We all agreed and decided that the coffee maker and supplies would be the best things for our family to work on together. A few days later, Mom found a coffee maker online, showed it to us, and with a few clicks it was on its way. We gathered the rest of the supplies and called the shelter to find a day that we could deliver them.

I drove my mom to the shelter — very slowly because she had baked fresh chocolate cupcakes for the women, and they were sitting on my clean leather seats. She had never been in the shelter before, but the whole way she talked about how excited she was to be able to check off something on their list.

When we took the gifts inside, the women were so happy. My mother was bright-eyed, carrying chocolate cupcakes into a shelter full of women she did not know. She stood by the front desk, thanking women for their compliments on her baking and talking to the volunteers as I filled out the donation sheet. As we left, I wished the women "Happy Thanksgiving," and we were met with a chorus of "Happy Thanksgivings" and "Thank Yous." My mother teared up as we walked through the rain to my car. I did not have to ask why; I knew that she did not cry out of pity. She did not cry out of sorrow or commiseration. She cried because she was thankful to have the opportunity to help someone.

I am thankful for my mother and the lessons she has shown me in love and compassion. I can say with certainty that I am not the only one whom she has made a better person.

— Cheyenne H. Huffman —

79

A Very Mary Pat Christmas

*Each day offers us the gift of being a special occasion if
we can simply learn that as well as giving, it is blessed
to receive with grace and a grateful heart.*
~Sarah Ban Breathnach

The doorbell rang and I waved thanks to the deliveryman as he walked away fifty pounds lighter. I sighed
when I saw the familiar, looping handwriting on the
colossal box.

Every December was the same.

"Greg, Mom's gifts are here. I need you to lug this inside, please!"

Greg moaned. "Another Mary Pat Christmas."

I rolled my eyes, remembering the conversation I'd had with Mom only a few weeks earlier.

"Mom, please don't send a million presents this year. We always end up throwing most of it away, and you can't afford it."

"You throw most of it away?" Her voiced dripped with hurt.

I backtracked. "Well, what I mean is that we just don't have a use for most of the stuff, Mom. And besides, how much do you spend? The shipping alone has to be astronomical. You and I both know you can't afford it. Please just... don't this year."

"But it's fun for me, baby. I love being able to spoil you all like that."

"You'd spoil us if you'd make something for us. Make a stuffed animal for the kids, or a pillow, or send us some banana bread. We don't need all that junk."

"Junk?" Drip. Drip. Drip.

Greg heaved the box inside and dragged it over to the tree. I grabbed the scissors and sliced through the tape, revealing a mountain of presents, each wrapped in shiny, stiff paper and tied with colorful coils of ribbon.

"Can you believe her?" I complained.

Ever the steady voice, Greg replied, "I know it's frustrating for you, Shan. But it makes her happy."

"But she can't afford it!"

"I know… but you can't make her stop."

"I know." I grabbed a gallon-sized garbage bag from the pantry. "You wanna try to knock this out before the kids wake from their naps?"

"Sure."

We knew better than to wait to open the gifts until Christmas morning. With two little kids, it made no sense to lengthen opening time by an hour. Especially when most of the gifts wouldn't be of interest to them, anyway.

The first thing I opened was a toothbrush. No enclosed container, no packaging… just a single toothbrush in a plastic baggie. I dangled it in the air for Greg to see.

We both burst out laughing, then tossed the contaminated toothbrush into the garbage bag.

Next, it was Greg's turn. He was shocked when he pulled out a pair of Beats earbuds.

"Shan, these are really nice earbuds. Oh, wait a minute…" Looking closer, we noticed the packaging had Chinese characters on it. "They're knockoffs," he said.

"Well, maybe they still work well?" I asked.

I plugged them into my phone but couldn't even bring them close to my head. The crackling would've deafened me.

Slowly, the garbage bag began to fill with a random assortment of items no one could ever use. Pens engraved with the name "Paul" (no Paul in our family), broken sunglasses, knitted leg warmers, every item from the Avon catalog, and a single, large marshmallow in another plastic bag. At one point we opened a gaudy, gold "family tree" necklace that looked like old-style rapper bling. I couldn't help but laugh when Greg slung it around his neck and broke out into "Funky Cold Medina." But it wasn't just that one necklace. Because Mom bought in bulk, we soon opened a second family tree necklace. And a third. By the time we'd opened our fifth identical necklace, we were rolling on the floor, holding our sides.

Finally, we came to the last present. It was enormous.

"You want the honor?" Greg asked.

"Let's open it together."

We ripped the paper, revealing a box with a lion's head on it. Looking closer, we realized it was a plastic fountain, to be mounted on the wall. Immediately, I called my siblings.

"Did you guys open your gifts from Mom?"

"Yeah… you?"

Suddenly we were all laughing. Each of us had received the fountain, the earbuds, Paul's pens, leg warmers… even the toothbrushes and marshmallows.

As we collected the items that we thought we could use or donate, Greg pulled aside a pair of adult-sized slippers that looked like dinosaur feet and said, "Keep or donate? They're way too big for the kids."

I considered them. "Let's keep 'em," I said. "They might like them someday."

Wiping our tears, we cleaned up before the kids awoke.

We didn't know it then, but that would be the last box we ever opened from Mom. Less than four months later, Mom passed away suddenly from a stroke.

At the funeral, my siblings gathered in a hotel room and talked about our Mary Pat Christmases. We laughed about how we all should've invested in Avon. How she had once given my brother and his family piles of presents when they visited her in Florida from Brazil, where they lived at the time. Not only could they not use all the gifts, but they had no way of getting everything home — so they ended up abandoning most of it at the airport. Laughter flooded the room as we shared our treasured memories, one silly gift at a time.

Suddenly, they didn't feel so silly. They felt priceless.

Right then and there, we decided that the best way to honor Mom each year would be to continue the tradition of a Mary Pat Christmas. We would take a ten-dollar budget, someone's name, and a limited amount of time in Walmart to shop for things Mom would've picked.

Somewhere, Mom was laughing in approval.

When we returned home, I was unpacking when I heard a little voice behind me.

"Aaaaaaarrrrrr!"

"Hmmm?" I said, not turning around.

"AAAAARRRRR! Look at me, Mama!"

I turned to see my four-year-old boy, hands clawed, teeth bared. And on his feet, a pair of adult-sized dinosaur slippers.

I began to cry as my baby T-Rex stomped away.

"Merry Christmas, Mom," I whispered. "Merry Christmas."

— Shannon Stocker —

Turn-About Thanksgiving

*Tell me and I forget, teach me and
I may remember, involve me and I learn.*
~Benjamin Franklin

My daughter, Katie, was in third grade when she became an American. Oh, she may have been a legally born citizen for nine years, but this was when her heart became quintessentially "American."

Katie's class had been studying the Pilgrims and how they had only survived through the friendship of the Native Americans. My daughter was fascinated by how the Wampanoag people had taught the English how to use fish as fertilizer and grow native corn. Her imagination was stirred by the additional suffering and hardship averted by this act of kindness from the original Americans. She also learned Thanksgiving was a feast of appreciation that we repeat every year in honor of this act of kindness.

To celebrate their studies, the class was going to create their own Thanksgiving feast and had agreed to try some of the recipes from that first celebration. Katie and her best friend, Vera, were on a team together. Their job was to make corn on the cob. Best friends since kindergarten, they were a study in opposites. Vera was a tiny, black-haired beauty with dark eyes and a rich, brown complexion. Katie was tall and blond, reflecting her English heritage, with hazel eyes and golden skin.

As the girls worked, talk turned to family feasts and what everyone was doing for Thanksgiving. Vera was silent in class, but later confessed that her mom "wasn't sure" about Thanksgiving.

Vera's mother had come from Mexico and was part Native American. After working as a veterinary assistant for decades to raise her large family as a single mom, Vera's mother was going blind, had consequently lost her job, and was struggling to provide for her youngest three kids. Decades of giving to others and sharing all she had had created a large network of supporters who felt honored to give back to this remarkable woman and her children. But despite their help and her church's help, times were hard. Vera confided in Katie that not only would she not be having a feast for Thanksgiving, but she might not even be eating.

Katie was appalled and came home determined to do something about it. She emptied her piggybank while her sister and brother chipped in as they could. Too often our family had been the recipients of others' charity; now it was our turn to give back.

We bought a turkey and fixings for mashed potatoes, gravy, stuffing, and sweet potatoes. In honor of their class project, we bought corn on the cob. We baked pumpkin pies and made cranberry sauce.

The Wednesday before Thanksgiving, I made our family feast (except the turkey), packed it in aluminum tins and stacked it all in the refrigerator.

Thanksgiving morning, we were all up at the crack of dawn to create a new feast for Vera's family. We put their turkey in to bake and began making all the sides so they would be warm and fresh.

With her brother, sister and me, Katie directed the cooking as we sang and danced and played in the kitchen, so pleased at the wonderful surprise we were preparing for Vera's family.

"You know what's funny?" Katie asked as we chopped and measured and stirred.

"No, what?" I asked.

"It's turn-about," she said.

"What do you mean?"

"Well, the Native Americans helped the English Pilgrims on

Thanksgiving, right?" Katie ventured.

"Right…"

"Well, now the English get to help the Native Americans!" Kate said, laughing at her own joke.

Soon, we had beans and corn, sweet and mashed potatoes, pie and cranberry sauce all packaged up and smelling of sweetness, spices, and love. The beautiful, hot turkey was centered on a plastic platter and surrounded by carrots and onions. We'd replaced Vera's turkey in the oven with our own and set it to roasting while we headed over to Katie's friend's house.

Everything had been put in cardboard boxes so we could play a game of "Ding-Dong Dash" to deliver it. And, with her brother and sister, Katie quietly sneaked up to Vera's door, going around the side of the house so as not to be seen from the picture window in the living room, and silently set the boxes on the stoop.

Her brother and sister circled back and got into the car. We started the engine with the passenger door open so that Katie could jump in, and we could drive off.

Then Katie looked to the car for the "high-sign" that we were ready to go. She'd been hunched down on the stoop to make sure no one could see her standing at the door.

As we signaled, Katie reached up, rang the bell — and ran! She jumped in the car, and off we drove. Just as we turned the corner, Katie's brother called out, "They've opened the door!"

And our deed was done.

We never told a soul. And, in fact, I changed Vera's name here so as to not give us away.

When Vera came back to school, she did ask Katie if she knew anything about her special delivery.

"How could we help you, Vera?" Katie replied. "You know we can barely take care of ourselves."

And, with that, Vera dropped it.

But what I can't drop is what happened to my daughter that day. For that was the day she exhibited all the best traits of Americans — caring, compassion, loyalty, resourcefulness, and kindness… above all else, kindness.

Yes, Katie may have been born a citizen, but it was on Thanksgiving of her ninth year that my child really, truly became an American.

— Susan Traugh —

A Modest and Moveable Thanksgiving Feast

Thanksgiving, after all, is a word of action.
~W.J. Cameron

We had finally decided to skip our traditional family dinner and make the pilgrimage to Macy's Thanksgiving Day Parade with our five-year-old daughter, Kerry. We never anticipated what Kerry would take away from the experience, or how it would affect our lives for years to come.

We caught the dawn train from Poughkeepsie to Grand Central along with hundreds of other excited celebrants. Like many other families we packed a small backpack with sliced turkey sandwiches and juice boxes; eating on the fly in New York City is expensive and complicated, unless you settle for pretzels and roasted chestnuts from a street vendor. Kerry was wide-eyed and a little overwhelmed. This was not your ordinary outing with Mom and Dad.

As the train pulled into the terminal, everyone rose and stood in the aisle anxiously waiting to disembark and head toward the parade route along Fifth Avenue. Rather than have our diminutive daughter jostled by the crowds, we waited until everyone had stepped off onto the pandemonium of the platform. As we walked up to the entrance to the terminal Kerry spotted a homeless woman sitting in the shadows, invisible to all except my curious daughter.

"What's that?" she asked. Linda and I looked at each other, caught off guard by the need to explain something very different than the happy scene we were about to join. During our first years of parenthood we'd discussed how we would explain such nearly ineffable topics as God, death, and eventually sex and love. But homelessness? We weren't prepared. We gave as simple and honest an explanation as we could muster and continued on to the parade.

The following year, we decided to attend the parade again. So the night before Thanksgiving we went shopping for sliced turkey for sandwiches. Again, Kerry caught us off guard.

"Can we bring some sandwiches for those people?" she asked. We knew immediately whom she meant. How could we refuse? More importantly, why would we refuse? This was a golden opportunity to honor Kerry's sense of charity. Our six-year-old daughter was teaching us an important lesson. We bought five pounds of sliced turkey, two loaves of bread and a can of cranberry sauce. What are turkey sandwiches on Thanksgiving without the tangy-sweet taste of cranberry sauce? That night we prepared and packed two-dozen sandwiches into our now overstuffed backpack.

The next morning we took the train into Manhattan again but there was a different excitement brewing in our little family. We waited until all the other families had left the train and hustled off to the parade route. Then we walked up the ramp toward the terminal, scanning the shadows. There was a homeless man sitting in the same spot as last year. We stopped and extracted the first of the little feasts from the pack. Without a word of instruction we handed it to Kerry. She walked over to the man slowly, standing still until he looked up at her. She reached out and handed the sandwich to him. Neither spoke a word. Then we were off to the parade, stopping along the way to distribute the rest of the sandwiches, except one for each of us. Somehow, no giant Thanksgiving sit-down feast ever tasted as good as those sandwiches.

Over the next decade we took a hiatus from the parade and shared the day with our families. And then, one year, our extended families couldn't get together for Thanksgiving, so we decided to resume our Manhattan parade tradition. This time, Kerry was bringing a boyfriend along.

We were still inside the terminal when Kerry spotted the first homeless man sitting motionless in a dark corner. She extracted a sandwich and took it over to him, as usual not exchanging a word. She must have prepped her boyfriend; he wasn't as perplexed as we expected. Not only did Kerry fulfill her sense of kindness and generosity but she also passed on her good example. She's a thirty-year-old mother now with three daughters of her own. They haven't made it to the parade yet. I hope they ask us to come along when they do. There's nothing like sharing a turkey sandwich with new friends.

— Thom Schwarz —

82

Christmas Promise

*Because that's what kindness is. It's not doing
something for someone else because they can't,
but because you can.*
~Andrew Iskander

C hristmas Promise began more than twenty years ago.
Three women started it, one of whom was a teacher who
asked the children in her first-grade class to write letters
to Santa. Those letters launched the program.

Christmas Promise is not a governmental program. It is not a church
program, though it is non-profit. It is not advertised or promoted; it is
secret. There is no paid staff. No gasoline reimbursements, no lunch,
nothing. One local golf course hosts a fundraiser in September. All
the money goes to Christmas Promise.

A person can select one family and buy for the whole family. The
gift giver takes the gifts to Christmas Promise and the program wraps
and delivers them. Christmas Promise might also decide to add to
the gifts.

Everything from office space to wrapping paper to gifts is donated.
Some local companies send their staff over to spend an afternoon
wrapping gifts. Once they are introduced to the program, those people
will often return to help on their own time.

In 2013, 254 families were recipients of Christmas Promise. The
families are nominated by individuals familiar with the secret program — teachers at low-income-area schools, clergy, ministers and so

on. It doesn't matter how many kids are in the family and no family is on the list more than one year. No family knows or suspects they are going to receive anything. Everyone living in the household receives a gift, even grandparents.

Families don't get cell phones or laptops. They get basic needs, like warm clothes, blankets, pajamas, books and games. Additionally, stockings for homeless children and adults are filled with toothbrushes, toothpaste, hand cream, tissues, and other items that most of us don't think of as luxuries. Over four hundred backpacks are filled with pencils, paper, crayons and books.

Many of the families receive specific requests. One little boy asked for warm socks for his father so that he could go out and get a job. Another child wanted "bug shampoo" (the teacher wrote that he had lice). Another child wanted something for his mother who has four children and only one job. The letters the kids write are heartbreaking. One little girl asked for nothing for herself; many of the kids don't. They ask for items for their parents, brothers and sisters.

There are more than sixty men who grow white beards to deliver carloads of toys and food. Yes, they wear the requisite costume! The Santas report back to the office after finishing their Christmas Eve deliveries and volunteers get letters describing the Santa experience. The letters explain how grown men break down and cry. Each Santa delivers to four or more families in a specific area. They sometimes have to go back (fully costumed each time) until they catch the family at home. Since no one knows they are coming, deliveries can be a challenge.

This is Christmas at its best. This year I am making doll clothes for the program. I have purchased twelve dolls, and they all need shoes, pajamas and dresses. Any donations are appreciated. And if you'd like to help wrap packages after Halloween, I'll show you where to do it and help you get started. You won't feel like a bit player. Not even a second player. You will feel like the top elf in Santa's workshop. Because that's how it makes you feel. A little help goes a long way.

—Linda A. Lohman—

83

Making Christmas Hope

Christmas is the one day of the year that carries real
hope and promise for all mankind.
~Edgar Guest

The holiday season was approaching, and our economy was still in a downward spiral. For several months, I had been attending a new church. Reverend Lori's messages were of everyday spirituality, and humanity to our fellow people, and hope, especially in these trying times. Her messages always inspired me and I wanted to follow up and make a difference in someone's life.

So many people this past year had lost faith and, more importantly, hope for a brighter future. People were feeling desperate. The streets were becoming more dangerous. I was thinking about the homeless, how they continued to find strength to go on, and how they would spend Christmas this year.

Across from my church was a park, and as fall came and went, I noticed a larger number of homeless people making their home there. I wanted to make their Christmas special this year, and hopefully remind them of Christmas pasts with their family and friends before hard times came their way. Yes, food and cash would help, but they could receive those any given day, and I wanted to make Christmas Day different.

I bought some Christmas gift bags in bright colors with Santa's face and "Ho-Ho-Ho" written across the front. Wanting to be practical yet capture the spirit of the holiday, I purchased Santa candy, peppermint candy canes, individual bags of nuts, cookies, and bright red tissue paper. Okay, this was a start, yet it wasn't special enough in my mind. Then I saw the fluffy little brown and white teddy bears with red bows around their necks.

Most of the homeless at this park were grown men. Would they like my gifts? My friends Marlene, Jerry, Ken and I assembled the bags. Christmas music playing loudly in the background, our hearts felt open and right about our mission. Placing the sparkly red tissue paper inside each bag first, followed by the candy and snacks, the cuddly bear, and a couple of dollars as a gift, we twisted the tissue paper sealing all the treats inside. Early Christmas morning, we set out to the park, stopping at a local Dunkin' Donuts to pick up coffee and doughnuts for the men too.

Never having done this kind of community outreach before, we were not sure how we would be received. The next hour was beyond our wildest expectations. As we approached the park, we saw a few more people than we anticipated, and we said to each other, "I hope we have enough bags." We were then spotted, and twenty or more people approached our car slowly, some walking, some limping, some jogging, still not knowing what to expect as we opened the door. They looked so tired as their eyes scanned the huge bag carrying all our goodies.

We had expected to hand out bags to everyone right there by the car and leave, but the men walked us over to a pavilion where most of them gathered to eat, sleep and just hang out for the day. Once there, we started to pour hot coffee and pass out doughnuts.

No one asked what was inside the bags. Everyone was patient as they took a cup of coffee and a doughnut, sitting down, savoring every sip and bite. As we said "Merry Christmas" to each, their responses of "Merry Christmas" back to us began to strengthen. They started to smile and their eyes brightened. We started to hand out the bags. Some got two bags by mistake and they turned and gave their extra to someone else, saying "Merry Christmas," happy to share their treats.

One younger man, seeing the teddy bear, looked up and said, "I have myself a teddy now." He put it inside his shirt pocket and patted it gently, his eyes gleaming.

Their resilience inspired me that morning — how they put aside their hardship for a couple of hours, opening their hearts, forgetting their troubles as they shared what they had. As we drove away, our own hearts were filled with gratitude and hope for brighter days ahead, and as we looked back, the group gathered under the pavilion waved until we were out of sight.

— Paula Maugiri Tindall, R.N. —

84

'Tis Better to Give than to Receive

Families are like fudge... mostly sweet with a few nuts.
~Author Unknown

I n late November, right after Thanksgiving, thoughts of dread and gloom used to start to invade the minds of my family. It's not that we didn't enjoy all of the holiday festivities. It's just that the holidays meant gift giving. And gift giving meant gift receiving. And receiving gifts from my Aunt Beadie was always interesting.

My Aunt Beadie was a really nice person and we did love her. She did tend to be a bit eccentric and always exaggerate the truth... just a tiny little bit. Like the time she told us she thwarted a bank robbery that was in progress and single-handedly detained the robber until the police arrived. Or the time she came screaming down the stairs at my house claiming that there was this huge hole in the floor of my son's closet and that both of my sons were going to fall through it down into the dining room below. Why hadn't any of us ever even seen this huge gaping hole in our floor? Why hadn't my kids fallen through it before? And then there was the time she swore she could hear the conversations going on in my neighbor's house through the heating ducts in OUR living room. She talked to her dog, too. And of course the dog answered her.

Aunt Beadie raised gift giving to a whole new level, or should I say lowered gift giving to a whole new level. The gifts she gave defied all common sense. Why would my two young sons, ages five and eight at the time, need valets? Now I'm not talking about the living breathing kind of valet who brings you breakfast in bed or irons your newspaper, but the piece of furniture kind of valet on which you hang your suit jacket and tie when you come home from work so they won't wrinkle. The kind that has a special safe place where you can put your cufflinks and tie tack so you won't lose them. What was Aunt Beadie thinking? But, I have to tell you, we did actually use those valets. They made a great tent frame. If you place them just so far apart and drape an old sheet over them, voilà — you have a tent.

The matching Hello Kitty nightshirts she gave to my husband and me one year were quite lovely. They were a kind of brown color with the perfect Hello Kitty logo right there on the front and they each came with matching coin purses. Fetching. She had bought both nightshirts in a large size… a child's size large. Not that we would have worn them anyway. And our boys would not have been caught dead wearing Hello Kitty nightshirts. We donated them, and the coin purses, and I'm sure two little girls were delighted to receive them.

One year we got a talking alarm clock. It didn't have a clock face but instead spoke the time in a very loud voice so you wouldn't have to put your glasses on to read it. That could possibly have been useful… if we spoke Russian.

We all got matching terry cloth shower wraps one year that were monogrammed with initials — not *our* initials but still quite lovely. The boys used them as Superman capes. Never mind about the very tasteful pink flamingo that she got for our yard one year. Now the Magic-8 Ball was actually quite useful. I used to ask it whether or not I should cook dinner. I loved it when the answer was, "My reply is no."

What do you say to a loving relative with the worst taste in the world? She would sit right there while we opened her gifts, with a big smile on her face. A mere thank you just didn't seem adequate. So we learned to ad-lib — meaning we learned to lie. "Oh Aunt Beadie, this is amazing. Thank you so much. I have never seen anything quite like this. Oh, the colors are dazzling. I just know this will come in so handy when… oh, I just love it!"

When Aunt Beadie reached her mid-eighties, she decided to stop shopping. No longer would she buy us useless gifts that we would never use. She started giving away useless gifts from her own home — all of the junk that she had been collecting for years and years. Old jars, some without lids, cracked dishes, ashtrays (for our non-smoking household), and much, much more. But the best of all was the jewelry.

None of her jewelry was real. Aunt Beadie knew that. And we knew that too, but she didn't know that we knew. She always claimed everything was real. The set of six huge spider pins was one of my favorite gifts. They were gold (gold-colored metal) with jade (cloudy green glass) centers. I hate spiders! The pins creeped me out — they went right in the trash but I wrapped them in newspaper first to be sure they wouldn't escape. The "ruby" earrings were so ugly and so heavy I was afraid they would pull my ear lobes off if I even tried to put them on. And where could I possibly wear them? Trash! Immediately! And how about the tiara? Please don't forget about the diamond (clear glass) and emerald (green glass) tiara. Now that was a keeper. I actually wore it… to a fiftieth birthday party when I went as the prom queen!

Sadly Aunt Beadie passed away a few years ago. Not to worry. Her daughter, my cousin, has taken up right where Aunt Beadie left off. Ethel is very busy "finding treasures" in Aunt Beadie's closets and drawers to wrap up and give to us as tokens of love. And although our sons are grown and have families of their own now, they still dread the "special gifts" they know that they, and their children, will receive. I, too, can hardly wait to see what is in store for us this year.

— Maddie Sohn —

Chapter
10

Around the Table

85

Try It, You Won't Like It

It isn't so much what's on the table that matters,
as what's on the chairs.
~W.S. Gilbert

My kids act like I'm trying to poison them if they see anything in the kitchen that contains high fructose corn syrup. So I read labels, and buy only organic products when I know they are coming to visit. My sister's nutritionist has an ever-changing list of food prohibitions for her—right now it is bread, dairy, and chicken. Chicken? My stepdaughter doesn't like meat... except bacon. Her boyfriend doesn't eat animals... except ones that swim. My stepson doesn't eat strawberries, his dog must have organic pumpkin once a day, and his girlfriend can't eat dairy or gluten. One of my kids hates raisins. They both loved raisins until I hired a really weird nanny when they were little. She didn't like raisins and she convinced the kids they didn't like them either. A dislike of raisins eliminates a lot of things that are usually served to small children—very inconvenient. Now one of them eats raisins again, too late for me.

My father-in-law must have white bread and plain lettuce at every dinner. So I have to make sure we have a head of iceberg lettuce and some plain white rolls when he comes. My sister-in-law and niece don't eat dairy or gluten. After trying many stores, they have found the best salmon at one particular seafood shop in our town, but I never remember which one, so I always worry I am serving salmon from the wrong place. And what if my salmon was in the same truck as the salmon that ended up at the wrong store? Do they separate families?

Sometimes, I would like to separate from my family, especially when I am hosting a large family event and have to juggle the conflicting and ever-changing needs of so many people. I frankly think this is all ridiculous. There are lots of foods I hate — olives, cherries, avocados, sushi — but I just keep my mouth shut. That's right — I don't eat the offending items and I don't say anything. Once I had a hard time keeping my cool during a business lunch as I sat in a very authentic Japanese sushi restaurant in midtown Manhattan watching Japanese businessmen scarf down slithery slimy sushi. I kept drinking Cokes to soothe my stomach, as I was nauseated just from looking at the sushi. And this is the Iron Stomach that did not get sick in India, Turkey, Bolivia, or the Amazon.

But my entire family's list of dislikes added together is nothing compared to those of my father. He has never tried any kind of soda or any alcoholic beverage, but he knows he doesn't like them. Can you imagine he has never had even a sip of wine? And he didn't drink beer in college or in the Air Force? He has never tried a bit of Indian food, Chinese food, Japanese food, Thai food, Mediterranean food, or any ethnic food whatsoever. He is eighty-one years old, but he has never in his life tried pizza or pasta or rice. He knows he doesn't like them. His face goes pale at the sight of salad dressing, even oil and vinegar. He orders plain steak at restaurants and if they bring it to the table with a little butter sauce on top, he looks stricken and sends it back. The amazing thing is that his sister has the exact same taste in foods. She has never tried any of the foods that he has never tried. They were raised back in the 1930s, when many Upper East Side New York families had cooks, but they have never tried ninety percent of the foods that the rest of us eat. What did the cook actually cook?

When Dad traveled to China for a week, despite the fact that his group was being feted all over the country as visiting dignitaries, practically with state dinners, he brought an entire suitcase filled with

Sara Lee coffeecakes to subsist on. Basically, he doesn't like any dish in which different types of food are touching each other. I have joked that I should serve him his dinner on one of those compartment plates, like we use for little kids, so that each food is walled in, safely protected from the other foods.

The most stressful family event for me is Christmas Eve. We have been hosting Christmas Eve at our house for the last ten years or so, and we usually have more than twenty people, seated at three tables in three different rooms. It is chaotic, but lots of fun. Promptness is not my family's forte, and multi-tasking in the kitchen is not fun on a holiday, so I plan a menu that does not require precise timing. That usually means stews, beef and peppers, or pasta sauce, since I can cook them for four, five, or even six hours without worrying.

Every Christmas Eve I have to go through the list of food issues and prepare accordingly. I need iceberg lettuce for my father-in-law, a steak ready to broil for my father, something gluten free for my sister-in-law, niece, and stepson's girlfriend. Bread without raisins for one of my children, I forget which one. No strawberries in the dessert. Something besides chicken for my sister. Something that swims for my stepdaughter's boyfriend. The list goes on....

But despite the extra planning for the finicky tastes of my family, we have a great time and the "afterglow" from Christmas Eve lasts throughout the season. With my parents getting older, I am just thankful to see them around the table. And last Christmas Eve, in an act of great paternal love and sacrifice, Dad announced that he would not require a separate steak, but would eat my beef stew, even though the beef and the carrots and the onions and the potatoes were touching each other and he had never tried beef stew before in his life. I think my mother convinced him that since he liked the four items that were in the stew, he should give me a break from broiling the steak-for-one while trying to feed twenty other people. I watched him that night and saw that he did manage to get some of it down, which I really appreciated. I didn't tell him that I had poured a little red wine in the pot!

— Emma Dyson —

86

Hum

Love makes your soul crawl out from its hiding place.
~Zora Neale Hurston

oul food (n) traditional southern African American cuisine. Ever since I was a child, I've hummed when I'm eating. Let me rephrase that: I hum when I eat GOOD food. I'm talking that fresh out the oven, skin still cracklin', pot bubblin', beans so green you can taste the soil that gave them life, good food. I come from a family of good cooks. Soul-food cooks.

Grandmama cooks with love and taught all nine of her children how to do so, who in turn taught their children, my generation, how to do so. And we will teach the next generation.

It had been a while since I had had soul food. I'm horrible about attending family gatherings and don't really know many other Black people in my town. I keep to myself most days. So my access to that good food is limited. Maybe once every other Mother's Day when I made it over to Grandmama's for the after-church meal. I always pile up my plate and dig in, humming the whole time. Aunt Algie has always teased me about it. I just tell her that's how you know it's good food.

So here we are, Thanksgiving 2020. Although it's the time of the year most people usually want to gather and visit with family and loved ones, gatherings have been advised against. And furthermore, I've recently had surgery and am under explicit doctor's orders to stay home. It's already been a long, lonely year, and this definitely isn't helping. So when Aunt Algie called and offered to bring me a plate of food from the dinner at Grandmama's house, I was beyond elated. All that good food delivered to my door with a face-masked hug from Uncle Paul to top it off? Grubhub, eat your heart out.

They swung by late in the evening on Thanksgiving Day. I met Uncle Paul at the door, we took a moment to catch up, and then he left. I had already eaten so I put the bag in the fridge, giddy at how heavy the container inside felt. I could have opened it and peered at my bounty, but the fat kid that I am, I was already imagining what goodies awaited me. It felt like it was Christmas Eve and I was a curious child, shaking presents, imagining what was inside. I didn't want to ruin that magic.

Dinnertime the next day finally rolled around. I had eaten a little earlier while catching up with a friend, but it was more of a snack than a meal. Did the job at the time, but by now I was starving. I hobbled to the kitchen on one crutch, opened the fridge, and pulled out the Walmart bag of deliciousness. One smaller Ziploc bag with four rolls and a stuffed Cracker Barrel to-go container were my prize. Have you ever noticed how it feels like time slows when you're waiting on something? It felt like I could have written this story in the time I stood there, watching that black container spin round and round. Almost in a trance, the gentle humming of the microwave guiding me in song, taking my mind far, far away....

After what felt like a century, it was time. I hobbled my way to the table and immediately started shoveling it in. Juicy, tender brisket cut thick. Mac & cheese so rich and cheesy. My god, the cheesiness. Gravy with the giblets over the stuffing. Creamy green bean casserole with those little fried onions on top that get a little soggy but somehow still stay crispy on the edges. But then the carrots stopped me in my tracks. All my aunties always made them the same way: cut into rounds and baked to tender, melt in your mouth perfection with butter and cinnamon. One bite, and I was a child again, sitting at the kids' table in the corner of Grandmama's kitchen, humming more and more intensely with every bite. And there's something about corn bread with that dense, cake like texture and actual corn in it that sets my soul ablaze. As I polished off that cornbread, I remained that child in the corner, my humming now something more of a victory song than a happy little tune.

By the end of the meal, I didn't feel quite as alone as I had when I began eating. I could feel the love of my family growing in me with every bite, soothing and warming my recently aching soul. I sat there, staring at the now almost empty to-go dish, with so much appreciation for that piece of plastic. Almost moved to tears with how full both my belly and my heart were in that moment. Still humming my victory song.

— Emmy Faith —

87

All by Himself

Concentrate on counting your blessings, and you'll
have little time to count anything else.
~Woodrow Kroll

My second year in college had started. I hadn't decided whether to fly home for Thanksgiving yet. Although I had missed the holiday the year before, and I didn't want to miss it two years in a row, I didn't have the money for the ticket, plus I wasn't sure I could get enough time off from my job.

All that wondering changed when my mom called. She got right to the point: "Your grandmother isn't doing well. Your dad and I decided I should fly out there for Thanksgiving." Mom was an only child, so that made sense to me. But I was not ready for what I heard next. "We decided you would want to come along so I covered your ticket."

My mom was a whiz at logistics. "I will fly from Alabama, and you can fly from Minnesota. We will meet in Northern California the afternoon before Thanksgiving. Your dad and the younger kids will stay home for Thanksgiving at our house. I will have all the holiday preparations done so they can just pop the turkey in the oven on Thanksgiving morning."

As always, Mom's plan went off without a hitch. I met her at the Oakland airport, and we took a taxi to our hotel.

When we got in the door, Mom promptly called my grandpa. "Would you like us to come over and get the holiday meal ready for tomorrow, Dad?" She was disappointed when she hung up the phone. "Your grandfather doesn't drive at night anymore, and your grandmother is already resting for the night. He will pick us up sometime tomorrow morning."

Mom was anxious to see her parents, especially her mother, who was really fragile. But Grandpa didn't show up until well after nine in the morning.

When we finally got to their house, we got to say hello and then Grandpa helped Grandma lie down again and banished us to the living room, telling us we would eat Thanksgiving dinner at noon. He went into the kitchen.

Mom paced the floor. Finally, I asked her what the matter was. She didn't appreciate the question. "He can't cook," she hissed. "How's he supposed to fix a Thanksgiving meal for us?"

I tried to reason with her. "Can't you smell dinner? It smells divine to me. Grandma is upstairs resting. Grandpa is the only one who could be cooking." But we couldn't see through the kitchen door.

She had an idea. "Let's sneak out the front door and see what's going on. Then we will know who is really cooking." Grandpa was very hard of hearing, so he didn't hear us leave. It was a crazy plan, but I followed her around the house to the kitchen windows. There we watched Grandpa fill water glasses and make coffee, undetected. "When did he learn to make coffee?" Mom asked out loud. We ran back around the side of the house and into the living room.

We should not have done that because it made Mom worse. "I tell you, he can't cook." She continued to pace in the tiny living room. Finally, Grandpa came through the kitchen door. It was almost noon by then.

Speaking directly to my mom, he said, "I am going to get your mother up and bring her down to eat with us. You two — go sit down at the dining room table. Stay out of the kitchen!" So we did.

When Grandma got situated at the table, Grandpa sat down and said grace. Then he got up and started making trips back and forth through the kitchen door: first he brought the water, then the coffee, then a couple of relish trays, rolls and individual lettuce salads he had poured out of one of those premixed plastic bags. You get the idea. It took forever because he moved slowly, and he only brought out a couple of things at a time.

Then we heard the oven door squeak open. Mom's eyes got big. She stopped answering Grandma's questions because she was listening so hard. The kitchen door opened again, and Grandpa came through with a potholder in each hand. He served Grandma first, with a flourish, and then Mom. The smell of the food was so good I didn't think I could wait any longer. Grandpa came through the door one last time and set hot food in front of me, and then himself. The food was still too hot to eat, so we sat in silence.

Finally, Mom spoke. "Wow, I can't believe it, this smells so good." I started shoveling food into my mouth, careful not to make eye contact with Mom. If I had, surely I would have choked to death from laughter. But I could tell by Grandma's eyes that she had been in on planning this Thanksgiving dinner.

You see, Grandpa had truly made the Thanksgiving dinner all by himself. He had heated and served each of us one of those TV turkey dinners on little metal trays. You know the kind: a little mound of stuffing with a slab or two of pressed turkey on top, a blob of whipped potatoes with not enough margarine and a pile of really bright green peas, but no dessert. It tasted as good as it smelled, and I really don't even like peas.

I guess it shows that it's who's around the table, not what's on it, that makes the food taste so good.

— Pamela Gilsenan —

Snaccident

I believe in a benevolent God not because He
created the Grand Canyon or Michelangelo,
but because He gave us snacks.
~Paul Rudnick

My sister's holiday feast was to die for. A cousin's delicious Death-by-Chocolate Fudge almost killed me. Starving, I sampled one piece after another. Then I recalled the trick of drinking lots of water to quell hunger pangs. Three glasses later, I helped myself to my uncle's homemade peanut brittle. Might as well enjoy. Who knows? This grandma might get run over by Santa and his sleigh on the way home.

Despite the munching, I found room for the main course, where even the vegetables were fattening. Who could resist sweet potatoes buried under mountains of marshmallows, broccoli smothered in cheddar cheese sauce, and homemade rolls dripping with honey butter? And then dessert came along and one sliver of my favorite homemade coffee cake topped with maraschino cherries quickly turned into three.

So stuffed that I could do Santa's suit justice, I was grateful when we finally moved away from the grazing table. While my elderly aunt entertained everyone with stories of the good old days, I absentmindedly reached over and grabbed a handful of nuts from the candy dish on the coffee table. When I bit down, there was a horrible crunching sound. I swallowed and worried I'd chipped a tooth. My throat burned, and tears streamed down my face.

Around the Table | 277

Mustering a weak cry, I whispered, "Water! Hurry!"

My brother-in-law raced over, ready to perform the Heimlich. Waving him away, I pointed to the potpourri centerpiece as I continued to cough and sputter. To be honest, the cinnamon flavor wasn't all that bad, but I'd recommend savoring the aroma instead.

When we got ready to leave, my sister held up the potpourri and giggled. "Would you like me to package the leftovers for later?"

"No thanks. Guess I'll never live this down."

The following afternoon, my husband walked into the room just as I lifted a floral centerpiece to dust beneath it and snickered, "Snack time already?"

— Alice Muschany —

89

Phantom's Thanksgiving

Fun fact: Most cats like their food at room temperature and won't eat it if it's too hot or too cold.

The first cat I ever had, a gift from my girlfriend, was a black kitten that came into my life because his previous owner (my girlfriend's co-worker) was looking for a new home for him. They had to give him up when they had a baby and the cat thought she was a plaything.

Phantom would lie asleep at the other end of the couch as I watched television, but would be waiting for me in the kitchen when I got up to get a snack. I never saw him run past me; he simply appeared in the kitchen before I did. He also developed the habit of finding ways to get to the human food he wanted so much. I swore he could walk through walls (or at least pantry doors).

Several years later, my now-wife and I moved to the other side of the country, to Los Angeles, to start a new job for me at a new school. The two of us and Phantom moved into our new home in August. My wife and I both came from big families and were used to large gatherings for Thanksgiving, so we were a little sad that we could not afford to fly back home for the holiday. Determined to make the best of the situation, we invited several friends in the same predicament over to celebrate "Friendsgiving" on that Thursday.

As the cook in our family, I spent the early morning hours preparing the turkey and a dozen side dishes, constantly shooing Phantom out of the kitchen. When our guests arrived, we asked them to help us keep Phantom away from the food. Eventually, he made such a pest of himself during dinner that I put him in the bedroom and closed the door.

After dinner, we left everything on the dining room table and the kitchen counter in order to go to the living room, watch some football, and relax after eating. A few minutes into the game, I heard a noise from the kitchen. With my wife and all of our guests sitting there, no one was in the kitchen, so I got up and looked down the hall. The bedroom door was open a crack.

Moving quickly to the kitchen, I could not believe what I saw. I had carved the turkey and left the uncarved part sitting on the counter. Phantom was sitting inside the remains of the turkey, very contentedly eating around himself. He was in the act of pulling some meat off the thigh I had not served.

"Phantom!" I yelled, startling some of the guests, who jumped up to see what was the matter. The cat simply gave me a look and kept eating. The guests, on the other hand, found it quite funny, although we now had a lot fewer leftovers.

I finally went over and removed him from his seat in paradise, cleaned him off (threatening him with a bath later) and set to work cleaning up. By the time I left the kitchen, he was contentedly licking himself clean on the couch in the spot I had vacated, no doubt enjoying the turkey flavor.

Phantom is gone now, but our friends still laugh about the year that we did not have a "turducken" but rather a "turkitten" for Thanksgiving dinner.

— Kevin Wetmore —

90

Christmas Our Way

The heart of every family tradition
is a meaningful experience.
~Author Unknown

I come from a long line of Puerto Ricans who celebrate American traditions and holidays like everyone else. At Christmastime, we follow the customs of decorating, trimming a tree, and baking. However, what sets us apart from most families is our Annual Pastele-Making Day.

Pasteles are a tamale-like dish that encompasses various ingredients, including potatoes, taro root, squash, plantains, green bananas, and yucca for the masa. The inside of the shell is a slow-simmered beef stew seasoned with red achiote powder mixed with cooking oil, for color and taste. Pasteles are an acquired taste due to the sour tang of the vegetables. To most of our guests, it is unpleasant, but for those of us who grew up eating this dish, it is wonderful.

Making this recipe is an arduous task that requires excellent leadership, organization, and tenacity. Only one person in our household fit that job description — my maternal grandmother. Mama had a shiny gray bob, never spoke English, never wore pants (only skirts and dresses), never drove, and never divorced my grandfather — who abandoned her decades ago. She always wore jewelry, hummed, and loved to read her Bible. She even had the resolve to return to school when she was in her forties to obtain her high-school diploma.

Mama loved to cook, and pasteles were her Mona Lisa, the pièce de résistance in her culinary repertoire. She was the master, and many people told her so.

Growing up, I remember Mama standing by the front door of the house with her handbag, waiting for someone to drive her to the market. Whoever drove Mama knew that the journey would consist of numerous stops at meat markets and small Latino grocery stores, all for the choicest ingredients. My brother, who could never speak a word of Spanish, usually "volunteered" for the job after Mama slipped him a twenty-dollar bill.

When Mama returned home with numerous bags of groceries, she instructed all of us to wash our hands and await further instructions. She then covered the dining-room table with newspapers, set out bowls on the table, and heaped all of the vegetables into the dishes for peeling and chopping. From there, she moved to set up station two, which consisted of meat preparation with sharp knives, heavy pots, spices, and mounds of the reddest ground chuck available.

When Mama nodded, we manned our stations. My sister and I peeled and chopped, and my mother prepped the stew. In the final position, Mama set up a food mill that attached with a clamp to the cutting board we pulled out from underneath our counter. There, my father would churn the cut vegetables to a smooth masa. Mama would assist him by adding warm milk and the achiote oil to the batter to form orange goo.

We were a finely-tuned machine. When things were going well, Mama would sing Christmas carols in her beautiful operatic voice. If things were moving too slowly, she would look at us sternly and tell us exactly what she thought. There were no excuses for doing a lousy job.

When the stew settled, and the masa mill stopped, it was time to assemble the packages. Mama replaced all the soggy newspaper and covered the dining-room table with an old tablecloth. Three chairs made up the assembly station, which encompassed a pot of masa, a pot of stew, a bowl of the red achiote oil, and three rolls of parchment paper. (While many Puerto Ricans swear by fresh banana leaves to encase the pasteles, Mama pooh-poohed the idea, stating that the banana leaves distracted from the taste.)

Mama sat down like a concert pianist ready to charm us with her talents. My mother and father sat on either side of her. Finally, Mama unrolled a cylinder of parchment paper, dunked her spoon in the red oil, and made a bull's eye right in the center of the sheet. My parents quickly followed suit on their parchment rolls. With a quick slap, the masa landed in the middle of the achiote, and the swirling continued, this time to make room for the stew. The yummy smell of garlic and onion from the meat hit our nostrils. We all longed for big, beefy pasteles, but she would have nothing to do with it.

To Mama, the determination of success was in the numbers. If she made fewer than 100 pasteles, she failed. If she mustered more than 100, it was a good day.

My older sister and I waited patiently to participate. When a stack of packages was ready, my sister and I went to work on tying bundles. We pulled the string from the roll, measured eighteen inches, and cut. On and on we would tug, measure, cut and then set aside 100 strings. When done, we dutifully bound two packages together and set them aside for counting.

As the years went by, we longed for promotion to assembly. My sister and I tired of cutting thread and bundling packages. Finally, when we were in our twenties, Mama promoted us to Assistant Pasteles Assemblers because she thought our parents were too slow.

We did this for years and grew to enjoy our special day with her. Years later, the doctor diagnosed Mama with Alzheimer's. She moved slower, forgot the achiote, and even stood in the kitchen staring into the open refrigerator. The year we placed her in a home, we quietly peeled our bananas, stirred the beef, and milled the orange goo. Tears rolled down our cheeks as we stretched the *masa* thin to make 100 bundles, just as she had.

It's been ten years since Mama passed, and we miss her. Although making Christmas pasteles is a laborious process, we still do it to honor her memory.

Even so, we changed a few things. My father retired the little food grinder for a state-of-the-art food processor, and we buy the meat already cubed. My niece now joins us on Pasteles Day. Although

I highly object to my mother allowing her to skip string cutting and move straight to assembly, I'm glad we can pass down the tradition to her. My niece may not make pasteles for her family, but she will always have a story about Mama to tell her children.

— Lizette Vega —

91

A Bountiful and Blessed Meal

*Within our family there was no such thing as a person who
did not matter. Second cousins thrice removed mattered.*
~Shirley Abbott

I grew up thinking I was related to the entire county. Seriously!
My mother was the fourteenth child in a family of fifteen. You
know your family is overly large when every possible crush
you have is heralded off-limits because "he's your cousin."
Needless to say, years later, all those cousins have married and our
family has expanded. Every year, we celebrate with a reunion and
Thanksgiving meal together, thankful for each other and the past
year's blessings. Last year's head count was 641 souls — all from Gerrit
and Rolena and their fifteen children.

Technically, we are a small village, and there are always new faces
and missed faces. When we walk into the reunion on Thanksgiving
evening, we are met with a loud hum of voices and laughter, the squeals
of children playing games, and the mixed smells of apple pie, pumpkin
pie, turkey and stuffing. We always serve buffet-style, with a notebook
at the beginning of the line in which the direct descendants are required
to sign our names, which of the original fifteen we belong to and how
many people we brought to the reunion.

So it happened that about a month after another epic Thanksgiving
reunion, just a few days before Christmas, my cousin, Teresa, was stopped

by a gentleman with two little pig-tailed girls in tow at a local store.

"Hello, I'm sorry, but I recognize you from the meal held on Thanksgiving," he said to her.

He went on to explain that the day before Thanksgiving, his wife had left him and his two daughters. Devastated but determined to uphold Thanksgiving for his children's sake, he had dressed and bundled up his daughters, intent on finding a restaurant for a Thanksgiving meal.

There were no restaurants open due to the holiday, but he noticed a large number of cars at the community center and deduced that there must be a community Thanksgiving meal. He took his daughters inside and was met with the crazy chaos of my very large family. They were greeted like they belonged and encouraged to take off their coats. The father pulled up a chair and watched as his daughters quickly took off with new friends to play tag in the gym. He knew a few of the others in the room, but most were strangers.

When the children were summoned from the gym to gather for the prayer and meal, he began to realize this might not be a community meal after all. He noticed families grouping together to get in the buffet line. But his giggling girls were hungry, and the food smelled amazing, so with two little hands in his, he joined the line. However, when he reached the notebook, his suspicions were confirmed.

It wasn't a community event at all. He and his daughters had just crashed a family event. So, he humbly wrote his name in the notebook and noted they were a party of three. He was certain someone was going to call him out on it, but no one said a word. His family enjoyed the meal, and then sat a while longer to have dessert and play a few more games. Then, he bid everyone "goodnight," to the dismay of his daughters, who begged to stay just a little longer.

At this point, Teresa smiled and hugged the newest unofficial member of our family. She told the man he was most welcome, and invited him to come again next year as our family blossoms in all sorts of ways. And, by our deduction, since he does live in our county, he most likely is a cousin anyway!

— C. Joy —

92

Christmas in Canada

Never worry about numbers. Help one person at a time,
and always start with the person nearest you.
~Mother Teresa

rian paced the floor as he prayed that they would be able to get out of their country unscathed. Even with the proper papers, many men who tried to leave were thrown in the army. Families were torn apart. Lives were shattered.

It was late November and Brian was waiting for his new employee, Alex, to arrive from Ukraine with his family. Brian had first gotten to know Alex when he hired a few students from Ukraine for his previous business. As he described him, Alex was "a computer nerd" just like him, and now that Brian was starting a new business he could use Alex's help again. Now Alex was married, with a six-year-old daughter, and Brian had undertaken to move the whole family to Canada permanently.

Our family had already gone through our cupboards, looking for those extra items we could donate to the young couple's new home. Who needs two electric mixers? And why did I need to keep that extra coffeemaker I had stashed away?

When the plane landed, Brian welcomed Alex with a warm handshake and a sigh of relief. He met his wife Marina, a tiny pretty lady, and their beautiful daughter Julia. Her eyes filled with wonder as she looked around the bustling airport, and she shyly hid behind her mommy's skirt.

They came with two suitcases. That was it. All their other belongings were left behind. It must have been so bittersweet for them, leaving their families and almost everything they owned to come to Canada for freedom and opportunity.

Brian set them up in a hotel for two days and helped them shop for food and other essentials. It didn't take us long to set up house for this war-torn family. Brian and his wife Shannon rented Alex and Marina a neat and clean tiny bungalow on the south side of town.

Alex gasped as Brian opened the door to their new home. Marina burst into tears, and Julia ran from room to room, delighted.

"How many people live with us?" Alex asked, as his eyes grew larger and larger with every room that they explored.

"What do you mean?" Brian asked, not understanding the question.

"At home we live in one room, in a tenement, with lots of other families," Alex explained.

"Who does that lovely green grass outside belong to? Can Julia go outside to play?" Alex couldn't believe his good fortune. He held his head in his hands and wept.

It didn't take them long to bring Julia to Colasanti's, a giant greenhouse filled with plants and video games, bumper cars, jumpy castles and loads of entertainment for young and old alike. They walked along the riverfront enjoying the sculptures and Julia ran and danced in the park near their house.

"Canada so good to us," Alex stated in his broken English. "We celebrate Christmas on December 25th like real Canadians. In the Ukraine, Christmas is celebrated on January 6th."

"They must join us," I exclaimed, already planning Julia's Christmas stocking.

"Mom do you have any idea how overwhelming all twenty-six of us are?" Brian asked. "We are so noisy. There are so many gifts and twelve children will be running around screaming their heads off and chasing one another from room to room. They are probably going to come in one door and run wailing out the other!"

"I thought that they wanted to experience a real Canadian Christmas!" I countered.

"But what about Secret Santa for the adults?" Brian asked.

"Ed and I will choose their names and surprise them. And please let me have the joy of buying precious little girly items for Julia!"

At 2:00 p.m. on Christmas Day the doorbell rang and the children and their parents started spilling into the house.

Meat pies, bread stuffing, mashed potatoes and gravy, sweet potatoes, cinnamon honey squash, corn, honey-laced carrots, shrimp rings, salsa, veggies, homemade buns, and cabbage rolls covered the counters and extra table. And the smells of honey roasted ham and succulent golden turkey were the crowning glory.

Alex, Marina and Julia brought a bottle of wine and some homemade fruit-filled buns, sharing their own special Christmas treats.

Even though she spoke little English, Julia was soon running around the house with our granddaughter Maya. She soon found herself sitting in a circle with the twelve other children as they opened their gifts. Julia was so excited. The very first present she opened was Ana's beautiful blue dress from the movie *Frozen*. She tried it on immediately and twirled and spun as we all applauded.

She then opened a doll, coloured pencils, crayons, pencil cases, books of all kinds, hair clips, lip gloss, fairy wings, an Ariel nightlight and a stocking filled with goodies. Julia squealed with joy as she displayed a Barbie, an Olaf and a princess T-shirt from her never-ending magic bag.

When the grownups played Secret Santa, Alex and Marina were astonished as we called their name and they got to open their special gifts.

First came their Santa stockings filled with a mug for each of them, tea towels, Canada socks, Canada hats and boxes of chocolates. Alex got a Nike Canada sports hoodie and Marina got a sweater, with matching hat and gloves.

As the parents gathered up their sleepy children and hauled all their loot to their cars, my husband Ed and I assessed the damage to the house. Leftovers, wrapping paper, tinsel and messy floors were our souvenirs of the grand celebration that had taken place. We hugged one another tightly, appreciating our time together, our affluence, and our family.

As Alex, Marina and Julia put their arms around me to say good night, I asked them, "Are you alright? Are you happy?"

They crossed their arms in front of their hearts and whispered, "Canada beautiful. Here we safe!"

— Barbara Bondy-Pare —

Chapter
11

Four-legged
Family Members

93

Bailey's Best Christmas

*Fun fact: Visitors to Kent, England, can visit the Dog
Collar Museum at Leeds Castle, which contains more than
100 dog collars dating as far back as the 15th century.*

I will never forget our Labrador Retriever's sixth Christmas. Our sweet Bailey was solidly built, with a shiny chocolate-colored coat and a happy smile. Adored by family and friends for his gentle disposition, he was the kind of dog that liked everyone. Useless as a watchdog, we always joked that if a burglar intruded, Bailey would just wag his tail and lead him to the silver.

Like any beloved child, Bailey had his own Christmas stocking. Nothing fancy, but it was always filled with some special treats for Christmas — usually something to chew on and a plush doggy toy, although most of the doggy toys seemed to go missing eventually.

But this particular year, Bailey's nose might have been a bit out of joint, because we had a new baby in the house. Anika was stealing some of the attention away from Bailey, who'd been spending a bit more time in the laundry room than usual, sulking.

My mother had knitted Baby Anika a beautiful Christmas stocking that I'd hung on the mantle with the other hand-knit stockings. But a few days before Christmas, that new stocking was missing. The rest were still in place — but Anika's was mysteriously gone. That's when I remembered that I'd spotted one of Anika's favorite baby toys out in Bailey's dog run a few days earlier. The plush yellow duckling that sang "Singing in the Rain" had been lying beak-down in the snow. I rescued the kidnapped duck to find that it was in good shape and still able to sing.

Curious about the missing stocking, I looked out the kitchen window. There, on the freshly fallen snow, I spotted the red-and-green sock. Relieved to find it was in perfect condition, I gave Bailey a good-natured scolding and then returned it to its hook with the others. That's when I noticed Bailey's stocking hadn't even been hung yet. Was he trying to give me a hint? So before long, Bailey's Christmas stocking was hanging too, and we all had a good laugh over it.

Christmas came and went, and the following weekend I joined my mother and sister for a little getaway. That evening, my sister asked if I had liked my Christmas present from her. Caught off guard, I tried to remember her gift, but came up blank. She described the packaging (she's known for beautiful wrapping) and informed me that it contained a very special handmade bracelet. "And there was something special in there for Bailey, too," she said with concern.

Suddenly, I remembered how Bailey had snatched Anika's duck and Christmas stocking and wondered if he'd taken anything else. It actually seemed out of character since he'd never been that kind of dog before. But having a baby around had been an adjustment for him. So I called home and explained the mystery to my husband. He promised to do some investigating and called me back a few minutes later.

Now, I must explain that Bailey's kennel wasn't just an ordinary kennel. It started with a doggy-door that led from the laundry room out into a pretty nice doghouse (with two rooms). And that led out into a large, fenced dog run that he could freely come and go from. Pretty posh for a dog.

"I found the wrapping paper and ribbon and box outside," my husband told me. "So I could tell Bailey was responsible." But he explained that the items that were supposed to be inside the box were missing. "So I crawled into Bailey's doghouse with my flashlight. I found the bracelet and a leather dog collar with beadwork that says

'Good Dog.'"

Of course, we had a good laugh over that one—the "good dog" that had stolen a present from beneath the Christmas tree. My husband reassured me that both items were in excellent condition. "He didn't chew them or anything. But what surprised me even more was that he'd decorated his doghouse."

"Decorated his doghouse?" I wondered if I'd heard him right.

"Yeah. You know the boxes of Christmas decorations that you'd left in the laundry room?"

"The ones that just had leftover decorations?" I asked.

"It looks like Bailey helped himself to some of those decorations. And he's put them in his doghouse."

"You're kidding!"

He laughed. "No, I'm serious. Bailey decorated his doghouse."

It took a few seconds for this to even register. "So Bailey found his Christmas present under the tree, opened it up, then took it into his doghouse that he'd already decorated?"

"And that's not all," my husband said.

"There's more?"

"Yeah. Bailey's got a collection, too."

"A collection?"

Now my husband laughingly described how Bailey had all his plush doggy toys lined up against one of the walls of his doghouse—all the toys that he'd gotten for previous Christmases that we thought had gone missing.

"They're all clean and in great condition," he said with wonder. "Almost as if Bailey and the toys were having a Christmas party together."

We had a good long laugh over that, and after I hung up, I told my mother and sister the story. We marveled over how Bailey had known which box actually contained a present meant for him and how he'd carefully opened it and taken it into his doghouse. And they could hardly believe that not only had he decorated his doghouse with Christmas things, but he had neatly arranged his stuffed pals against a wall, as if to celebrate together. I'm not sure what motivated him, but I think Bailey's Christmas was a good one. And the words on his new collar, "Good Boy," couldn't have been more fitting. He truly was a good boy!

— Melody Carlson —

94

Christmas Cat

Life constantly presents the greatest opportunity
brilliantly disguised as the biggest disaster.
~David Icke

We adopted a cat from a neighbor. She had a large litter of kittens, all of whom my kids would have happily adopted. Somewhat grudgingly, they were persuaded to settle for one beautiful, little tabby-colored creature. Being a new kitten, he came to us without a name. The search was on to find something suitable. We decided to wait a few days before deciding. There was no rush, and this would give us a chance to observe the kitten's nature and come up with something suitable.

After a week, there was still no name that struck us as appropriate. The kitten seemed to be a fairly calm creature with no obvious character flaws. There were lots of unsolicited suggestions, but none that seemed to be particularly obvious choices. The rest of the family decided to give our son the honor of naming the cat. It seemed to have taken a special liking to him. As it turned out, none of us was happy with his decision. Roosta didn't seem to be a suitable name for a cat, but we had agreed to let him choose. My son couldn't explain why he chose that particular name. Perhaps it came from his interest in reggae music. So, Roosta was to be the cat's name.

The kitten adoption had taken place in the weeks leading up to Christmas, a most exciting time for children and kittens alike. As in previous years, we had a freshly cut tree covered in sparkling, dangling decorations. Roosta spent many quiet hours learning how to decorate the tree. He watched closely as each decoration found its special place in the branches.

All was well until the day before Christmas.

Then, in the middle of the night, we were awakened by a loud crash. The whole family rushed into the living room. We arrived in time to see Roosta making a hasty exit. The tree, complete with water container, decorations and seemingly every last pine needle, was sprawled across the floor. That night of all nights, our new kitten had decided to see what it would be like to "roost" in the upper branches. He must have had quite a surprise when he discovered he was a lot heavier than a Christmas ornament.

We spent hours cleaning up the mess. The tree was a total wreck, way beyond salvation. Early the next morning, the debris was wrapped in plastic and taken down to the garbage room. We might be the first family in history who had to dump their tree on the day before Christmas.

In honor of his attempt to roost in the Christmas tree, we all agreed to change the cat's name. It went from Roosta to the much more appropriate Rooster.

—James A. Gemmell—

The Christmas Surprise

At Christmas, all roads lead home.
~Marjorie Holmes

Christmas day is always crazy at my in-laws' house. Gran and Pops McClanahan have four adult children: three sons and a daughter. All have married and together they have produced ten grandchildren — seven boys and three girls, ages twelve and below. I married their youngest son, Sam.

In the summers and at Christmas we all gather, driving from our various homes on the East Coast, to spend time together at Gran and Pops' nine-bedroom summer house in Narragansett, Rhode Island. Although it's a large house, twenty people make it feel smaller, create sporadic "sleeping" schedules, and usually offer grab-what-you-can eating arrangements. I am often reminded of the "Old Woman in the Shoe" nursery rhyme where "she had so many children she didn't know what to do."

But as unruly as it is for the adults, it is a blast for all the little cousins, and at Christmastime it's double the fun. The cousins have often not seen each other since summer and Santa is coming too!

Unlike some families, the McClanahans don't draw a single name out of a hat so each person only has to buy a single holiday gift — no, each family buys gifts for every other person. Gran and Pops love the over-the-top merriment.

Surprisingly, despite our five families, the McClanahans as a group only acquired one dog, a large Yellow Lab with a square mug named Rumbo, a resident of New Canaan, Connecticut with Gran and Pops most of the time. Rumbo was once considered my husband Sam's dog, since Sam was the one who spent the summer raising and training him back when he was a pup; but with our growing brood Rumbo officially moved to Gran and Pops' place, with us remaining occasional dog-sitters since we live nearby.

Two years ago, Christmas in Narragansett was like the previous ones—the kids were another year older, they still had boundless energy, and the promise of Santa energized them even more. Rumbo also had gotten older. He was nine and arthritic. He would wander around wagging his tail looking for a pat, but he spent most of his time away from the chaos of fast-moving children, snuggled in his well-worn dog bed.

That Christmas Eve we, not Gran and Pops, had brought Rumbo up from Connecticut. When we arrived and started to unpack I tossed Rumbo's dog bed under the huge, beautifully decorated Christmas tree. He looked the picture of doggie adorableness under the twinkling lights and ornaments, his large mug resting on the edge of his dog bed looking out at us.

By that evening all the other families had arrived, one by one, unloading more bedlam into the house. As the presents were added under the tree, Rumbo's bed shifted, but we all lavished him with a tummy rub and a quick snuggle as we scooted him this way and that. Giving us his normal "smile" and wag, he didn't seem to mind.

That evening we had a festive dinner, and after the cleanup, Gran let Rumbo out. We all went to bed, knowing we'd be up again in a few hours.

Indeed, at 5:30 the first of the kids awoke. One by one, the eager children herded their parents downstairs. Over the next few hours, seemingly hundreds of presents were torn open. Long-desired toys magically appeared, somewhat useless household items were passed among the parents, and laughter could be heard sprinkled between Christmas carols being played on someone's laptop. Paper and discarded wrappings were everywhere.

As I scanned the chaos I noticed Rumbo lying in his dog bed, wrapping paper scattered all around it. It was the first time I had focused on Rumbo since I had woken up, and I decided to give the guy a Christmas rub. As I walked toward him I wondered if anyone had remembered to feed him or let him out that morning. I didn't remember seeing him outside.

His eyes were open and I knelt down in front of him and pet his head.

"Merry Christmas, Rumbo!" I said, giving him a scratch.

Rumbo's eyes and mouth were open, and his long tongue was hanging out, but he didn't move. Suddenly I noticed that he felt sort of cold. As I looked into his unmoving eyes and held their vacant gaze, I realized that Rumbo… was dead.

"OMG!" I wanted to text somebody. What the heck was I supposed to do?

I knelt in front of him, blocking him from the rest of the room, as my brain went into panic mode. It was Christmas morning. I was in a room full of children and there was a dead dog under the Christmas tree. I touched his leg — yes, it was stiff, and rigor mortis had set in.

I actually laughed. I realized that it was a perfect McClanahan Christmas moment. Most people find squirming puppies under their tree, but here at the McClanahans… it's a little different. You always had to think on your feet around here.

I quickly deduced that this was a job for my husband — a "real" McClanahan. I stood up, casually pulled my husband aside, and gave him the facts. Word traveled fast through the adults. Each in turn looked over at the Christmas tree and saw Rumbo "asleep" underneath it.

I had recovered enough from the shock to ponder the details: Where does one take a deceased dog on Christmas? What happens when your vet lives three hours away? Who do you call? And then, how do you sneak a dead 120-pound dog out of a house full of ten children? If we chose to leave him where he was, when would one of the kids notice that Rumbo wasn't moving, or go over to pat him as I did?

Well, it turned out to be surprisingly easy. Each mom gathered her own brood to go do something "exciting" away from the family room, and the four dads got to work lifting the awkward, stiff dog, still in his dog bed, and placing him in the back of Pops' pickup truck. Someone grabbed a blanket and gently covered him.

And there Rumbo stayed on Christmas day, out in the fresh Rhode Island air.

It was a while before it occurred to one of the kids to wonder where Rumbo was. As a group we had decided not to tell them until Christmas was over. Our stock answer was to be "I don't know," which is normal since people never know where anyone else is in that house.

It certainly wasn't an easy decision to leave Rumbo outside, in the back of a pickup truck, on Christmas, of all days, but we told ourselves that our options were limited. We were sure that Rumbo — the kindest, and most gentle dog in the whole world — had joined Santa on his sleigh, and together they were finishing up the rest of Santa's Christmas deliveries.

— Claire Field —

Wreck the Halls

*Cats are a kindly master, just as long
as you remember your place.*
~Paul Gray

My wife and I unpacked several big boxes and con-templated the contents. The instructions seemed simple enough. Hopefully, this was going to be our salvation.

Christmas was coming and we were pulling out the decorations for the season. My wife Donna loves to decorate, and our place looks like something out of a designer magazine once she is finished. It makes the holidays even more enchanting. Or it did, until we adopted a litter of rescue kittens.

We've always had a large family of rescue animals call our place home, but we really bumped up our game once we moved to Italy. There were lots of stray cats that lived and bred in the balmy climate, making for more opportunities to bring some little furballs home.

More than any other beasts in our menagerie, our cats love it when Christmastime comes around. The bright lights, colorful decorations and twinkling tree are just some of the splendid attractions that make the season particularly fun for them. They grab at all the shiny, sparkly things with great enthusiasm.

Two years ago, Donna outdid herself and put up the best decora-tions ever. She had a big tree as a centerpiece, with smaller trees and decorations displayed throughout our living areas. It was as pretty as could be and she was proud of the results of her hard work.

A few months prior, a pregnant female found our rescue haven and soon bore five adorable kittens. By the time my wife started decorating for the holidays, the five scamps were just coming into their own. Even in balmy Italy, my wife would never dream of leaving new kittens outside in December. So they stayed indoors at night, admiring her decorating handiwork.

Kittens love to throw themselves into a tree and bat at the lights and decorations. Grown cats and dogs do not resist much either, so we made sure to close the doors to the decorated areas at night. We didn't want any damage to the Christmas décor, or to the animals who could injure themselves playing with it.

After finishing everything, the decorations looked fantastic. It was Donna's best result ever and the effect was stupendous. That evening, we enjoyed the twinkling lights while slurping eggnog and eating chestnuts in front of the blazing fireplace. Then we made sure to close the doors before heading to bed.

The door handles in Italy are built like a lever, so that a dog swatting it, or a cat hanging on it, can trip the latch and open the door. Because of this, we learned to lock the doors at night. But that fateful day, we must have forgotten one door. Intrigued by the Christmas decorations as they wandered around the house that night, one of the animals must have tried the door to the living room and managed to open it.

Needless to say, we found a disaster the next morning. All the decorations had been trashed, with our five new little kittens still playing in and around the large Christmas tree, which was now lying on the floor. The dogs all looked at us with guilty expressions on their faces. Happily, none of the animals had hurt themselves, but the beautiful decorating was destroyed. We didn't have the heart to begin all over again, so we salvaged what we could for the season and that was that.

Last year, we decided to do something unconventional. We ordered a variety of cat trees and adorned them with cat friendly decorations and treats. We figured that we could still have reasonably nice decorations throughout the living areas that would also serve as a kitty playground. We assembled the biggest cat tree as the main attraction, with smaller ones situated here and there for effect. We tied strings and treats to them for the kitties to play with and chew on. We even strung some twinkling lights around the room for an overall holiday effect. After all was said and done, things didn't look too bad. Then we picked up all the wrapping paper and boxes that the kitty trees came in and put them in the storage room.

Congratulating ourselves on our ingenuity, we broke out the eggnog, preparing for a relaxing evening in front of the fireplace. We patiently waited for the kittens to discover their new kitty climbing trees. As we sat down, some of the cats and dogs wandered in to sniff at the cat trees and kitty safe decorations. But no one stayed to play, and there was no sign of the kittens.

After an enjoyable evening in front of a cozy fire, we finally headed to bed. Curiosity got the best of us though, so we decided to see what the new kittens were up to first.

We found them all in the storage room. They were happily playing hide and seek amid all the empty boxes and packing material that we had just put in there.

Best kitty Christmas presents ever.

— Sergio Del Bianco —

Pointy Ettas

*I've seen a look in dogs' eyes, a quickly vanishing look
of amazed contempt, and I am convinced that basically
dogs think humans are nuts.*
~John Steinbeck

So here's the deal. I'm not the one who writes the holiday letter. I'm the dog, Kirby, the smart one in the pack. The female human, the human that the others call "Mom," is busy. She says she's doing holiday stuff, but between you and me, she's suffering from severe cookie overdose.

Look, it's been a stressful season. First of all, there's a dead, fat guy dressed in a red suit on the lawn. Now you'd think the humans would be upset, but each morning when I go out to bark at him, the female human yells, "For Pete's sake Kirby, it's just deflated." Believe me, I know dead, and that guy in the red suit isn't just deflated.

But here's the real problem. The dead guy comes back to life every night. And he looks really happy about it. There's a bunch of little skinny guys with him. I don't know much about fashion, but I wouldn't be caught dead in their pointy shoes. Anyway, being the defender of the home, I run outside when the dead guy stands up. And what do I get for it? I get yelled at. Even the wannabe-alpha male called "Dad" (my favorite human because he shares something called "fries") yells at me.

But you know what? It gets worse. The dead guy is bad, but there's also a deer out there. And that deer is really, really sneaky. He

Four-legged Family Members | 305

stands completely still all day long and then at night he lights up like Vegas and starts lifting his head up and down. I bark at him, too… but from a safe distance. Take it from me; you don't want to mess with a deer. Horns hurt.

Oh, and that's not all. There's also a huge pink bird out there that waves its head. It wears a hat like the dead guy and drags around a sleigh. Yeah, I don't get it either. I don't go anywhere near that pink bird. It scares me.

Inside there are all these red flowers around called Pointy Ettas. We had a really nice big one that looked and smelled good. So I ate it. It was all soft and chewy — not like the stinkbugs or mice I usually eat. But after I ate it I didn't feel so hot. Kind of like that one time I ate too many stinkbugs and threw up all over the couch. The female human saw the remains of the Pointy Etta and started freaking out and I ended up in the car. Fortunately I barfed up the Pointy Etta right as I got onto the leather seats, so I got to get out again.

After that I decided that if it smelled nice, I wouldn't eat it. So that's why I ate berry-looking things that were on the Christmas tree — which, by the way, isn't a real tree. So I ate those red things and they turned out to be something called Styrofoam. Then Dad said something about it "expanding in my stomach." I had to get in the car again. But don't worry, I barfed it up. This time on the female human. The female human said that she was really happy that I was okay, but her eyes were leaking water.

Just between you and me, it smelled really good in the car.

— Laurie Sontag —

The Gingerbread Massacre

The smells of Christmas are the smells of childhood.
~Richard Paul Evans

"Be sure to hang the delicate ornaments high," said Polly, my stepmom. "Jake might mistake the colorful glass balls for his toys and try to bite them." Jake was new to our family that Christmas. He was a beautiful brown-and-white puppy, with giant puppy feet and a supremely expressive face. And, of course, he was loaded with the puppy curiosity that makes everything a toy.

Two weeks before Christmas, we brought out the boxes of ornaments, many of which had been in Polly's family for ages. Among them were some handmade treasures, including a special box that held an entire gingerbread family. They were real cookies, hung with red ribbons, made with love by one of Polly's relatives many years earlier, and lovingly preserved.

Every now and then, I or one of my little sisters—Ruth and Sue—would pretend we were going to nibble one, knowing that Polly would say, "You'll break a tooth! They're so old that they're rock hard and tasteless." We didn't really want to eat them, but we enjoyed teasing Polly.

Since we didn't know how Jake would react to the ornaments or the tree, we were careful to put delicate or potentially dangerous ornaments up high. No glass balls or ornaments, nothing small enough to choke him, no tinsel or lights were within his reach. Jake sniffed the tree a lot, probably puzzled and delighted that the outside was inside. Those first couple of days, Polly caught him starting to lift a leg on the tree twice. But he learned quickly and settled for sniffing from a distance.

The weekend before Christmas, Dad and Polly had a great idea. "That new holiday movie is playing. Let's all bundle up and go see it at the drive-in." Excited, we jumped into the car with our blankets, pillows and bags of homemade popcorn, and off we went for a great evening.

A few hours later, we returned home and opened the front door to find… a terrible mess. No, it wasn't the Christmas tree. In fact, we weren't sure what it was. We stood just inside the door staring at big brown chunks of… something. We all looked at each other sideways, fearing the worst, and wondering who would be brave enough to see what it was. As it turned out, the mess was Jake's bed, which he'd destroyed. Left alone for the first time, he must've gotten bored, attacked it and left it for dead. We didn't know then that the bed was not the only casualty.

The next morning was Saturday, so we girls were in the living room. I waited for *American Bandstand* to come on, while Ruth and Sue watched cartoons. I noticed that they weren't sitting in their usual TV-watching spots. Instead, they were very close to the Christmas tree. We weren't allowed to touch any of the presents, but we could look. So Ruth and Sue "took inventory" frequently, checking carefully to see if more packages with their names on them had magically appeared.

"Nothing new for me," said Sue. "Just a new one for Dad." Ruth continued to look, leaning in every direction as far as she could, without touching. Then something caught her eye.

"Hey, who broke Gingerbread Baby?" she asked, accusingly.

That brought Polly out of the kitchen and into the living room fast. "Where? Show me!" Ruth pointed out the former baby cookie, which was now just a head, still tied to the tree by its red ribbon.

"Here's another broken one," said Sue. "It's Gingerbread Grandpa.

Or it was. Now it's just his head, hat and part of his bowtie."

That caused a flurry of inspection, and soon it was clear that four members of the gingerbread clan — Baby, Grandpa, Aunt and Uncle — were now just gingerbread heads.

"I didn't do it," I said, just in case anybody thought I'd had a midnight snack of rock-hard ornaments. Quickly, my sisters echoed me with denials of their own. In unison, we girls and Polly all looked at Dad. If anyone was famous for midnight-snack raids, it was him.

"Not me," he said. "I'm holding out for fresh gingerbread."

Polly stared intently at the gingerbread catastrophe. "Wait just a minute," she said as she realized that only the low-hanging cookies were affected.

As if in slow motion, she turned and said, "Jacob!" Until that moment, Jake had been sitting by Dad, looking happy as ever. Suddenly, his posture changed. Guilt spread over his face as surely as if he'd been caught with Gingerbread Grandpa's bowtie in his mouth. With his head bowed a little, he tried not to meet Polly's gaze, but it was clear what had happened. It was as if he were wearing a sign that said, "I killed three generations of an innocent family. Not sorry!"

We learned a lesson that year. To Jake, rock-hard, decades-old gingerbread cookies were just a different flavor of dog bone. Every Christmas from then on, when the ornaments came out, the first thing we did was hang the survivors of the Gingerbread Massacre, as well as the four gingerbread heads, high up on the tree, out of Jake's reach. And every year, he'd stare up longingly, as if remembering those tasty "dog treats" he enjoyed during his first Christmas season.

— Teresa Ambord —

Archie the Angel

The best Christmas trees come very close
to exceeding nature.
~Andy Rooney

I tiptoed to the corner of the living room. "Archie, where are you? Come out, come out, wherever you are!" I chanted.

Archie's loud purring had revealed his hiding place behind our freshly cut eight-foot Christmas tree, but he didn't realize we'd located his whereabouts. I peeked through the branches and spotted him rolling from side to side on the red plaid tree skirt — playfully sparring with a tiny tree branch that was touching his tummy. Archie's black fur glistened as he nestled close to a strand of twinkling miniature white lights my husband had just put on the tree.

Suddenly, Archie's purring became louder and he began to twitch and thrust about. Then he sprawled flat out on his back and lay motionless under the tree. I was stunned to watch our lively eight-month-old kitten become subdued and induced into a state of euphoria from inhaling the intoxicating scent of the fresh pine.

I motioned for my husband to join me. "Look at Archie," I whispered, "he's intoxicated from the fragrance of the pine."

"I think pine is the new catnip," my husband teased. "He can sleep it off under the tree."

The following morning, we'd hit the snooze button twice and were trying to steal another ten minutes of slumber. But Archie was wide awake and his noisy purring woke us up when he entered our bedroom. He was back to his energetic self, and leapt upon our bed and began jumping back and forth between our pillows — licking our faces and purring incessantly in our ears. There was no way to coax Archie to settle in with us and take a catnap before breakfast.

As I fed Archie his breakfast, my husband made us omelets. While we ate our breakfast, we compiled a list of things to do that weekend.

Before we left the house to run errands, we looked in on Archie, lying fast asleep in his bed. "He's such a good-natured little guy," I said. "How could anyone abandon such a sweet kitten?"

My husband gave me a hug and said, "Just be thankful he was dumped on our doorstep."

Indeed. I'd never forget that chilly, rainy Halloween night. It was long after the trick-or-treaters had stopped begging for candy at our door. My husband was sound asleep on the couch and I'd settled in to watch *The Addams Family* television marathon. Suddenly, tires squealed, a loud, gruff voice shouted, "Get lost runt!" and a vehicle peeled rubber down the street. Quickly, I turned on the porch light, opened the front door and discovered a soaked and crying black kitten underneath the porch swing. I scurried to grab a towel and scooped him into my arms. As I dried him, he arched his back and purred. After he was completely dry, I gave him a bowl of warm milk. He arched his back and purred as he lapped up the milk. When finished, he arched his back, meowed softly, rubbed against my legs and waited for me to pet him. He was so cute when he arched his back to get my attention — I decided to name him Archie.

Our four-hour shopping expedition that afternoon was a huge success. We finished the Christmas shopping for our parents and siblings, purchased a vintage metal angel tree topper and a red personalized Christmas stocking for Archie. On the drive home, we decided after dinner my husband would place the angel on top of the tree and I'd hang Archie's stocking from the fireplace mantel.

"Archie's probably pacing and meowing by his food bowl," my husband said, pulling into the driveway.

As we entered the back door into the kitchen, the sweet fragrance of pine filled our nostrils. "I love the smell of Christmas!" I said, with no sign of Archie waiting to be fed.

My husband headed for the living room. "Archie's sleeping under the tree. Let's feed him after we unpack the car."

To our dismay, when we returned to the living room twenty minutes later, Archie wasn't asleep in his favorite spot. Apparently, Archie had no plans to leave his new haven, the Christmas tree. Unbeknownst to us, he'd managed to climb limb by limb up the back of the tree. In a matter of seconds, the tree began to sway to and fro against the wall. Then we spotted Archie on a tiny branch in back of the tree, about a quarter of the way from the top of the tree.

"Archie, stop!" my husband shouted. "Don't go any farther!"

But it was too late; the branch made a loud cracking noise and tinkling sounds of tin ornaments rang in our ears as they tumbled to the floor. Archie dug his claws deeper into the tree trunk and the tree began to tilt forward. Fortunately, it was my husband to the rescue. He reached for Archie, tugging hard, forcing him to release his claws, as the tree, laden with lights, vintage tin ornaments and tinsel crashed to the floor.

"What were you thinking? You could have been badly hurt," my husband scolded, stroking Archie's head and shoulders to soothe his frayed nerves.

"The top of the tree was bare, and I believe Archie wanted to be our treetop angel," I chuckled.

While Archie ate his dinner, we lifted the Christmas tree back into the corner of the living room. Surprisingly, there were only a few minor adjustments to make to the branches of lights and tin ornaments — no breakage whatsoever.

After Archie's stocking was hung and the metal angel was placed on top of the tree, we couldn't help but admire our handiwork. "This calls for a glass of bubbly," my husband said. "You grab the champagne flutes."

Unaware that Archie was underfoot, my husband popped the champagne cork into the air and it grazed Archie's head.

"This sure hasn't been Archie the angel's lucky day," I said. "Do you think it's true that cats have nine lives?"

My husband laughed. "I sure hope so. I think Archie's going to need them."

— Georgia A. Hubley —

The Great Christmas Cookie Caper

A cat, after being scolded, goes about its business.
A dog slinks off into a corner and pretends
to be doing a serious self-reappraisal.
~Robert Brault, rbrault.blogspot.com

One of the most amazing gifts I've ever received came in the form of a grossly overweight six-year-old Golden Retriever named Nemo. Nemo was owned by the neighbors of my wife's hairdresser. For a variety of reasons, the dog's weight was allowed to balloon to over 170 pounds. The vet told the owners that the dog would likely die soon if something wasn't done about his weight.

I'm not normally much of a volunteer, but in spite of the fact that we were in the midst of adapting to a rambunctious six-month-old Golden Retriever puppy named Molly, I offered to do what I could to help Nemo. Something about his story touched my heart.

The original arrangement was for Nemo to alternate weeks between our house and that of his owners. We were both to do our best to get him out walking and monitor his food intake. Since I enjoy walking anyway, it wasn't hard for me to incorporate Nemo into my routine. It seemed that his owners had trouble finding the time to do their part. I was just about ready to give up on the deal when they asked if I'd adopt Nemo. I felt I shared a bond with the dog and was happy to take him full time.

Of course I had to get my wife's blessing and convince her of the benefits of having two big dogs in our house. It really didn't take much effort since she seemed to like Nemo too. Molly enjoyed having him around, and except for the occasional turf battle, the transition went smoothly. Nemo became an official member of our family.

We watched Nemo's food intake closely and walked him three or four times daily through all kinds of weather. His diet consisted of three cups of dog food per day, and his treats were mostly bits of raw fruits or vegetables. It took nearly two years to get Nemo below one hundred pounds, but he did it!

There was one major bump in the road for Nemo. When he was around eight years old, he tore his right ACL and had to undergo surgery. This injury probably resulted from being so overweight for so many years. But Nemo endured the discomfort and pushed through the arduous, boring, and likely painful rehabilitation regime. Within six months he was back to his old self.

What we found in Nemo was a gentle, wise soul who had the heart of a warrior. One day while on a walk an unfamiliar dog approached us in a very aggressive manner. In the blink of an eye Nemo positioned himself between Molly and me and the other dog so he could meet the charge head-on. He quickly ran the aggressor off. As I said, our gentle giant has the heart of a warrior.

Nemo embraced his new active life with enthusiasm, and begrudgingly put up with the reduced rations. But while Nemo lost — and kept off — over seventy pounds, he certainly didn't lose his deep affection for food! Given an opportunity, our boy has proven many times that he can and will eat just about anything. One of the more notable incidents was what we now refer to as the Great Christmas Cookie Caper.

One of my wife's holiday traditions includes baking hundreds of intricately decorated Christmas cookies for get-togethers and gifts. She would put some cookies on foil-wrapped trays and store them on our porch until needed. We never had a problem with this arrangement until one holiday season.

One night, after we had been asleep for a few hours, Nemo let me know that he needed to go outside. He barely made it out the door before his bowels exploded! This scenario repeated several more times during the course of the night. It was very unusual for Nemo to be ill and we could not figure out what was wrong. The next day I noticed that the door to the porch was slightly open.

As soon as I walked onto the porch I saw why Nemo had been sick. I remembered that I snagged a couple of cookies after lunch the previous day and I must not have secured the porch door after my cookie raid. Nemo was obviously presented with an opportunity he couldn't resist. By the looks of the demolished trays, it appeared that Nemo indulged himself with about one hundred very fancy cookies!

A quick call to the vet put us at ease when we were told that our big boy might be uncomfortable, but would be in no serious danger. As best as we could tell, our little Molly had taken no part in the Great Cookie Caper and she seemed to enjoy being the "good dog," even if just for one day.

As for my wife, I'm still trying to make it up to her.

— Jim Carey —

Our Family Christmas Card

*Fun fact: In Icelandic folklore, a person who doesn't
have at least one new item of clothing for Christmas
will be taken by a horrible Yule Cat.*

L ast year, Art and I decided to dress in matching holiday sweaters and, along with our three cats, snap a "family" Christmas picture. Mailing it out as a Christmas card to relatives and friends sounded like fun, especially considering all the kids' pictures we've received over the years. We'd accumulated many cute cards to display along with hideous ones of babies, animals and people. This card, including our feline family, would be payback. It was a good idea, but not so easy to pull off.

Our first challenge was finding two identical holiday sweaters we both liked and would wear while taking our picture. We shopped in the men's department of a large store for a better selection of colors and patterns, and because Art wouldn't be caught dead in women's clothes.

The first sweater to catch my eye was navy blue, trimmed in white, displaying a beautiful wintry snow scene. It was a frontrunner. We continued our search, looking for something more colorful. The next one we liked was a white cable turtleneck sweater. Not colorful at all, but a perfect winter sweater. The final sweater in the running consisted of a red background with two white reindeer on the front, surrounded by a swirling snowflake design. We agreed this was the one.

Now the search for our sizes began. There were many in large sizes, less in medium and very few in small. After looking through hundreds of sweaters, I couldn't believe we found a small petite in the men's department for me. "A Christmas miracle!" I shouted loudly. Embarrassed, I hid behind a stack of sweaters.

Next, I stopped at the Dollar Store and picked up three red bows. I planned to tie them around our cats' necks as bowties. It would be easier than trying to keep small Santa hats on their active heads.

Picture day finally arrived. Art set up his camera and timer in front of our living room couch, while I corralled the three cats into the room. We wore our matching sweaters; the cats wore their red bows. If only it were this simple. Art held Daisy, our youngest striped kitten, on his lap while I held Oliver, a seven-year-old, gray-and-white male, and Ginger, a twenty-four-year-old tuxedo cat.

Daisy was the first cat to get fidgety and run away. While Art was chasing after her, the timing device went off. I was left sitting there with two cats on my lap in a firm grip with a surprised look on my face. Our second attempt was even worse. The camera didn't work, and when Art left the couch to fix the flash, it went off unexpectedly. This picture showed the tail and rear end of Daisy, and Art's crotch. Not a great family image for a Christmas card.

In the next shot, Oliver and Daisy had both run off, leaving me with poor old Ginger, who was happy to be sitting on my lap, or any lap, sleeping. By our seventh attempt, we decided to give up on the cats and take only our picture. We were both tired from the constant running back and forth chasing cats and adjusting cameras, and perfectly content sitting back and relaxing on the couch. I'm surprised we didn't fall asleep like Ginger.

Our final picture turned out well. We shot it holding photographs of our three cats. I was elated just to be smiling and not trying to restrain a runaway cat.

— Irene Maran —

Meet Our Contributors

We are pleased to introduce you to the writers whose stories were compiled from our past books to create this new collection. These bios were the ones that ran when the stories were originally published. They were current as of the publication dates of those books.

Mary M. Alward lives in Southern Ontario. She has one grown daughter and two grown grandsons. When Mary isn't writing, she loves spending time with her family, reading, crocheting and spending time with friends.

Born and raised in northern British Columbia, **Marty Anderson** has raised four daughters and now currently resides with his wife in a remote community where the Wi-Fi is slow so no one is tempted to move back home. His hobbies include hiking, dog walking, shoveling snow and listening to his wife.

Teresa Ambord is a full-time editor/author for a global business publisher. That's how she pays the bills, but for fun she writes stories about her family and pets. She lives in the rural northeastern corner of California with her posse of small pets. They inspire her writing and decorate her life.

Anastasia M. Ashman is an award-winning producer of cultural entertainment. Co-creator of *Tales from the Expat Harem*, a travel collection recommended by *The Today Show*, she's scripting a film about bridging her radical West Coast family and traditional Near East in-laws at a palatial Istanbul wedding. Her microblog is www.twitter.com/thandelike.

Elizabeth Atwater lives in a small Southern town with her husband Joe. She discovered the joy of reading in first grade and that naturally seemed to evolve into a joy of writing. Writing brings Elizabeth so much pleasure that she cannot imagine ever stopping. She sold her first story to a romance magazine when she was seventeen years old.

Caitlin Quinn Bailey is the communications coordinator for a nonprofit and has always been a writer, thanks to the incredible support of her family. On April 24, 2010, her dad will give her another priceless gift — walking her down the aisle on her wedding day. Thanks, Dad. E-mail her at caitlinqbailey@gmail.com.

Candy Allen Bauer has written dozens of short stories and has been featured in *Working Mother* magazine and on MSN Family. She is currently working on a compilation of short stories about growing up poor in Southern West Virginia. Candy lives on the Eastern Shore of Maryland with her husband Andrew and their five children.

Tamara Bell left her career as a real estate agent in 2018 and is currently living her life-long dream of writing and working at an antique shop. She and her husband Paul have resided in Cooperstown, PA for thirty-eight years where they raised two daughters. Tamara is an avid supporter of animal rescue and historic preservation.

Cynthia Bilyk is currently working on her bachelors in psychology. She recently quit her job and became a stay-at-home mom. She enjoys reading, the outdoors, and volunteer work. Please e-mail her at ufodonkey@gmail.com.

Barbara Bondy-Pare has four children from her first loving husband, Ronald M. Bondy. Since he passed away from lung cancer, she has married a high school classmate, Eddie Pare. Their twelve adorable grandchildren keep them young, active, and entertained. Barbara is all about love, family, and hugs.

Jamie Cahill is a freelance writer and a reader for Chicken Soup for the Soul. In her freelance career, she's written about everything from oil markets to French pastries to blockchain technology. She lives in Greenwich, CT. When she's not busy with her three children, husband and dog, she loves to travel and read.

Barbara Canale is a freelance writer and columnist for *The Catholic Sun*. She has been published in *Chicken Soup for the Veteran's Soul* and *Chicken Soup for the Adopted Soul*, and is the author of *Our Labor of Love; A Romanian Adoption Chronicle*. She enjoys biking, skiing, and gardening.

Christopher E. Cantrell has several diplomas from the Tennessee College of Applied Technology. He teaches Industrial Maintenance in Middle Tennessee and was in the maintenance field for twenty-four years. He and his high school sweetheart started dating at sixteen and have been married since 1991. They have two children, and love to travel.

Jim Carey lives in Sheboygan, WI with his wife Janet and their two Golden Retrievers — Molly and, the star of the story, Nemo. Jim is a practicing chiropractor and the author of the Civil War novel, *Echoes from Home*.

Melody Carlson is one of the most prolific novelists of our time. With more than 250 books published and sales topping 6.5 million, she writes primarily for women and teens. And every year she publishes a Christmas novella. She's won numerous awards, including a RITA and Romantic Times Career Achievement.

Kristen Clark is a speaker, writer, and gratitude expert. Her articles on marriage and relationships have appeared in numerous journals, magazines, and compilation books. Along with her husband, Lawrence, she also writes for and manages Hiswitness.org and NewBeginningsMarriage.org. E-mail Kristen at kristens@hiswitness.org.

Maril Crabtree lives in the Midwest and enjoys writing about her far-flung and amazing family. Her award-winning poetry and creative nonfiction have appeared in numerous journals and anthologies. More of her work may be seen at www.marilcrabtree.com.

Anne Crawley has been teaching English to seventh-graders for thirty-four years and still enjoys it every day. She lives in rural Pennsylvania with her husband and two daughters, plus two cats and three dogs. She loves to read, write, swim, and spend time with her family, especially her mother who lives nearby.

Jennifer Clark Davidson grew up as the middle child in her family, with an older sister and a younger brother. She and her husband have been married for thirty-six years, and have two married children, two in-laws (considered their third and fourth kids), two beautiful grand-daughters, and two grand-dogs. She is currently setting up a podcast.

Sergio Del Bianco has a background in fine arts and psychology. He is an artist and writer interested in the intersection of art, psychology, and the humanities. He resides in Europe with his spouse and growing family of rescue animals. E-mail him at sergiodelbianco@yahoo.com or through Twitter @DelBianco97.

Judy Ann Eichstedt is the mother of six children and one grandaughter. A freelance writer and homeless activist, Judy is the coauthor of a book of poems titled, *Weary Souls, Shattered by Life*. Please contact her at judea777@msn.com or www.wearysouls.com.

Sue England credits Clare Bolton (Aurora Cultural Centre) and Isobel Warren for inspiring her to resurrect her creative spirit. She is a member of Writers' Community of York Region, a Realtor with Royal LePage with her life partner Steve, and is writing a story for children.

Claire Field received her B.A. degree from the University of Vermont. She is married and the mother of three kids. She is a full-time homemaker, hockey mom and coach. She enjoys traveling, skiing, skating and playing tennis and paddle tennis.

Lynne Foosaner is a political activist, freelance writer, and grand-mother, not necessarily in that order.

H.M. Forrest is a freelance writer and editor who lives with her teenage son and exotic pets. She enjoys traveling with her son. Her stories have appeared in the *Chicken Soup for the Soul* series, *Writers Weekly*, and *Winter Whimsy*. She recently completed her first young adult fantasy novel. E-mail her at HMForrest1@gmail.com.

John Forrest is a retired educator, who writes about the excep-tional events and wonderful people that have enriched his life. His anthology, *Angels Stars and Trees: Tales of Christmas Magic*, is in its third printing. He lives in Orillia, ON, with his wife Carol. E-mail him at johnforrest@rogers.com.

Karen Foster is a freelance writer, blogger, and speaker. Her devotions and true first-person stories have appeared in multiple magazines, ezines, and anthologies. Karen has also served as a jail chaplain for women inmates. In addition to being a military spouse, Karen served as an Air Force Public Affairs Officer for ten years.

James A. Gemmell can be found most summers walking one of the Caminos de Santiago in France or Spain. His other hobbies are writing, playing guitar, drawing/painting, golfing and collecting art.

Ellen C.K. Giangiordano graduated from Temple University School of Law in 1990 and was a litigator for eight years in Philadelphia before returning home to raise her five children. Ellen enjoys cooking, sewing, weight lifting, yoga, spending time with her family, and reading the works of John Paul II. Ellen and her family now live in Georgia.

Pamela Gilsenan has five adult children and assorted grandchildren. She lives in the Colorado Rocky Mountains. Thanksgiving is her favorite holiday.

Lori Giraulo-Secor is a single mom in western New York with two beautiful children, Adam and Leah. She writes nonfiction short stories and children's poems. She's inspired by her family and is working to compile their funniest moments for a novel. Read Lori's blog at http:// loridreams.blogspot.com or e-mail her at Lsecor1@rochester.rr.com.

Rose Godfrey is a speech pathologist, writer, and mom to twelve children. She enjoys traveling the USA in a vintage RV, pinning projects she'll never complete, and finding a few moments of solitude amongst the chaos. Rose writes about travel at learningacrossamerica.com.

Cindy Golchuk lives near Las Vegas, Nevada, with her husband, her not-so-angelic grandson, Zack, and two dogs who rule the house with iron paws. In her spare time she enjoys reading, walking with friends, rewriting her three manuscripts geared toward a female readership and polishing her three book series for tweens.

After a twenty-year nursing career and fifteen years in radio, **Pamela Goldstein** turned to her passion — writing. She has three manuscripts and three plays under her belt, and several short stories published in the *Chicken Soup for the Soul* series and other anthologies. Her latest story is in the magazine Madre Natura. E-mail her at boker — tov2002@yahoo.ca.

T'Mara Goodsell is a lifelong dog lover who writes and teaches in St. Charles, MO. She is published in several *Chicken Soup for the Soul* books as well as other anthologies, newspapers, and publications.

Rose Hofer studies nursing, business, and literature at Front Range Community College. She grew up with her six siblings in Oregon and Colorado. She loves reading, writing, and helping others. She plans to continue writing and hopes to complete her first novel in the coming years.

Georgia A. Hubley retired after twenty years in financial management to write full-time. Vignettes of her life appear in various anthologies, magazines and newspapers. Once the nest was empty, Georgia and her husband of thirty-six years left Silicon Valley in the rearview mirror and now hang their hats in Henderson, NV. E-mail her at geohub@aol.com.

Cheyenne H. Huffman is a journalism student at King's College, from which she will graduate in 2019. She enjoys writing, crafting, and volunteering in her community. She would love to continue writing inspirational and feel-good stories documenting her life and its many lessons.

David Hull is a retired teacher who enjoys writing, reading, and spoiling his nieces and nephews. He lives in Holley, NY.

Michelle Jackson has a master's in psychology and is living in Arizona with her husband and three dogs. Her articles on family relations have drawn over 400,000 readers. She frequently answers family relation questions through her articles in an online publication.

Lynn Johnston has been sharing the amusing, moving lives of the Patterson family with millions of readers since 1979 in her award-winning comic strip, *For Better or For Worse*. Nominated for a Pulitzer Prize, Lynn has received the Order of Canada and claims a star on Canada's Walk of Fame. Visit her at www.fborfw.com.

Ruth Jones lives in Cookeville, TN, with her husband Terry and a very fat cat named Annabel.

C. Joy lives in the Midwest, nestled among cornfields and cows. Mother to five children, grandmother to three, she enjoys gardening, reading, knitting, and traveling.

Vicki L. Julian, a University of Kansas graduate, is the author of four inspirational books, various newspaper and magazine articles, and a contributor to six anthologies. She also writes a faith-based blog and a Christmas-themed children's book is soon to be published. Learn more at vickijulian.com.

Tom Kaden is counselor at Someone To Tell It To—www.someonetotellitto.org. He is a graduate of Messiah College and Asbury Theological Seminary. Tom and his wife Sarah and their four children live in Carlisle, PA.

Leslee Kahler received both her BS and her BA from Eastern University, and her Master's from Villanova. She has a son and a daughter and lives on a small farm in rural Pennsylvania with her family and eight rescue cats. She works as the ESL assistant at the local high school and hopes to be a novelist one day.

Wendy Keppley, a Florida native, counseled troubled teens and taught college courses for high school honor students. She enjoys family, playing with her grandsons, and living in the woods near Tampa, FL. Wendy also loves writing, kayaking, reading, yoga, exploring waterfalls, and oneirology. E-mail her at wendykep@gmail.com.

Jacqueline Davidson Kopito received her Bachelor of Arts degree from Syracuse University and a master's degree in Corporate and Public Communication, with honors, from Seton Hall University. She is a member of the Writers Guild of America. She lives with her husband and two sons in Short Hills, NJ.

Jeanne Kraus is a retired elementary educator who taught in Florida for over forty years. She now lives in Tennessee and continues to write short stories and poems for anthologies. She has been published in other *Chicken Soup for the Soul* books and is an author of three children's books and a Boomer Humor book for women.

After thirty-plus years as a communications professional and corporate wordsmith for a Fortune 500 company, **Mitchell Kyd** has begun a new journey as a freelance writer and tale weaver. Her stories reflect the humorous and sometimes poignant moments of life in rural Pennsylvania. Please e-mail her at mitchellkyd@gmail.com.

Beth Levine is a freelance writer whose work has been published in many national magazines (*Woman's Day*, *More*, *Good Housekeeping*). She is the author of two nonfiction books, and she thinks Christmas cookies are a very good idea. To learn more about Beth visit her website at www.bethlevine.net.

Linda A. Lohman retired after forty years in the accounting profession to write slice-of-life short stories. Knowing that truth is always better than fiction, she has over 150 Chicken Soup for the Soul books in her collection. She loves Chicken Soup — the books and her mom's soup! E-mail her at lindaalohman@yahoo.com.

Irene Maran is a freelance writer and storyteller. Her stories revolve around family, animals and everyday topics humorously expressed in two bi-weekly newspaper columns, *The News-Record of Maplewood and South Orange* and *The Coaster in Asbury Park*.

Patrick Matthews is the president of Live Oak Games, and designer of the award-winning game *StoryTellers*. He's also the author of "DaddyTales," a newspaper column about his life as a dad.

Marie Loper Maxwell is the mom of many, lover of learning and devourer of books. She spends most of her time with her husband and seven children reading, writing and making memories.

Stefano Mazzega has been a forensic scientist with the RCM Police for almost thirty-four years. He is the General Manager of the forensic laboratory in Vancouver. He is nearing retirement and hoping to transition to a career in writing. Stefano writes humour and suspense.

Rosemary McLaughlin has loved stories and storytelling since she was a little girl — writing plays for her friends to perform. After thirty-five years as an English teacher and reading her students' writing, she is now retired and doing her own writing and enjoying her family. She is proud to be part of the *Chicken Soup for the Soul* series. E-mail her at Rosemarymclaugh@gmail.com.

Paula Meyer received her Master of Education degree from the University of Manitoba in 2011. A Vice-Principal in Winnipeg, she is a mother to three amazing women who have taught her so much about the importance of community. Paula enjoys travelling adventures and reading. E-mail her at pmeyer@mts.net.

Cynthia Morningstar received her Bachelor of Music in Piano

Performance in 1979. She has worked as a librarian for a number of years, and has directed her church choir and taught piano. Her husband, Mark, is a pastor in Indiana. They have three daughters: Amanda, Beth, and Jill. Contact her at cbmorn@hotmail.com.

Tolly Moseley is a publicist and freelance writer in Austin, Texas. She and her blog, Austin Eavesdropper, have been featured on About. com, G4TV, in *Rare Magazine*, and in *The Daily Texan*. Thanks to her aunt, she now knows how to decorate the perfect Christmas tree. Contact her at tollymoseley@hotmail.com.

A visual artist by training, **Susan Mulder** left a career teaching and speaking in her field to pursue new directions. A chronic maker of handcrafted goods, book nerd and doting Mim (as her "grands" call her), she also loves to cook and writes a little here and there. Susan resides in Michigan with her husband and an ornery cat named Bo.

Alice Muschany lives in Flint Hill, MO. She loves retirement. It's true — every day is Saturday. When she's not spending time with her grandchildren, she's busy hiking, taking pictures, reading and writing. E-mail her at aliceandroland@gmail.com.

N. Newell worked for BC Tel/Telus for thirty-four years and won several service awards for his work. He is now retired and lives on Vancouver Island.

Lisa Peters lives in the New England area and is a writer, wife and mother of two children diagnosed with special needs. She shares her humorous and heartwarming life experiences on her family blog at www.onalifelessperfect.blogspot.com.

Changing seasons, unexpected blessings, love that lasts forever... these are a few of **M. Jean Pike's** favorite things. With a writing career spanning two decades, she has eight romance novels and over two hundred essays and short stories in print. Visit Jean's blog at mjeanpike.wordpress.com.

Evelyn Pollock's career included teaching, educational politics, and human rights consulting. She retired to Horseshoe Valley to write and paint. She is active in local writers' groups and in the arts community. Since retiring, several of her short stories and a book of her art have been published. E-mail her at pollockconsulting@bellnet.ca.

Connie Kaseweter Pullen lives in rural Sandy, OR, near her five children and several grandchildren. She earned a B.A. degree, with honors, at the University of Portland in 2006, with a double major in Psychology and Sociology. Connie enjoys writing, photography and exploring nature. E-mail her at MyGrandmaPullen@aol.com.

Lea Ellen Yarmill Reburn resides in beautiful central Ontario, and was born and raised locally. She is married, a dog lover, a caregiver to many, and loves to write true life experiences — some typical and some not! She has previously been published in several periodicals and newspapers. Guardian Angels Copyright ©2009 by Lea Ellen Yarmill Reburn, first published in *A Cup of Comfort for a Better World*, Copyright ©2010 by F+W Media, Inc. Reprinted with permission from the author and publisher. All Rights Reserved.

Janet Ramsdell Rockey has contributed to various *Chicken Soup for the Soul* books, *Heavenly Humor* collections (Barbour), and has authored two devotional books (Barbour). She lives in Florida with her family and two precocious cats.

Maureen Rogers is a transplanted Canadian who still loves to visit her homeland. Her writing projects include fiction, poetry and essays. She has been published online, in newspapers, anthologies and in *Chicken Soup for the Coffee Lover's Soul*, *Chicken Soup for the Soul: My Resolution* and *Chicken Soup for the Soul: My Cat's Life*. E-mail her at morogers@gmail.com.

Kathleen Ruth received her B.A. from St. Catherine University in St. Paul, MN and her M.A. in TESOL from the University of Central Florida. She taught in Minnesota and Florida, Bangkok, Thailand and Beirut, Lebanon. She loves reading, traveling, and embracing multiple cultures. Kathleen has five children and ten grandchildren.

Melanie A. Savidis received her Bachelor of Arts from Allegheny College and her Masters of Education from the University of Rochester. She teaches in the Rochester City School District. Melanie and her husband Mike have three sons. She enjoys writing, playing music and traveling.

John M. Scanlan is a 1983 graduate of the United States Naval Academy, and retired from the Marine Corps as a Lieutenant Colonel aviator. He currently resides on Hilton Head Island, SC, and is pursuing a second career as a writer. E-mail him at ping1@hargray.com.

Thom Schwarz, RN spent most of his most formative years working in the emergency room and at the bedside of his hospice patients. He wants to be just like his kids when he grows up. E-mail him at thomapl@Yahoo.com.

Troy Seate is an alumnus of Texas Christian University and lives in Colorado. His memoirs, essays, and fiction reflect his love of nature and its creatures.

Drew Sheldon was raised by a single mother in a time and place where that was highly unusual. That led him to follow an uncommon path through life and he's now aspiring to be the kind of writer his mother would like. He lives in the Pacific Northwest with his girlfriend and their blended family of fur-babies.

Stella Shepard is a journalist/photographer living on beautiful Prince Edward Island and married to Reg Phelan. Her son, Joshua, is daddy to seven-year-old Damian, who is a joy and a blessing. Stella's articles have been published in magazines, books and newspapers. She has just completed her first manuscript. E-mail Stella at rphelan@pei.sympatico.ca.

Lori Slaton is originally from Long Island, NY. She is the mother of two teenagers and currently lives near Atlanta, GA. Lori enjoys writing as a hobby and hopes to fulfill her goal of completing the novel she began writing years ago. E-mail her at lori_slaton@bellsouth.net.

Mary Smith is a regular contributor to *Angels on Earth Magazine* and *Guideposts Magazine*. She resides in Richmond, VA with her husband Barry. They have four grown children, two biological and two adopted. Mary loves writing for the Lord, walking, and gardening. Please e-mail her at stillbrook@comcast.net.

Laurie Sontag is a California newspaper columnist and author of the popular blog, Manic Motherhood. Her work regularly appears in books, magazines and on the Yahoo Shine Network for Women. You can see more of her work at www.lauriesontag.com.

Suzette Martinez Standring is syndicated with GateHouse Media and wrote *The Art of Column Writing* and *The Art of Opinion Writing*.

The unseen world sends powerful messages and she listens. Learn more at www.readsuzette.com.

Heather J. Stewart grew up in Waverley, NS. She grew up with a love of learning, reading, and writing. After teaching for ten years in Thompson, MB, she returned home and now teaches at Brookhouse Elementary. Besides writing for her students, she enjoys cultural events and musical pursuits.

Shannon Stocker is a coma survivor and RSD/CRPS advocate. Shannon has previously written for the *Chicken Soup for the Soul* series, writes picture books, blogs, is a musician, and is currently writing her memoir. Her world revolves around Greg, Cassidy, and Tye. Follow her crazy life at shannonstocker.com and on Twitter @iwriteforkidz.

Sue Summer writes for *The Newberry Observer* and *Newberry Magazine*, co-hosts a radio show for WKDK-AM, and is artist-in-residence with the S.C. Arts Commission. She graduated from USC and is author of the most widely read unpublished novel in history. She and her husband Henry have three children and one adored grandchild.

Deborah Tainsh, widow of a U.S. marine and mom to two sons, the oldest KIA in Iraq, is a published author of four military family books and one children's book. She enjoys giving inspirational talks, teaching writing workshops, mentoring at-risk youth, traveling, camping, hiking and continued writing and learning.

Paula Maugiri Tindall, RN, writes her stories and finds her inspiration from personal life experiences and through nature while overlooking the lake where she resides in Florida, completing her first book. Her work has been previously published in *Chicken Soup for the Grandma's Soul*. She can be reached at lucylu54@aol.com.

Award-winning author **Susan Traugh's** work has appeared in several *Chicken Soup for the Soul* books plus local and national magazines. Her young adult novel, *The Edge of Brilliance*, and her special education teen series, *Daily Living Skills*, can be found on her website at susantraugh.com. Susan lives in San Diego with her family.

Lizette Vega received a Bachelor of Arts degree in Christian Ministries from The Master's University in California. She is the author of *NINE! The Nine Virtues Known as the Fruit of the Spirit*, and two children's books, *Alligator Loose in the City!* and its sequel *Alligator Loose in the Train Depot!*

Bettie Wailes owns Wise Owl Tutoring in Winter Park, FL. She is a marathoner, working toward completion of 100 marathons. She has two children, five grandchildren, and two great-grandchildren. She has written *The View From the Back of the Pack*, a memoir about her running life, to be published soon.

David Warren has been writing part-time for three years. This is his second story to appear in the Chicken Soup for the Soul series. David has also appeared in *Grand* magazine and is the author of *Mealtime Guests*, a nationally released children's book. David resides in Kettering, OH with his wife Angela and daughter Marissa.

Christy Westbrook enjoys writing inspirational stories about everyday life. She loves spending time outdoors with her family and friends. She lives in Lexington, South Carolina, with her husband, Thad, and their two daughters, Abby and Katie. She wishes to thank her wonderful critique group for all of their support.

Kevin Wetmore is a writer, actor, director and comedian originally from Connecticut but now calling Los Angeles, CA home. He is the author or editor of over a dozen books and several dozen short stories, and a Professor at Loyola Marymount University. Learn more at www.somethingwetmorethiswaycomes.com.

Helen Wilder, a former kindergarten/first grade teacher in southeastern Kentucky, is married with one daughter, a son-in-law, and a grandpuppy, Paco. She is passionate about teaching young children, storytelling, journaling, reading, scrapbooking, and writing.

Ann Williamson received her Master of Arts in Creative Writing from Regis University in 2008. She was inducted into Alpha Sigma Nu, the Jesuit Honor Society and was published in *Apogee*, the Regis literary journal. She is a devoted grandmother and an avid reader. You may contact her via e-mail at anngracewilliamson@hotmail.com.

A video producer/director living near Toronto, ON, **Jamie Yeo** received his Bachelor of Applied Arts degree in Radio and Television Arts from Ryerson Polytechnical. A pioneer in multimedia development he began his early work in interactive laser videodisc. He lives with his partner Marilyn Cameron. E-mail him at jamieyeo@rogers.com.

Meet Amy Newmark

Amy Newmark is the bestselling author, editor-in-chief, and publisher of the *Chicken Soup for the Soul* book series. Since 2008, she has published 194 new books, most of them national bestsellers in the U.S. and Canada, more than doubling the number of Chicken Soup for the Soul titles in print today. She is also the author of *Simply Happy*, a crash course in Chicken Soup for the Soul advice and wisdom that is filled with easy-to-implement, practical tips for enjoying a better life.

Amy is credited with revitalizing the Chicken Soup for the Soul brand, which has been a publishing industry phenomenon since the first book came out in 1993. By compiling inspirational and aspirational true stories curated from ordinary people who have had extraordinary experiences, Amy has kept the thirty-year-old Chicken Soup for the Soul brand fresh and relevant.

Amy graduated *magna cum laude* from Harvard University where she majored in Portuguese and minored in French. She then embarked on a three-decade career as a Wall Street analyst, a hedge fund manager, and a corporate executive in the technology field. She is a Chartered Financial Analyst.

Her return to literary pursuits was inevitable, as her honors thesis in college involved traveling throughout Brazil's impoverished northeast region, collecting stories from regular people. She is delighted to have come full circle in her writing career — from collecting stories "from the people" in Brazil as a twenty-year-old to, three decades later, collecting stories "from the people" for Chicken Soup for the Soul.

When Amy and her husband Bill, the CEO of Chicken Soup for the Soul, are not working, they are visiting their four grown children and their spouses, and their five grandchildren.

Follow Amy on Twitter @amynewmark. Listen to her free podcast — Chicken Soup for the Soul with Amy Newmark — on Apple, Google, or by using your favorite podcast app on your phone.

Thank You

We owe huge thanks to all our contributors and fans. Here at Chicken Soup for the Soul we want to thank our editor Kristiana Pastir for reviewing our story library and presenting us with hundreds of holiday stories to choose from for this new collection. Publisher and Editor-in-Chief Amy Newmark made the final selection of the 101 that are included here, all personal favorites, and Associate Publisher D'ette Corona created the manuscript. None of these stories appeared in previous Chicken Soup for the Soul books about the winter holidays. They were compiled from our books on other topics.

The whole publishing team deserves a hand, including Senior Editor Barbara LoMonaco, Vice President of Marketing Maureen Peltier, Vice President of Production Victor Cataldo, and our graphic designer Daniel Zaccari, who turned our manuscript into this beautiful, entertaining book.

About Toys for Tots

Your purchase of this *Chicken Soup for the Soul* book supports Toys for Tots and helps create Christmas miracles for children who might not receive gifts otherwise!

Toys for Tots, a 76-year national charitable program run by the U.S. Marine Corps Reserve, provides year-round joy, comfort, and hope to less fortunate children across the nation through the gift of a new toy or book. The gifts that are collected by  Marines and volunteers during the holiday season, and those that are distributed beyond Christmastime, offer disadvantaged children recognition, confidence, and a positive memory for a lifetime. It is such experiences that help children become responsible citizens and caring members of their community.

For over seven decades, the program has evolved and grown exponentially, having delivered hope and the magic of Christmas to over 291 million less fortunate children. Now, in its 76th year, the Marine Corps Reserve Toys for Tots Program also provides support year-round to families experiencing challenges and exceptional circumstances, thus fulfilling the hopes and dreams of millions of less fortunate children nationwide. The Marine Toys for Tots Foundation is a not-for-profit organization authorized by the U.S. Marine Corps and the Department of Defense to provide fundraising and other necessary support for the annual Marine Corps Reserve

Toys for Tots Program.

You can learn more about Toys for Tots by visiting their website at https://www.toysfortots.org.

Sharing Happiness, Inspiration, and Hope

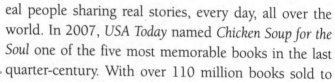eal people sharing real stories, every day, all over the world. In 2007, *USA Today* named *Chicken Soup for the Soul* one of the five most memorable books in the last quarter-century. With over 110 million books sold to date in the U.S. and Canada alone, more than 300 titles in print, and translations into nearly fifty languages, "chicken soup for the soul®" is one of the world's best-known phrases.

Today, thirty years after we first began sharing happiness, inspiration and hope through our books, we continue to delight our readers with new titles, but have also evolved beyond the bookshelves with super premium pet food, television shows, a podcast, licensed products, and free movies and TV shows on our Crackle, Redbox, Popcornflix and Chicken Soup for the Soul streaming apps. We are busy "changing your life one story at a time®." Thanks for reading!

Share with Us

We have all had Chicken Soup for the Soul moments in our lives. If you would like to share your story, go to chickensoup.com and click on Books and then Submit Your Story. You will find our writing guidelines there, along with a list of topics we're working on.

You may be able to help another reader and become a published author at the same time! Some of our past contributors have even launched writing and speaking careers from the publication of their stories in our books.

We only accept story submissions via our website. They are no longer accepted via postal mail or fax. And they are not accepted via e-mail.

To contact us regarding other matters, please send an e-mail to the webmaster@chickensoupforthesoul.com, or write us at:

Chicken Soup for the Soul
P.O. Box 700
Cos Cob, CT 06807-0700

One more note from your friends at Chicken Soup for the Soul: Occasionally, we receive an unsolicited book manuscript from one of our readers, and we would like to respectfully inform you that we do not accept unsolicited manuscripts, and we must discard the ones that are sent to us.

Chicken Soup
for the Soul

Changing lives one story at a time®
www.chickensoup.com